FROM CREATION TO RE-CREATION

God's Actions on Behalf of Sinful Humankind,
From Creation to the Re-Created in Jesus Christ

DANIEL LAZICH

WESTBOW
PRESS®
A DIVISION OF THOMAS NELSON
& ZONDERVAN

WestBow Press books may be ordered through booksellers or by contacting:

WestBow Press
A Division of Thomas Nelson & Zondervan
1663 Liberty Drive
Bloomington, IN 47403
www.westbowpress.com
844-714-3454

ISBN: 978-1-6642-4273-9 (sc)
ISBN: 978-1-6642-4272-2 (hc)
ISBN: 978-1-6642-4274-6 (e)

Library of Congress Control Number: 2021916441

Print information available on the last page.

WestBow Press rev. date: 09/22/2022

To the Savior of the world

ACKNOWLEDGMENT

My sincere gratitude to Eugene Theodore for his selfless support and encouragement throughout the preparation and publication of this book. Also, gratitude to my wife Sue for being patient and supportive in this effort.

CONTENTS

INTRODUCTION

Within the last forty years, scientific discoveries and knowledge about our universe contain unprecedented theological implications. They imply that the Creator exists, more so than ever before. These discoveries have developed a worldview that challenges both theologians and scientists to engage in a mutually fruitful dialog.

Scientists in quantum cosmology have observed and studied regions of our universe that humankind did not know existed until recently. Others have investigated the exotic subatomic world of particles to discover how our universe functions. The knowledge gained from these studies has been unimaginable just a few decades ago.

Information presented here is in general terms to facilitate understanding by all readers, hopefully. A detailed information presented in precise scientific way can be found in numerous reports and publications in the field of quantum physics, quantum cosmology, and the anthropic cosmological principles.

The new knowledge and discoveries about our universe imply that we, humankind, reside in a universe that is fine-tuned to our existence and that it gives the appearance of a unique one. There is a convincing indication that an all-knowing intelligence selected a type of universe that would be suitable for the carbon-based intelligent life, humankind, specifically. Our new knowledge and understanding leads to a possibility that the Ultimate Intelligence, the Creator, who possessed all knowledge, selected the essential parameters of our universe. The basic parameters of our universe appear to be fine-tuned to our existence and no other intelligent life.

This treatise will refer to God, the Creator, as the Absolute (Unchangeable) Intelligence for ease of understanding.

The new knowledge about our universe implies that our universe may be one of an exceedingly great number of universes. Regions of spacetime may not be the only regions within God's dominion. There could possibly be an infinite series of regions in God's dominion. However, humankind cannot research such possibilities.

Our universe is certainly not an ordinary or routine one. The construction and the functionality of our universe also indicates that it was not made by accident. In contrast, studies and observations of our universe imply that the Creator selected it before initiation of its beginning. An intelligence that possessed all knowledge, possible, about our universe must have selected the value of its critical parameters before its creation.

New knowledge about our universe reveals the nature of our reality in stark contrast to classical understanding. Quantum cosmology and anthropic cosmological principles contain unprecedented theological implications concerning the Absolute Being, the Creator. These implications indicate that a truthful reassessment of Christian theology's relationship to classical philosophy could be beneficial. Such a reassessment would enable a theological worldview that is more proper and in line with the now known facts of our universe and its Creator.

Ancient-time and the classical worldview do not fit well with the observed facts of our universe and its nature. The ancient-time worldview is highly limited and local. The austere nature of the ancient worldview is not a deliberate attempt to promote a particular view. We should not fault the biblical and ancient epic authors for writing in the way that they did. In ancient and biblical time, authors did the best that they could have done. Their ability to discover and grow in knowledge was highly restricted.

The classical worldview is highly deterministic because classical philosophy is deterministic. Therefore, ancient-time and the classical worldviews are not suitable for understanding the current nonlocal reality, as advanced studies imply. The world view enabled by recent discoveries is nonclassical, nondeterministic, and universal. Therefore, both theologians and scientists would benefit more from a global perspective than a local one. A descriptive interaction with our reality, rather than a proscriptive one, would help all humanity.

However, such a reassessment requires acceptance that human beings have three parts that are unique to carbon-based intelligence (or carbon-based life). These parts are the human spirit (intelligence), the body, and the soul.

In classical philosophy and theology, the human soul represents human identity. The nonclassical worldview and understanding suggests that the human spirit (intelligence) is the human identity. As we shall see, in the chapter on creation, that when the Creator placed the spirit into the human body, man became a living being. Therefore, the human spirit is the motive force for human life. In its biblically based role, the Holy Spirit resides in yielded believers and communicates to their human spirit, influencing correct thinking and a proper decision-making process. The human spirit, in the Bible, and intelligence, in physics are one and the same part of the human being.

Quantum cosmology and anthropic cosmological principles describe the Absolute Intelligence as the Final Observer, which is the Biblical Creator. Individual intelligent inhabitants of the universe are local observers. They collectively act as the interior decorators of their observed dwelling, the spacetime region. Final Observer coordinates the observations made by the lesser individual and collective observers into one whole structure.

Therefore, it appears that for a universe such as ours to exist at all, the Final Observer must have it in his mind continually. In human terms, the Final Observer must have the universe and its inhabitants in his memory always. If the Final Observer were to forget us for a fraction of a second, we and our universe would cease to exist. The description of the Final Observer in anthropic cosmological principles conforms well to the Judeo-Christian concept of God, the Creator. Despite efforts to the contrary, the quantum definition of the Final Observer is not going away.

Readers of biblical verses and narratives would benefit from the distinction between the experience of faith and the intellectual analyses of faith-based experience. Theologians would do well to rely less on local experience, which may influence a subjective worldview. Local and subjective interpretations of religious experience can produce greater detail of ever-diminishing reality. While it may lack detail, a global worldview may help reconcile locally perceived conflicts. Such a worldview can reinforce the realization that God acts in life and experiences of yielded believers, here, now, and whether they notice it or not.

The reading and interpretation of biblical texts and narratives have varied historically. Because there is only one Absolute Being, there is only one truth. Adaptation of a global and nondeterministic worldview could help theologians and individual believers achieve a more uniform understanding of religious experiences. However, when addressing faith experiences, yielded believers must be aware that faith-based religious experiences do not lead to salvation, regardless of how noble they are. Faith-based religious experiences must be a witness to the salvation that we have now, in Jesus Christ, our Lord. In general, we should avoid strict literalism. It only serves to cause rise to controversy and unfruitful debates.

Historically, theologians and scientists were unwilling to engage in constructive dialog. The natural tendency is to attack the other side's view believing it will reinforce one's personal view and subjective conclusions. A person cannot prove himself right by attempting to prove others wrong. However, both theologians and scientists see and study the same nature. There is one Creator and therefore, one creation. There is nothing in all of God's creation that promotes conflict. Nature itself prefers an honest dialog while respecting necessary diversity. Nature, as we see it now, prefers unity in diversity. However, such unity must stand on the foundation of one truth, which is Jesus Christ.

As it stands today, the world is vastly different from the world in biblical time. Information and knowledge that were available in the ancient and biblical time do not compare with the modern-day world. The strict adherence to a local deterministic worldview can influence our interpretation and understanding of the Bible and science. However, Christians should adjust their worldviews and the way that they understand science to conform to modern-day knowledge. Theologians should adopt this adjustment. Christians can adjust their worldview without sacrificing the universal truth presented in the scriptures.

The need for theological discourses, analyses, and presentations that consider the most advanced discoveries has never been greater. There is a real need for the religious worldview to be updated so that it reflects the most advanced findings concerning the Final Observer the biblical Creator. Ancient-time people and authors of the biblical-creation narrative developed their cosmological understanding based on limited local observations. Ancient-time people did not have adequate means to probe further and discover more. Therefore, they had limited ability to advance in knowledge and understanding.

Considering the recent discoveries concerning our universe's existence, the time to present the Judeo-Christian Creator is now. Everyone would gain a better understanding. Understanding the Creator's work of bringing our universe into existence will enable us to have a clearer understanding of God, who prepared everything that humankind needed before he created it.

In its present state, the world needs a theological and philosophical foundation that conforms to the scriptures without ignoring or downplaying the significance of scientific facts and the voice of nature. Opposing science because we do not trust scientists does not promote a serious, logical, and fruitful dialog. Science cannot and should not echo theological concepts verbatim. Likewise, theology should not strive to shape scientific understanding to make it conform to preferred theological conclusions.

Scientific undertaking in the field of quantum physics and quantum cosmology reveal profoundly theological implications. Quantum cosmology and the anthropic cosmological principles only study our universe's creation and its carbon-based life, not the creation week. Shockingly for many, quantum cosmology concludes that our universe was created from nothing. Quantum cosmology also supports the conclusion that the Ultimate Intelligence, the Final Observer, initiated our universe's creation. The Final Observer had all knowledge about our universe before he created it. Quantum cosmology maintains that the very beginning of our universe, was based on a set of laws and parameters which were determined and put in place by the all-knowing Intelligence before the beginning of time, (the universe).

The studies and analyses that are relative to anthropic cosmological principles imply that our universe was founded on the principle of selfless love, or the biblical agape. This indication is indisputable confirmation of the Judeo-Christian concept of God, the Creator. He is love. These are significant, and unprecedented theological implications Christians should explore in depth and honestly.

The scientific discoveries in the twentieth century changed our perspective of the heavens forever. Humankind now has sufficient physical evidence that our universe was created from nothing, which was accomplished by the All-Knowing Creator. Our universe is a book that was written by the hand of the Creator. In an unprecedented way, this book, written by the Creator, describes him in grander way that no human being ever could.

Neither science nor theology should conduct its research and study with presupposed outcomes and results. Everything must be examined and evaluated with an open mind and a firm intent to discover what is right.

All knowledge that exists comes from God. Therefore, all resulting knowledge and understanding by created intelligence should glorify God and present him in the true light.

A way of thinking that is shaped by a particular social and religious setting should often surrender to rigorous analysis and research that is not based on rigid presuppositions. The current composition of our universe has not been there from time immemorial, and it will not remain so for eternity.

Currently, we see only a part of the actual reality in which we live. We can only see our past and travel into the future, which we cannot see. Yet our all-inclusive universe is only a speck of dust in God's infinite dominion. Therefore, we must accept that what we learn and observe applies only to us, the intelligent processing of information in our universe, and not to any other intelligence in another region of the Creator's dominion.

Science and theology can reinforce each other beneficially. Scientific studies and research address physical matters. Theology addresses the human spirit and the spiritual needs of people. However, both can find a mutual reason for research and study. Human beings are made as an order of spirit (intelligence) that functions through human mind, brain, and free will. However, looking to the heavens, both the physical and spiritual nature and needs can be satisfied.

Often, theologians include the biblical reality of a Savior and salvation when discussing creation. Study of creation is concerned with the physical and material. It addresses what we can see, touch, and physically explore.

However, humans cannot see and experimentally research the salvation of sinful humankind. What God accomplished on our behalf in the body of Jesus Christ on the cross at Golgotha is apart from every law known to humankind. The great exchange of humankind's spirit, through the body of Jesus Christ on the cross is so wonderful that it is incomprehensible. Neither theology, science, nor philosophy could explain it fully.

God created a new humankind in Jesus Christ to preserve humanity. He gave humankind a new spirit, or life, to replace the life that had sinned. This treatise will explore the re-creation of humankind later.

The salvation of sinful humankind is an inexhaustible subject. If all created intelligences were to explore the facts of salvation together, they would never exhaust all the knowledge that is contained in the salvation of humankind. God alone knew what had to be done to save sinful humanity.

Even if salvation on the cross, at Golgotha, is based on some law, we cannot know and understand it. Such a law is well beyond our capability to understand. Our brains cannot process all the information concerning the salvation of humankind. The only possible conclusion is that God saved humankind because he loved it unconditionally and selflessly. God is love eternal.

The creation of our universe and humankind in it reveals agape, which is selfless love. God carried out all his actions and interventions in the history of humanity because he has always loved us selflessly. In the past, God acted with the intent to save fallen humankind and restore it to him as his children, in the fullness of time.

The section of this treatise that addresses the re-creation of humankind will explore salvation in more detail. If we could put together the vocabulary of all possible created intelligence, we could not find adequate words to describe our God and Father. The heavens declare the glory of God. His glory is his selfless love.

SECTION 1

SECTION II

1

The Beginning

"In the beginning God created the heavens and the earth."
(Genesis 1:1 NIV)

UNDERSTANDING THE SPECIFIC events, their sequence, and mechanics of creation is not essential concerning our salvation. Exhaustive concentration on the mechanics and sequence concerning the creation process often diverts our attention from its message. The message presented in the biblical narrative of creation is especially important. It reveals the nature of God, our Creator. Therefore this author will address the message first.

The biblical narrative about the creation week opens with a stand-alone sentence which does not specify when the heavens and the earth came into existence. However, we should not claim that the authors of the biblical account erred. They had to describe the creation week in the only way they could have done it. They did it in the only way the people could understand. They described it based on the knowledge and experience available at their time. Even the best attempts by modern-day science cannot describe our universe at zero time.

"In the beginning," is usually applied to the beginning of the universe. However, the very beginning of our universe is beyond our ability to discover, understand, and describe. Recent discovery concerning the beginning of our universe reveals an unexpected probability. Our universe began apart from all laws that are known to humankind. The implication is that beginning of our universe may have conformed to a law that is not in the universe that the quantum law orders. Could it be "In the beginning God..."?

People in ancient time did not know that the universe existed. Therefore, the authors of the biblical narrative of creation did not describe our universe's creation. They only described the preparation of the planet Earth for humankind.

The ancient Babylonian creation epic names the beginning as the beginning of their gods. However, it does not specify when or how did their gods come into being. Authors of the biblical account of the act of creation were familiar with Babylonian epics. The authors of the Babylonian epics wrote them before the biblical-creation narrative. In contrast, the biblical account of creation attributes the act of creation to one eternal God, who has no beginning or end. The authors of the biblical account of creation adopted and modified parts of the ancient epics by concentrating on one God rather than on many gods. The assertion that one and only God created all was more important to the biblical authors than a detailed description of how he did it.

Both the biblical-creation narrative and Babylonian epic assume that earth, which was covered with water, existed before God (or gods) created its functionality. The assumption that something existed before the first day of creation week applies to the planet Earth only. The Jews and Mesopotamians believed that the earth is the only inhabited place outside heaven. Humankind cannot know whether or not something existed before the creation of our universe. To maintain that biblical narrative of creation assumes that something did exist before the preparation of planet Earth is inappropriate.

The two biblical narratives of creation assert that the Creator transformed the preexisting disorder and chaos into functional earth and an order. Disorder and chaos were not conditions of God's Creation before the first day of the creation week. They depict the regions of human ignorance. After an intelligent observer obtains sufficient knowledge about these regions, the observation of disorder and chaos goes away. The lack of knowledge about anything appears as chaos to humans. Therefore, both the biblical and ancient creation accounts describe the transformation of the non-functional to something usable.

Authors of the biblical account and the ancient-time epics begin their narrative by describing the existence of darkness and disorder. Darkness and chaos were forces that opposed what God or gods determined to make. Therefore, to subdue the evil force of darkness and transform the disorder into order requires extraordinary power. The authors of the biblical account of creation asserted that only the God of Israel had sufficient strength, knowledge, and power to transform chaos into a functional earth.

The People in ancient time—Jews included—did not have knowledge about the universe that we have today. The ancient time's people had limited knowledge of cosmology and a very local and limited worldview. They could not have acquired the knowledge that humankind has today because knowledge increases with time. Also, an increase in knowledge requires more than visual observation. It requires proper facilities and instrumentation to probe, experiment, and investigate.

In ancient time, the people believed that heavens and the earth were the only inhabited places in God's dominion. The people thought that no other heaven or earth existed. Therefore, the biblical account of creation lacks detail, and it does not include decorative words and flowery descriptions. Other biblical references to creation, recorded in Psalms, Proverbs, and Isaiah, are more decorative. However, these references are limited in scope, concerning the acts of creating. Other biblical references to creation aim to portray God's unmatched majesty as the Creator whom the nation of Israel worshiped. They do not describe the mechanics of creation itself.

God created the universe and functional earth before the creation of humankind Therefore, humanity cannot analyze and understand the events that happened before its history began. Nevertheless to their credit, the authors of the biblical narrative of the creation activity preserved the true knowledge about God. There is only one God who is supreme over all Creation.

The biblical-creation narrative answers the question of who created, and what was created? It does not describe the *how*, or the mechanics of creation. Therefore, the Bible's readers should consider the time, geographic location, and culture to which the biblical creation account's authors belonged. Authors of the biblical narrative of creation were familiar with the ancient Near-East cultures. The familiarity with these cultures had an unavoidable influence on their ways of thinking.

The Jewish people originated from Mesopotamia. However, the Jewish narrative of creation week departed from the ancient creation epics and stood apart from the surrounding nations' norms. The authors of the biblical narrative of creation aimed at making their account of creating uniquely Jewish. They believed that God's chosen people had to stand apart from the surrounding nations.

Nevertheless, the authors of the biblical creation account and the rest of the scripture had an affinity to the culture and concepts of the region that the Jews originated from, which was Mesopotamia. Accordingly, they may have contrasted their account of creation to the familiar Babylonian epics.

Therefore, the readers of the biblical narrative of creation should keep this contrast in mind always. Attempt to inject concepts based on modern-day knowledge and understanding into the biblical account of creation would be unproductive and perhaps inappropriate. The proper and fruitful reading of the biblical account of creation should concentrate on the message it conveys. Concentration on the mechanics and chronology of creation of the universe and Earth does not contribute to the proper understanding of the message. It may also lead to misrepresentation of the Creator and his accomplishments. The readers of the biblical account of creation should aim to ensure credibility.

What Message Does the Biblical-Creation Narrative convey?

The central message of the biblical-creation narrative is that God is love. This treatise answers the above question first because the message that the biblical account of creation conveys is especially important. Other aspects concerning the act of creation are discussed later in this treatise. By faith, we must accept the biblical assertion that one God made everything that exists. Creation, as presented in the Bible, can neither be proved nor disproved.

By faith we understand that the universe was formed at
God's command, so that what is seen was not made out
of what was visible. (Hebrews 11:3 NKJV)

Our faith or trust in our Creator must win over perceived physical facts. To accept that God the Creator made everything that exists is more important than any other aspect of creation, people may debate. Discussions and debates concerning the sequence and mechanics of creation may be amusing, but they are neither essential nor useful. God is love, from eternity to eternity.

The biblical-creation narrative's chief aim was to present the one God—the God of Abraham, Isaac, and Jacob—as the Creator of the functional residence for the humankind that he loved. The God of Israel was the Creator because no other gods existed. However, the biblical-creation narrative did not claim that the message contained in it came by revelation.

The Jewish exegetes referred to the biblical account as a narrative. The authors of the biblical account of creation presented their understanding and description of God's interaction and relationship with the Jewish nation. They forcefully uplifted the all-knowing and powerful God of Israel. They affirmed that only the God of Abraham, Isaac, and Jacob was powerful enough to transform the chaotic world into a functional and enjoyable residence for humankind. They presented the all-knowing God who, before creating the universe, decided that he would, at just the right time, prepare the functional earth for humankind he loved.

The God of Israel is the only powerful enough to separate light from darkness and establish their inviolable boundaries. The God of Israel's people is the only one who established laws to govern the universe and the Earth that he prepared for humanity.

Furthermore, he did it alone and without any help and or advice. The God of Abraham, Isaac, and Jacob is so powerful and full of knowledge that he neither needed help, advisers, nor partners. He is the Only God. No other God existed before him because he had no beginning. Even if God the Creator wanted to consult someone, no one was there to ask.

God himself asserts the same in the Scriptures. God, the Creator, is the Absolute Spirit who has absolute power.

> This is what the LORD says—your Redeemer, who formed
> you in the womb: "I am the LORD, the Maker of all things,
> who stretches out the heavens, who spreads out the earth
> by myself." (Isaiah 44:24)

Modern-day knowledge about our universe implies that there could be only one Absolute Intelligence. If more than one was to exist, our universe could not exist. There is but one God. Human beings cannot verify such an assertion; however, it is something to contemplate always. God, the Creator, is much more than the human mind can understand and express. Humankind can describe the Creator only in terms that are applicable to our universe, where carbon-based life is. The things that we know and see are but a speck of dust in God's infinite dominion.

Humankind does not need a frequent reminder concerning this fact. Humanity always has the nature to contemplate. Even on the earth, altered by the violent geologic upheaval, there is sufficient reminder that only one God could have accomplished such a creative act. The God of Abraham, Isaac, and Jacob, the Creator of all, is incomparable.

> "To whom will you compare me? Or who is my equal?
> says the Holy One. Lift your eyes and look to the heavens:
> Who created all these? He who brings out the starry host
> one by one and calls forth each of them by name. Because
> of his great power and mighty strength, not one of them
> is missing." (Isaiah 40:25–26 NIV)

The one and the only God, the God of Israel, created all visible and invisible things. He accomplished it by himself, without assistance from another, and without anyone's advice. It is so because he is the all-knowing God.

In the biblical-creation narrative, the Creator is God, who has no beginning and no end. He has neither a past nor a future. God always *is*. God is in the eternal present in relation to the universe of spacetime and matter. He existed before creation and before anyone else lived. Therefore, God did not consult anyone else because no one else existed.

God, the Creator, determined when and what he will create before he made anything.

> Who can fathom the Spirit of the LORD, or instruct the LORD as his counselor? Whom did the LORD consult to enlighten him, and who taught him the right way? Who was it that taught him knowledge, or showed him the path of understanding? (Isaiah 40: 13-14 NIV)

The biblical account of the creation week presents this kind Creator, the one and only God, and the God of Abraham, Isaac, and Jacob, who spoke, and it came into existence. He did not need to exert physical labor to fashion the world. God did not rely on trial and error. He did not need to experiment. The Creator commanded it to be and it was. Everything came into existence exactly as he decided in advance.

The Babylonian creation epics maintain that many gods took part and collaborated in the creation of the world. Even though the biblical account of creation displays some affinity to the ancient Mesopotamian epics, the authors of the biblical narrative deviated from the traditional concepts of their own culture. They, in contrast to the Mesopotamian culture, forcefully asserted that no other god could have done the things that the God of Israel had done.

They aimed to clarify that the God of Abraham, Isaac, and Jacob was the only God. There was no other. He was the only one who could take something that was unusable and transform it into a fully functional world for humankind. He did so because he loved the people that he created.

The central message that the authors of the biblical narrative of creation presented is the nature of one God, the Creator of the heavens and the earth. The biblical description of creation asserts that the God of Abraham, Isaac, and Jacob is the Creator of all that exists, and he loves his creation selflessly. Before he began creating anything, the Creator decided that he would create humankind in the fullness of time. God, the Creator, loved humankind. Therefore, he made it in his image.

He also determined before creating the universe that the humanity that he loved would reside in comfort, beauty, and functionality which was beyond the human ability to secure. The one and only God, the

Creator, made everything that humankind might want, admire, and enjoy. Humankind did not have to supply food and comfort for the biblical God, the Creator, as the ancient epics claims.

The only thing that God, the Creator, required from the people was their loyalty. Our loyalty to God is the only way that we can have a successful eternity. Our life is from God, and we live in him. Apart from him, humankind could not exist. This treatise will address the fact that humanity did not honor its purpose.

The ancient-time creation epics, such as the *Enuma Elish*, present a view concerning gods that is in stark contrast to the biblical-creation narrative. The ancient and polytheistic creation legends assert that gods created the heavens and the earth as their residences. They made the earth a place where they could grow food. The Mesopotamian gods, however, desired services, and adoration. In time, however, the ancient nations' gods concluded that they should not labor for their own needs, so they made people as their slave laborers.

The ancient epics present gods who created comfort for themselves instead of the people who served them. They made the people supply housing, food, and all the support that the gods might need. The people had to pamper their gods. They believed that with excellent service and adoration, they would influence their gods to bless and protect them. The people always had to satisfy their gods to secure their blessing and protection. However, it often did not work.

In ancient time, the people wanted their gods to reside among them. If their gods were among them, the people thought, they could provide for their god's needs with less effort and more appropriately. So, they built temples for their gods in their communities. People invested much of their time and means to satisfy their imaginary gods' needs. They believed that if they pampered their gods, their gods would have a vested interest in protecting and blessing them. Such a practice resulted in many gods, and different religious orders, and traditions.

In ancient time, the people had to love their gods who did not love them in return but punished them whenever they felt like doing it. The gods of ancient-time's people were always guided by their feelings. Today, one often wonders how things have changed.

In contrast, the God of Abraham, Isaac, and Jacob always loved his people, even though they rebelled against him and often went their ways. He created them because he loved them. The biblical-creation narrative presents a benevolent God, the Creator, who cares for his creation.

Through his prophets, God reminded his people that he loves them forever.

> The LORD appeared to us in the past, saying: "I have loved you with an everlasting love; I have drawn you with unfailing kindness." (Jeremiah 31:3 NIV)

The biblical account of creation distinguishes itself from the other ancient epics by presenting a God who is intimately involved with his people at their level. The biblical-creation narrative's central message conveys the awe-inspiring majesty and unchallengeable sovereignty of the God of Israel.

For the authors of the biblical-creation narrative, the God of Abraham, Isaac, and Jacob is the Creator of the orderly and functional dwelling for the humankind that he loves. Therefore, he is the rightful owner and ruler of all creation. The biblical description of the creative activity assures its readers that their awesome God is the Creator of all that exists. The biblical Creator loves and cares for all his creation. The ancient creation epics do not and could not make such a claim.

2

Creation according to Biblical Cosmology

FIRST, THIS TREATISE on creation addresses the message embedded in the biblical-creation account. It addresses the contrast between the biblical and ancient Mesopotamian creation epics, mainly the *Enuma Elish*.

Next, this treatise considers the distinction between the ancient-time epics and biblical accounts of creation. Even though the biblical narrative displays an affinity to the ancient epics of creation, the Creator that they present is different. The biblical narrative of creation presents God, the Creator, as the only one who could have created order and functionality out of disorder. It emphasizes that the God of Israel created all that exists because he loved humankind and wanted it to have everything it needed for an enjoyable life with him. However, the ancient-time creation epics present gods who collaborated on creating a residence for themselves and then created the people to serve them as slaves.

The readers and students of the biblical narrative of creation week should not read it while employing modern-day literary tools. The authors of the biblical narrative and the ancient epics alike did not have knowledge concerning the rules associated with modern literature. To apply modern-day rules and methods to a critical analysis of ancient writings does not contribute to the best possible understanding. Readers and students of ancient-time writings concerning the world's creation—the biblical narrative included—should place themselves in the ancient-time writer's place. They should aim to understand how and what the authors of the biblical and ancient epics understood, to bring out the probable message contained within them.

The ancient-day cosmology had a narrow scope and lacked a broad-based observation. In ancient time, people did not possess the means and technology to properly study the universe and the world. They relied on a limited worldview, which was biased by local experiences and observations. We should not fault them for presenting the subject of creation in the way that they did. They presented it in the best way available to them.

Accordingly, the author of this treatise will present the biblical narrative concerning creation with an ancient worldview in mind. Likewise, these treatises will present the modern-day worldview as is and without bias. The message concerning the Creator and not the mechanics of creation is the aim of this treatise.

The ancient-time creation epic concentrates on the creation of function and not the material aspects of the world. The biblical-creation account alludes to the material universe and includes the chronology of events concerning functional Earth's creation. The ancient worldview employed by the authors of the biblical narrative of creation displays a tension between it and the worldview supported by quantum cosmology (This will be addressed later).

Therefore, the readers of the biblical narrative of creation would benefit more by concentrating on who created all that exists and not on how the Creator accomplished it. Concentration on mechanics and chronology tends to cloud the understanding. We do not serve our God, the Creator, by infusing modern-day knowledge about our universe into the biblical narrative of creation. Likewise, to insist that the biblical account of creation is an exact description of the creation's events raises credibility issues.

Our universe displays the most excellent majesty, knowledge, and power of our Creator. Modern quantum cosmology cannot and does not dispute it. As presented in the biblical account, the mechanics and the chronology of the creation events do not contain enough detail to help an in-depth understanding. It is not wrong to discuss the mechanics and chronology of creation. However, the readers should not treat it as doctrine.

Reading the biblical-creation narrative with rigid literalism presents tension with modern-day observations and knowledge. Such tension is not beneficial.

Modern-day study of our universe employs the most advanced instruments and methods. We see our universe as it actually is now. Our universe has not changed from what it has been in the time when authors wrote the biblical account. Modern study and observations do not support such a rigid view concerning the creation. However, as stated earlier, we must trust the Creator. God, the Creator, made our universe as we see it today; therefore, we must avoid holding biblical narrative as a dogma.

The biblical-creation narrative departs from the ancient-time epics by presenting the seven-day-creation week. The authors of the biblical-creation narrative did not say the reason that they did it. As stated earlier, the biblical-creation narrative does not claim a divine revelation. Therefore, the biblical-creation narrative authors may have based their description on prior knowledge or tradition, which they chose not to reveal. However, students of the Bible must accept the seven-day creation week. Seven-day-creation is important because it relates to the re-creation of humankind.

While modern-day science could not prove the seven-day-creation week; however, it does not negate it either. God did not need six days to create Earth's functionality. The Creator had the power and knowledge to create everything that exists by a single command instantly. The readers and students of the biblical-creation narrative should avoid conclusions based on anthropic nature and characteristics. God, the Creator, does not need to see a process. God creates by a decision and command and not by following the order of steps.

Why did the Creator choose six days of creation followed by a day of his rest? We do not know, and we cannot know it at this time in our history? We must accept it by faith and trust God. He knows what he is doing.

The biblical-creation account does not state that the day of the Creator's rest was the same as the days of creation. The Creator did not return to his creative activity concerning Earth because everything that was needed for humankind had been done. Therefore, his rest is eternal. Because God's rest is forever, the authors of the biblical-creation account did not say, "And there was evening, and there was morning the seventh day," as they did for other days. The day of God's rest is a twenty-four-hour day. However, his rest is forever.

The readers of the biblical-creation narrative would benefit by contemplating the significance and the meaning of God's rest rather than on the human need for rest from physical labor. The Sabbath rest that we are to seek is in the Lord.

> Truly my soul finds rest in God; my salvation comes from
> him. (Psalm 62:1 NIV)

Jesus told us, "Come to me, all you who are weary and burdened, and I will give you rest." (Mathew 11:28 NIV) Therefore, the seventh day of the creation week honors God's rest. Those who honor it visibly testify that they are resting in the Lord. Their physical rest is incomplete and temporary. People only pause from their labor, but they do not rest. However, our rest in the Lord must be permanent.

The six days of creation followed by the Creator's rest do not present tension with the quantum cosmology. It is a matter of preference and belief. Because the planet earth has experienced violent geologic upheaval, much of the information concerning its origin, structure, and function was lost and it is irrecoverable. Earth's current geologic composition and shape do not supply sufficient and exact information to describe creation's mechanics and methods. The geologic formation of the planet earth cannot supply the information necessary to address the chronology and the way that the Creator accomplished it. Earth's current shape and appearance do not reflect the way it was during the six-day creation and before the flood. It has changed significantly since the creation week.

Ancient-time cosmology held that the Earth was in the center of God's dominion. The heavens and the Earth made up God's dominion, the ancient times people believed. In ancient times, people believed that they and the earth were the only object of God's attention. They understood that no other populated world existed.

As ancient times people understood it, Earth was a circular disk that floated on the water that was underground. They did not define what supported the underground water. They did not know. Over the earth was a dome or the sky. The people believed that the Creator attached the sun, the moon, and the stars to the inside of the dome, or the sky.

Above the dome, the people believed that there was a large body of water because the sky appeared blue. They perceived that water on earth appeared blue. This perception led them to believe that was water above because it was blue. The people did not know why the sky was blue. They did not know that above the surface of the Earth, there was an atmosphere. They took for granted the air they breathe. They did not know they breathed air.

The people believed that above the water, there was a solid surface, which separated God's residence from the water below. Both the biblical account of creation and ancient-time cosmology placed God above the dome. Polytheistic peoples believed that the gods lived above the water. People also believed that Gods descended to the Earth through a gate in heaven. Heaven was attached to the planet's four corners to hold it up like a tent. The ancient-time people did not define how could the flat circle of the earth also have four corners.

Both ancient-times and biblical cosmology considered the planet earth as the only inhabited place outside of heaven. In biblical time, the people believed that the sun, moon, and stars orbited the earth. This concept persisted until a few centuries ago.

The ancient time's people thought that the Earth was a substantial part of God's kingdom. The heavenly beings, therefore, directed all their actions toward the Earth. There was no other place where God and the heavenly beings could go outside of heaven. They believed that God's throne was located somewhere in heaven.

However, God, through the prophet Isaiah said, "Heaven is my throne, and the earth is My footstool" (Isaiah 66:1). The entire heaven is God's throne, and the planet earth is where his feet rest. Therefore, heaven and the Earth are a unified whole, as asserted by ancient cosmology. Most of the knowledge about our universe has been obtained within the last four decades. We live in a privileged time of humankind.

The authors of the biblical account of creation could not see our universe as we observe it today. They did not know that a universe of size and complexity like ours existed. The universe that we observe today would have appeared strange for the people in ancient times. They based their descriptions on the knowledge they and their society had in their time. Therefore, the readers of the biblical-creation narrative should not infuse modern-day science and knowledge into it. Humankind today knows more about our universe than it knew in its history.

Modern science discovered the laws that order the universe. Humans did not invent the laws that order our universe. Modern-day knowledge stems from advanced observations, analyses, and simulations. The ancient time's people did not have the tools that are available to us. Our observation of the order and functionality of our universe does not fit ancient-time cosmology. Likewise, we could not modify ancient-time cosmology to fit modern-day observations. We would benefit by considering the current worldview which is supported by the observational evidence, when describing the Creator of our universe and humankind.

Neither ancient time nor modern-day people could understand the things that happened before the creation of humankind. Our brain cannot process the events that occurred before the creation of humanity. The sixth day of creation week is when human history began. What happened before the sixth day is a period apart from humankind's history. Someone must describe it precisely and in sufficient detail. However, even when explained the human brain could not process the mechanics of the creation that occurred before the creation week's sixth day. Conclusions concerning the things that transpired before the sixth day of creation are, by nature, speculative.

Moreover, the mechanics and sequence of functional Earth and humankind's creation do not have a salvific purpose. A correct understanding of the mechanics and sequence of creation is not imperative. Our salvation was accomplished through the body of Jesus Christ, not through the creation narrative.

As stated earlier, modern-day cosmology does not dispute the six-day creation week. The question of the reason for six-days persists. As described in the biblical-creation narrative, the six-day-creation sequence raises questions when reading it with rigid literalism. The conflict arises because the authors of the biblical-creation account based it on the limited ancient cosmology. Modern-day readers of the biblical account of creation should be aware that the authors relied on ancient cosmology and how the people in ancient times understood the world around them.

How did the authors of the biblical creation narrative think? What and how did they understand the world? What could they understand? These should be the criteria when reading the biblical creation narrative. Presenting the biblical account of creation as modern cosmology creates doubt as to its correctness and credibility.

A proper reading of both the biblical account concerning the creation and modern-day-cosmological description relative to creation avoids most tensions. However, the best practice is to read and consider the message embedded in the biblical account of creation. The biblical narrative tells us that the one and only God created it all. Moreover, as stated earlier, this is the central message that we should get from the biblical account concerning the six-day creation week. God, the Creator, loves us. Concentration on the mechanics concerning the six-day creation infused with modern-day scientific worldview does not improve humanity's understanding of our universe and creation.

The authors of the biblical-creation narrative described the mechanics and sequence of creation as seen from the earth's surface. They did not have the means to see it another way or from different angle. Therefore, they presented the narrative in the best way they could within the limits of ancient-time cosmology and knowledge. The sequence of events associated with the biblical-creation narrative does not match what we observe today. However, modern-day cosmology and the biblical-creation narrative agree concerning the origin of our universe. Both assert that our universe began by creation from nothing.

The tension may arise from conclusions concerning what came into existence from nothing. Also, what is 'nothing'? Both the biblical account of creation and quantum cosmology point out that our universe began under law that was different from the laws that govern our universe. Humankind cannot access the information concerning the law that governed before the initiation of our universe. Therefore, the beginning of our universe occurred outside of our universal sphere. A set of things to consider, which are aimed to mitigate the perceived conflict, will be presented later.

The biblical creation account addresses the Earth's function rather than the material aspect of our universe. Neither the biblical nor ancient narratives address the particles, atoms, and molecules of matter relative to our universe. They assume that matter itself existed without saying whether it had a beginning. Also, neither the biblical nor ancient narratives define the concept of something coming into existence from nothing.

What does it mean? What is existence? Readers of the biblical-creation account feel the need to supply an answer. However, we do not have reliable knowledge to find an answer. Is such an answer essential, the readers must conclude for themselves? The biblical account of the creation activity presents the nonfunctional earth before the act of creation that transforms it into a suitable and enjoyable dwelling for humankind.

The authors of the biblical-creation narrative assert that God, whom the Nation of Israel worships, is the only one powerful enough to bring something into existence from nothing. He is the only one who has the necessary knowledge that is required for such a creative activity.

> Now the earth was formless and empty, darkness was over
> the surface of the deep, and the Spirit of God was hovering
> over the waters. (Genesis 1:2 NIV)

The authors of the biblical account of creation wrote the account in Genesis in the past tense. They may have believed that Earth existed at the beginning; that is, before the six-day creation began. The authors did not describe the beginning because they believed that something existed before the command "Let there be light" by the Creator.

However, the authors of the biblical account of creation assumed that the formless earth was God's property. They emphasize that the Spirit of God hovered over the waters. By hovering above the water, the Spirit of God signified that the Earth was God's property. However, the planet earth was not yet suitable for the carbon-based intelligent life God determined to put on it. The earth's condition was such that only the God of Israel could transform into a fully functional home for humankind.

Nevertheless, the biblical-creation-narrative authors followed the ancient cosmological concept that something existed before the six-day creation. They describe the invisible, formless, and empty planet Earth. Two forces dominated the formless planet earth: water, and darkness. These two forces were the unconquerable foe for the people living on the Earth in ancient time. These forces opposed the life that the Creator determined to place on Earth. Darkness and Water presented a significant barrier to the people's movement in ancient time. They had to stay close to the place of their residence because of the unconquerable foe.

The people living in ancient times did not have adequate means to overcome the water's obstacles and the darkness. The authors of the biblical-creation narrative viewed the primeval earth as chaos and without order. In the tradition of the ancient Near-East, to say that a deity subdued the chaos was to give him the highest praise. It was so because people living in the ancient world viewed deities to be the same as human beings. Their gods were like people, only more powerful. So, when their gods accomplished something that humans could not do, people would shower them with praise and gifts.

The authors of the biblical account of creation asserted that the God of Abraham, Isaac, and Jacob was the only one who could overcome the evil force of chaos and bring order into existence. In doing so, the authors followed ancient cosmology's concept of the Absolute Being.

> And God said, "Let there be light," and there was light.
> God saw that the light was good, and he separated the
> light from the darkness. (Genesis 1:3–4 NIV)

God began ordering the earth and adding functionality to it by issuing the above command. He first removes the darkness so that that the things he commands into existence will be visible.

The authors of the Hebrew creation narrative relied on a worldview based on ancient time cosmology. Therefore, they employed anthropomorphism in their description of God, the Creator, his creative works, and his interaction with humans. They did not know that the universe we observe today existed. They could not have known it because human knowledge increases at a specific rate, which is established by the Creator. The lack of knowledge about things beyond the local horizon does not present the biblical-creation narrative's authors negatively. They did not have the means humankind has today. They could not have possessed the same means we have today. Furthermore, they had limited methods for increasing the knowledge.

The authors of biblical account of the creation week continued by describing the sequence of events associated with Earth's ordering. They described it in conformity with the ancient worldview. Chapter two of Genesis presents another view of the activities that are related to the six-day creation. The authors did not have other means by which to explain it. However, to their credit, they upheld God's unmatched power, knowledge, and majesty. The authors held on to the message that only the God of Abraham, Isaac, and Jacob, by his supreme power, that could have transform the formless and useless Earth into the most proper residence for humankind.

The biblical creation narrative concludes with God making the man, the humanity, in his image.

> So God created mankind in his own image, in the image
> of God he created them; male and female he created them.
> (Genesis 1:27 NIV)

Making the man was the climax of the six-day creation week. God did not command humankind into existence by saying, "Let there be man," He made a man from the earth's dust. The authors of the biblical-creation narrative did not consider man as an ordinary creation. God gave spirit, the intelligence, to man; therefore, man is in his image. The man was in God's image. Therefore, the creation of humankind is the crowning act of the six-day of the creation week.

> Then the LORD God formed a man from the dust of the
> ground and breathed into his nostrils the breath of life,
> and the man became a living being. (Genesis 2:7 NIV)

The breath of life is the spirit of humankind.

> The Spirit gives life; the flesh counts for nothing. (John
> 6:63 NIV)

God gave one spirit to the entire humanity in the first man Adam.

3

Creation according to Quantum Cosmology

QUANTUM COSMOLOGY CONCERNS with creation of our universe and not the Earth's functionality. The key point it presents is that our universe is by creation from nothing. The concept concerning the human *intelligence* in quantum cosmology, and human *spirit* in the Bible, are the same. The Creator gave the spirit to humankind. He did not make it from matter. Therefore, human intelligence (or human spirit) is not subject to the physical laws that governs our universe. However, it is subject to the law of intelligence. All humans have the same intelligence (same spirit) but different experiences and knowledge.

Human intelligence does not vary with time; however, human knowledge and the things that they experience vary among individual members of humanity. Human knowledge increases with time; however, it does not make humans more intelligent. An increase in knowledge only alters the things that humans experience. God gave one intelligence (spirit) to all humankind and not to everyone separately. The spirit (or intelligence) is the element that makes humankind in the image of God. Human beings process the information by a system of logic which is ordained by God. God is Spirit; therefore, he gave the spirit (intelligence) to humankind as its identity. The Final Observer in quantum cosmology and God in the Bible are the same.

Difficulty with the above assertion arises from the classical worldview. For centuries, humans maintained that the reality in which we live is local. Such an assertion implies that humans living in different localities on the planet earth live in separate realities. If so, then people in each local region would have different human intelligence (spirit). If it were so, more than one Savior would be necessary.

However, the discovery of quantum mechanics theory began to change our understanding of reality. Reality experiments in quantum cosmology have demonstrated that our reality is universal. The universality of reality applies to our whole universe, not only Earth. Universal reality implies that all humans have the same intelligence. They have the same spirit. Human spirit resides in human mind. The human mind is inextricably tied to our universe. They are inseparable because they are made of same matter. Therefore, the biblical assertion that God created all of humankind in one man (Adam) is correct. All human beings inherit their human nature from the first man (Adam).

As stated earlier, the readers of the biblical-creation narrative should consider the limits of ancient-time cosmology. In the present, humankind has limitations, of which we should be aware of always. The worldview based on the limited ancient-time cosmology needed the sequence of events that associated with the planet's ordering and making it suitable for humankind.

Modern-day knowledge about our universe is much higher than what the people in ancient time had. The knowledge we have acquired about our universe within the last four decades is much more than humankind had in its history.

The current worldview, enabled by quantum physics and quantum cosmology, does not reconcile with the worldview held by the authors of the biblical and ancient-time's accounts of the creation. The six-day creation itself is not in a particular dispute. It must be accepted individually. However, the mechanics of events associated with the six-day creation present a logical conflict with the current knowledge, which is based on observation. Nevertheless, the concept that is relative to the Absolute Intelligence, God, does not represent a significant conflict.

21

The conflict between science and theology centers on the nature of the Absolute Spirit (Intelligence). Quantum cosmology's concept of the Absolute, the Creator, is in more significant terms than the modern-day Christian concept. The biblical account of the creation week and quantum cosmology agree that our universe has been created from nothing. The ancient-day author declared, "The heavens declare the glory of God" (Psalm 19:1). The glory of God is his selfless love. The knowledge that humankind gained about our universe within the last four decades leads modern-day experts to conclude that our universe's very foundation is agape (selfless love). This development raised the question "Why?" What leads some of the modern-day experts to such a conclusion? These questions will be explored, in brief, in the remainder of this chapter.

In most cases, the students of the Bible read the biblical account of creation with strict literalism. They concentrate on the sequence of events and the mechanics of the creation account. The series of events and the mechanics of creation as presented in the biblical narrative reflect the ancient worldview. Only such a view was possible in biblical time. The authors of the biblical account of creation did not insist that the sequence of events and the order associated with the creation week are invariant. The authors of the book of Genesis employed varied ways to present the same message.

Christians should avoid the use of human analogy when describing God, the Creator. Humans should never view God as a physical Being, who has physical properties, or employs physical activity to create things. The biblical creation-narrative states, "God said" or "God commanded." Therefore, the creation accomplished by God is an intellectual activity. God did not have to exert physical force to create. He commanded, and it was. Such an approach was standard practice in ancient days. Biblical-narrative's authors often used a metaphor, metonym, or allegory to convey their message. The limitations of ancient cosmology resulted in a lack of detail. The authors of the biblical account of creation did not have another choice.

Christians should read the biblical account of creation to learn about the Person who created the universe and brought order to the planet Earth, and not the way that the Creator accomplished it. The Bible asserts, and science confirms, that the Creator has all knowledge about our universe.

The Creator had to have all knowledge about our universe before he created it. All events that have occurred, and will ever occur in our universe were a reality in God's mind before he created the universe. The very fabric of our universe affirms the need for an all-knowing creator. Without him, the universe would not exist. The Creator must observe our universe as a concrete reality continuously. If not, the universe would cease to exist instantly. This message should be the guiding principle when reading the biblical account of the creation week.

Both the Bible and modern-day science lead us toward the common ground when we read them with an open mind. Here science refers to quantum cosmology, quantum physics, and the anthropic cosmological principles. This treatise proposes things to consider which could be useful for Bible and modern-day science readers. This author found these to be useful. Following these minimizes the conflict and in some cases, eliminates it. These are the recommendations by this author. Not all Christian thinkers will agree with it.

Things to Consider

The Ultimate Intelligence Referred to in Quantum Physics and Cosmology and the Final Observer Referred to in Anthropic Cosmological Principles Are the Same

Some scientists refer to God as the Absolute or Ultimate Intelligence. The scientific definition of the above reveals God's same nature, as it is presented in the Bible. The Judeo-Christian concept concerning the Absolute Being is real. Each of the names above refers to an all-powerful and all-knowing being. Modern-day cosmology seems to imply that an all-knowing intelligence ensures the existence of our universe and humankind in it. Human beings must limit their definition of the Creator's activity to actions related to humankind and our universe only. We are not capable, and it is inappropriate to attribute to the Absolute human ways and methods.

God Established Specific and General Laws Before He Began Creating

God brought our universe into existence following the laws he ordained before creating our universe. Advanced knowledge based on observation lead to such a conclusion. God knew the kind of universe that was suitable for humankind before he created it. The Creator knew all histories and events that concern us and our universe before he initiated it. All humankind's thoughts throughout its history were known to God before he created anything.

> "Can you fathom the mysteries of God? Can you probe
> the limits of the Almighty?" (Job 11:7 NIV)

Those who read the biblical account of creation cannot add an event or a history that God did not know before he created our universe.

The laws that govern our universe are the prerequisite to creation, as ordained by the Creator. The law that ensured the proper beginning of our universe and its internal laws is not in our universe. Therefore, humankind cannot know the nature of the law that is not in our universe.

God, the Final Observer, Does Not Violate, Suspend, or Manipulate the Laws He Established before He Began Creating

Information obtained through advanced study and observation of our universe implies that if God, the Final Observer, were to violate the law that he established before creation, we and our universe would instantly cease to exist forever.

> If it were his intention and he withdrew his spirit and
> breath, all humanity would perish together and mankind
> would return to the dust. (Job 34:14–15 NIV)

God, the Creator, acts in the interest of a successful eternity for his creation not just to show what he can do. God, the Creator, is all-knowing and has all power. However, he is not a show-off. With God, it must be right or not at all. Human beings would do well to adhere to the same principle. The apostle Paul did.

I have the right to do anything, you say—but not everything is beneficial. I have the right to do anything—but not everything is constructive. (1 Corinthians 10:23 NIV)

God, the Final Observer, is Knowledge

God, the Final Observer, does not have to learn anything new because he is knowledge. All knowledge originates with God. He does not learn or experience something new because he is eternal. God is eternal because he has thought an infinite number of thoughts, per the quantum cosmology's perspective. Every possible thought by all created intelligence, and all events in God's dominion are in the absolute present to God. No past and no future; only the eternal present. All existence is in him. Apart from him, nothing could exist. God is eternal because he is timeless. There is no passage of time for him because he created the time.

The Creation of Our Universe and the Carbon-Based Life Are Separate Events

The carbon-based intelligent life must have a suitable-sized universe for it to thrive. The anthropic cosmological principles imply that our universe is the minimum size needed for the beginning of carbon-based intelligent life. The most advanced measurements have determined that our universe is 13.8 billion +/- 200 million light-years in radius. Anthropic principles imply that this is the size of the universe what we precisely need. Such a conclusion may be a subjective one because we are here to see it.

Nevertheless, the cosmological principles imply that the carbon-based intelligent life must arise in just the right universe and at just the right time. Only an all-knowing intelligence could have determined the size and time that would be exactly right for the carbon-based intelligent life. An all-knowing intelligence had to determine it before creating the universe. Indications are that humankind lives in the only type of universe where it could prosper. There is no other type of universe that is suitable for humankind.

Accordingly, our universe had to come into existence first, then the galaxies, then the solar systems, and then the planets. Only a planet that was located at exactly right orbit around an exactly right star could support the carbon-based intelligent life. Only a planet that orbits in the habitable zone, around the main-sequence sun, has the necessary characteristics needed for carbon-based intelligent life (humankind).

Suitable conditions for carbon-based intelligent life may be very rare. Earth may be the only planet in our universe suitable for carbon-based intelligent life at this time. Therefore, in just the right time, known to God the Creator only, God prepared the planet Earth for the humankind. He had determined before he created our universe when and where to prepare a planet for the humankind that he would put on it. Only when the new heaven and the new earth come will we know if another planet could be made suitable for humankind.

The Creation of the Universe Is the Creation of Time

God created time in the beginning. Therefore, time is the beginning of the universe. The Bible confirms it.

> By faith we understand that the universe was formed at God's command, so that what is seen was not made out of what was visible. (Hebrews 11:3 NIV)

The New International Version translates the Greek word *aionas* as the *universe*. However, the Greek word's first meaning is an indefinite amount of time, eternity, or ages; therefore, the more accurate translation would be *times* or *ages*. The results of advanced studies and research show that the beginning of our universe is, in fact, the beginning of time. The very beginning of our universe has been initiated in conformity with laws that are not known to humankind. The Absolute Intelligence, the Creator, started our universe's beginning in conformity with laws not known to humankind. Therefore, the beginning of the material universe is the beginning of what humans can study and understand.

Whether time existed before the beginning of our universe, we could not say. Whether or not time (in whatever form) existed before creation could not be determined. Carbon-based intelligent life may never know it. Eternity will tell us all we need to know.

However, God created time; therefore, time may not have an infinite past, only the indefinite future. Time and space are no longer separate characteristics of our universe. In quantum cosmology, *spacetime* is the universe. However, humankind does not know what time and space are. There are no known particles that mediate or carry time and space. The discovery of spacetime's nature of would be a giant leap for humankind. However, it could be also a dangerous leap.

Spacetime Came into Existence by Creating Something from Nothing

The current knowledge concerning the beginning of our universe indicates that the moment of time's creation conforms with the law not known to humankind. Only the Intelligence that had all knowledge about our universe before its creation, could have selected the beginning of spacetime. Therefore, the intelligence that chose the laws which govern spacetime must be outside of the created universe of spacetime.

The universe began with rapid expansion of spacetime which released the pure energy, from which the matter, in the form of the hydrogen atom, came into existence. Our universe is expanding at light's speed. Therefore, the energy it releases must slow down to below the light's speed to generate the hydrogen atoms.

The fusion process inside stars creates all other elements of matter in our universe. The creation of matter from expansion of spacetime continues in conformity to the equivalency of matter and the energy formula presented in the general theory of relativity. Therefore, humans can calculate the quantity of matter created out of energy by employing the same formula. Our universe continues to expand at the speed of light, based on the best measurements and observation. Therefore, it creates matter from energy continuously.

The continued expansion of spacetime releases pure energy, which becomes mater in the form of a hydrogen atom. The observed matter's estimated density and the rate of expansion in our universe are known. Therefore, scientists can calculate the rate of continuous creation of matter.

The expansion of the universe creates a significant amount of matter from energy continuously. Therefore, based on what we know about our universe, the matter is not from nothing but energy. The energy is from the expansion of spacetime. Spacetime is by creation from nothing. The expansion of spacetime releases pure energy. The expansion of spacetime comes from nothing and is expanding into nothing. Humankind cannot yet define nothing from which spacetime expands. However, the nothing does not imply vacuum. Nevertheless, our universe continues to grow at the rate that is suitable for carbon-based intelligent life.

The Creator made biological life and humankind out of the matter, which existed before the first day of the creation week, as shown by the six-day creation account. The creation week did not happen at the very beginning of the spacetime's universe. The six-day creation week became effective at just the right time and at a place the Creator determined before creating our universe. We cannot conclude biblically or by science, that our universe was created on the first day of the six-day creation week.

Also, there is neither biblical nor extrabiblical assertion that our universe's creation was concurrent with creating Earth. Likewise, there is no biblical support for the conclusion that the creation of the Earth and its functionality were concurrent during the seven-day creation week. Both Bible and ancient epics conclude that Earth existed before the command, "Let there be light."

Humankind Is a Unique Order of Intelligence (Spirit) Living In a Unique Universe

No created intelligence is like us, and no universe is like ours. The possibility exists there is an infinite number of created orders of intelligence. However, human beings could not know anything about them because they are different intelligences inhabiting homes designed for them. We could neither conclude nor theorize whether diverse created orders of intelligence inhabit regions outside heaven. Also, we could not conclude that other created orders of intelligence have a material form.

The Bible and ancient epics speak of the existence of various orders of angels. Jesus spoke of angels; however, he did not speak about other orders of created intelligence inhabiting regions outside heaven. If they exist, they must have a home suitable for them. Therefore, we cannot deny the probability that varied inhabited regions outside of heaven exist. Other created orders of intelligent life could not reside in our universe. It is a certainty that we are a unique order of intelligence, that is unlike no other.

Human beings should not even attempt to describe the various orders of intelligence. Current knowledge about our universe indicates that humankind can only live in this universe and no another. We are the only created beings inhabiting the universe of spacetime and matter. Based on our limited understanding of intelligence law, multiple orders of intelligence sharing the same habitable region would violate intelligence law. Influence among separate orders of intelligent beings is not allowed in our universe. Also, intelligent influences among human individuals, here on Earth, violate the law of intelligence. However, we are not alone. God is with us here, now, and always because he is Sovereign.

Humankind Was Made in the Image of God, the Final Observer; However, God, the Creator, is Not In the Image of Man

All created orders of intelligence are made in the image of the Creator. However, he is not in the image of any of the created orders of intelligence. God, the Final Observer, is the Absolute Spirit (Intelligence). Therefore, he can take the form of all created intelligence simultaneously, and yet at the same time, he is not in the form of any of them.

As said earlier in this chapter, our spirit (our intelligence) is from God. Thus, we are made in his image. However, we are not an absolute order of intelligence. We have our limitations. God, however, is not limited. To attribute to God a physical form and location within the universe of spacetime and matter is highly inappropriate. Created human beings should be careful of how and what they say about God, the Creator, and what they attribute to him.

All Humans Are a Single Order of Spirit (Intelligence)

At the creation, God gave the whole of humankind one spirit in the first man Adam. The advanced experiments and study in quantum physics imply that all human beings have the same intelligence (the same spirit).

The difference among humans is the knowledge and experience, that individual members of humankind acquire.

The spirit (intelligence) of humanity cannot increase, decrease, or change because spirit is not made of matter. Human intelligence does not vary. Our intelligence cannot be accurately measured by material means because our intelligence is not from matter. Knowledge does not make one intelligent, regardless of how much one learns. Intelligence acquires knowledge; however, the knowledge cannot obtain intelligence. Human intelligence determines how humans apply their knowledge. The spirit, or intelligence, is from God; the knowledge is by human effort.

With God, the End Does Not Justify the Means

In his actions, God does not rely on feelings. He is the Absolute Spirit. The Spirit is not made of matter. Therefore, we must not describe it in the form of physical manifestation. Human emotions are chemistry made of matter; therefore, feelings are a human characteristic that we cannot attribute to any other intelligence.

God acts at just the right time, which is known to him only and is in conformity to the plans he made before his creation. He always acts in the best interest of his creation because he loves it. God works in ways that guaranty a successful eternity and not the preferred present of expediency. The Creator always acts in way that is best for his Creation.

The Implications in Quantum Cosmology

The theological implications in quantum cosmology are astounding. They are unprecedented. This treatise will not address information and research in geology because of questions that are relative to the reliability and the sufficiency of data.

Earth has experienced a violent geologic upheaval in recent history. The violent geologic upheaval altered the earth's equilibrium.

In contrast, our universe is still made of the same composition and function as when it came out of the hands of the Creator. Humankind's deliberate intelligent decision in Eden impacted Earth; however, it did not alter the universe. Our decision in Eden subjected biological nature to decay. However, it did not change the nature of our universe. Accordingly, our universe and the planet earth wait with longing for the day when the consequences, which resulted from the human decision in the Garden of Eden, will no longer exist.

For the creation waits in eager expectation for the children of God to be revealed. We know that the whole creation has been groaning as in the pains of childbirth right up to the present time. (Romans 8:19, 22 NIV)

Certainly, theology and quantum cosmology cannot always agree. However, theologians and scientists can learn and gain insight from each other. Both, however, should be aware of the specific role each plays. Science cannot dictate theology, and theology cannot shape the meaning of scientific discovery.

The readers of science and theology should concentrate on various references to God, the Creator, and the creation. However, quantum physics, theology, and philosophy cannot describe the God's nature. Vocabularies of all created intelligence put together would not provide enough adequate words to describe the Creator. Human beings would do excellent service to God by restricting the scope of their imaginary description of him.

The results of scientific study concerning our universe compel scientists to consider the possibility that the Judeo-Christian concept concerning the Absolute Being is correct. What cosmologists conclude concerning the Absolute Being or the Final Observer displays a thought-provoking similarity with the Judeo-Christian concept.

Not all scientists are happy with the implications of the study and experiments. They hope for a desired answer to the puzzling implications in quantum cosmology and anthropic cosmological principles. However, the hoped-for answer did not show itself yet. Accordingly, some scientists admit that our universe is too strange to have a logical human solution. Therefore, they accept the probability that our universe began by creation from nothing and that it is governed by the laws established before the creation.

Why are the scientists reconsidering the traditional scientific position concerning the origin of our universe? For decades, the original big bang theory was the ultimate explanation of the beginning of our universe. However, the advanced simulations of the beginning of our universe identified a critical weakness in the original big bang theory. Scientists did not possess the means to evaluate the original big bang at its introduction. The original method could not create accurate image of the universe that we observe. Also, part of the problem was classical science's assertion that our universe is static. Famous scientist Einstein believed so, possibly because of his upbringing.

However, more advanced studies and observations confirmed that our universe is not static as originally believed. Advanced astronomical instruments confirmed that our universe is expanding at a phenomenal speed. The observations at various wavelengths of light confirmed that our universe is expanding at the speed of light; that is180,000 miles per second or 300,000 kilometers per second in vacuum.

Ongoing observations and studies indicate the possibility that the expansion of our universe is accelerating. The acceleration of our universe's expansion may be necessary to ensure the predetermined release of energy. Accordingly, scientists conclude that our universe must have started from a small region and grew to the today-observed size.

Initially, the big bang theory appeared successful. Observations of our universe have confirmed some of the predictions made by the original model. However, when scientists, employing advanced computing instruments, analyzed our universe near the first second of its existence, they verified that the primordial explosion of matter could not result in the universe we see today. When scientists tried to analyze and explain what happened in the first 99/100 of a second of the universe's existence, the big bang began to fall apart. It could not account for the observed large-scale structure of our universe. The difficulties associated with the original model compelled scientists to upgrade the original big bang theory. They still call it the big bang model; however, it is a fundamentally different. Still, it is not the best, model of our universe's beginning.

In the search for a better explanation of our universe, scientists turned to grand unified theories. Unified theories explore the possibility of uniting the parts of what we know about the physical world into one set of equations and formulas. Pursuing the unified approach, scientists, successfully resolved some of the original big bang's mathematical obstacles. The new approach could probe much farther back in time than the earlier method could.

Dr. Alan H. Guth, who is currently at the Massachusetts Institute of Technology, proposed a new model of our universe's origin. The new model is called the "inflationary universe theory." It explains the phenomena of nature back to one-tenth of a trillionth of a nonillionth of a second after the initiation of our universe (That is 1×10^{-43} second or number 1 preceded by forty-two zeroes after the universe's origin). The surprising revelation was that the new model postulated that our universe began by creation of spacetime from nothing. The new model is still the best description of our universe's observed phenomena and their extension to a beginning.

According to the new model's logical progression, our universe began with a rapid expansion of spacetime from nothing. This conclusion accords with the biblical statement, "In the beginning God created the universe" (times, ages) (Hebrews 11:3).

We say spacetime because the best studies and analyses available today show that space and time are so inextricably intertwined that they cannot be separated. Space cannot exist without time, and time cannot exist without space. Logical reasoning leads to a reliable conclusion that neither the energy nor the matter could exist in the absence of spacetime. Based on observations, the initial rapid expansion of spacetime has slowed down to the speed of light (300,000 kilometers or 186,000 miles per second. There is an indication, as stated earlier, that the expansion of spacetime may be somewhat accelerating. The possible acceleration is currently under study.

The Creator established laws before the creation of the universe. At the initiation of spacetime expansion, God activated these laws to govern the newly growing universe.

The expansion of spacetime releases pure energy. When the released energy slows down to slightly less than the speed of light, it becomes matter in the form of hydrogen atoms. Hydrogen is the dominant form of matter in our universe. Accordingly, the universe of spacetime and matter is also known as the hydrogen universe. Hydrogen gas, which consists of hydrogen atoms, coalesces under the influence of attraction (gravity) into the galaxies' core.

Matter impacts the spacetime, which could be the cause of observed attraction. In turn, the deformed spacetime determines the way that matter moves. The galaxies' core releases its excess matter, which becomes the arms of a galaxy. Following the laws that the Creator established before creation, galaxies' formation initiates the formation of stars, the Suns. The formation of stars leads to the formation of solar systems and planetary complexes, which are guided by God's planetary law that he established before creating the universe.

In the biblical account of creation, God separated the light from the darkness and established their boundaries. The implication of this act may show that darkness already existed. Suppose we were to apply the creation narrative only to the planet earth's preparation for carbon-based intelligent life. In that case, the existence of darkness before the dictum "Let there be light," is possible. However, if we were to apply the creation from nothing to the entire universe, neither light nor darkness, which are made of matter, existed before the beginning of our universe.

Quantum cosmology and the anthropic cosmological principles imply that neither light nor darkness existed before the Final Observer, God, commanded the universe into existence. The expansion of spacetime released energy, which became matter in the form of hydrogen atoms. The hydrogen atoms fused into helium, which formed the galaxies and stars. The fusion process in the stars released light that filled the entire universe. The Creator created our universe from nothing. Darkness in the universe of spacetime and matter is the shadow that is cast by galactic and solar system bodies. If the galaxies and suns were absent, there would be total darkness. Such a universe would cease to exist.

Through the prophet Isaiah, God indicated that he created both light and darkness.

> "I form the light and create darkness, I bring prosperity
> and create disaster; I, the LORD, do all these things."
> (Isaiah 45:7 NIV)

Whether they have positive or negative nature in human terms, all thoughts had gone through the mind of God before he began his creating activity. God is absolute and sovereign. Therefore, human beings blame him for everything. Some go further and claim that God took what those other gods did and made it better to show them how they should do it. Some even claim that Satan attempted to create a world for himself, but it did not work well, so God corrected it.

However, God, the Creator, did not correct the things that those other deities or heavenly beings did. Everything that exists was created by one and only God, the Creator. He created everything from nothing. He did not correct what some other deity or heavenly beings did. God the Creator is the only One. No intelligent beings existed before him; therefore, nothing could have existed either. God, through the prophet Isaiah, insists.

> "I am the LORD, and there is no other; apart from me there is no God. I will strengthen you, though you have not acknowledged me, so that from the rising sun to the place of its setting people may know there is none besides me. I am the LORD, and there is no other." (Isaiah 45:5–6 NIV)

Anthropic cosmological principles imply that there could be only one Absolute or Final Observer. The existence of more than one absolute intelligence is contrary to the laws that govern our universe.

Only the main-sequence stars, such as our sun, can support a planet suitable for carbon-based, intelligent life; as far as we know. The world's scientists are studying the possibility of other options. The main sequence of stars is the most populous sequence in our universe. A habitable planet must orbit the main-sequence star in the life zone of such a star. Our star's habitable zone encircles the sun at 94 to 95 million miles, approximately, from its center. Furthermore, only one planet can revolve in the life belt of the main-sequence star. Earth orbits the sun in the life or habitable zone.

All events, their sequence, and their order must follow the laws that the Creator established before creating the universe. There are no exceptions. Therefore, the star that supported the planetary system had to be created and fully functioning before the planet Earth could be transformed into a functional place that was suitable for carbon-based intelligent life.

The formation of the solar system guided by the Creator's laws, which were established before creating the universe, presents considerable tension between science and the sequence presented in the six-day creation narrative. However, if we were to consider the possibility that the observer of the six-day creation account found in the biblical narrative observed the sequence of creation while standing on the earth's surface the tension eases.

An intelligent, local observer on the earth's surface and the intelligent, local observer located above the planet would observe the same events but in a different order.

In either case, an intelligent observer must possess sufficient knowledge about the universe of spacetime and matter to accurately describe the mechanics of preparing a planet for intelligent life. If an intelligent observer does not possess sufficient knowledge about the universe of spacetime and matter, he could not accurately describe what he observed. Authors of the biblical narrative did not possess all necessary knowledge about our universe. They could not have possessed it.

Therefore, to describe the preparation of a planet for intelligent life accurately, unintelligent observer must have existed before the solar system was founded. However, humankind was made on the sixth day of the creation week and not before God created the universe and our solar system. Therefore, human description of the sequence of events associated with creating functionality on a planet would be highly limited.

Advances in observation of our universe lead to another surprising implication. A Creator who possesses all possible knowledge about the universe—past, present, and future—must exist. If not, the universe would not exist either. Also, the Final Observer must always have us and our universe in his mind for us to live. If he were to forget us for a fraction of a second, we and our universe would cease to exist.

4

The Fine-Tunned Universe

THE MOST PUZZLING discovery about our universe is the observed critical fine-tuning that has been done on the basic parameters that govern our universe. They appear to be fine-tuned to support the carbon-based intelligent life specifically and exclusively. As stated earlier, God, the Creator, has made our universe, with humankind in mind. Also, indication is that humanity can only function in this universe and no other. Our universe's nature at atomic and subatomic levels shows that only the All-Knowing and All-Powerful Intelligence could have created the universe that we observe today. The biblical Creator is all and only.

Recent advanced observation and analyses concerning our universe indicate overwhelmingly that physics and associated laws exhibit very precise coincidence concerning the requirements necessary for carbon-based intelligent life in it. The puzzling part is that the critical and essential parameters' precision is extremely sensitive to even a minute variation in their value. Some experts object to the conclusion that our universe is showing us that it was created for carbon-based intelligent life and no other. They contend that such a claim is subjective because we, for whom the universe was made, are making such a conclusion. Humankind is the carbon-based life for which our universe was tailored. Therefore, human beings cannot conclude otherwise. Human beings could observe and describe only the essential parameters tailored for them specifically.

What would be the consequence if only one of the essential parameters was slightly different? We cannot answer this question precisely. We cannot answer the above question because the Creator determined the precise values of critical parameters before creating the universe. However, the probability is that the universe and we, who live in it, could not exist ever. The essential parameters with their precise values were selected by an all-knowing intelligence, who was not in our universe. The critical parameters were functioning with now-observed values and precision before our universe's initiation and before humankind's creation. Nevertheless, our universe is showing that it is uniquely suitable for humankind and no one else.

How did the critical parameters become what they are today exactly? Did a primordial law exist that ordered such suitability? If such a law did function before the creation of our universe, who established the law? Opinions vary, and there are many proposals concerning this subject. Shockingly, even the lack of a natural answer testifies to our universe's uniqueness and its suitability for humankind only. Of course, this claim cannot be verified by an experiment. Even if we could employ the entire observed universe as a laboratory, we could not generate sufficient data to verify the critical parameters' implications. Even if such data were to become available, the human brain could not process it because it originated before human history began.

The Final Observer, the Creator, did not choose the essential parameters' critical values from a set of unknown parameters. The Creator possessed all possible knowledge before he began creating. Therefore, he knew which precise values of the essential parameters were suitable for humankind before creating the universe and humanity. The Creator acted in ways that were beneficial for a successful eternity, our universe and humankind.

The Creator always has an infinite choice. Even so, he chooses what is beneficial for humankind and eternity. When we begin with All-Knowing Creator, the questions concerning our universe's uniqueness become less than incomprehensible.

Six most prominent and critically fine-tuned parameters govern the expansion and operation of our universe. A few other vital parameters that play a significant role in the process of our universe exist. However, the six are cited as extremely critical and essential for our universe's and humankind's existence in it. The implication in the six critical parameters is puzzling. The six critical parameters are not part of any scientific theory. They were not predicted by theory but discovered by scientists who study the universe.

The six essential parameters are mathematically non-dimensional, which means that they do not have units. Therefore, the six critical parameters do not depend on or relate to each other. They do not depend on or relate to any other number or parameter in the universe of spacetime and matter as well. The choice of the value of the six critically tuned parameters is not subject to any law known to humankind. The implication is that the six critical parameters' value had to be selected by the Intelligence, who possessed all knowledge about our universe before creation.

The Six Critical Fine-Tuned Parameters

The Ratio between the Electromagnetic Repulsion and the Gravitational Attraction

All the atoms of matter possess two forces. Their role is related to the atom's stability. They are electromagnetic repulsion and gravitational attraction. An atom consists of protons, neutrons, and electrons. Neutrons do not have an electric charge. Protons, however, have a positive electric charge of one electron volt. Therefore, if there are two or more protons in an atom, they must repel from each other due to electric charge, as the law requires. However, because of their mass, protons are attracted to each other when they are in an atom, due to gravitational effect. Both forces in an atom follow the same law exactly. Because they follow the identical law, one would think their influence is identical. This interaction among protons is the same regardless of the distance between them.

The puzzling fact is that the electromagnetic repulsion force is much stronger than the gravitational attraction, and yet, the atoms are stable. Since the repulsive force is stronger than the gravitational attraction, the atom should fall apart, as logic maintains. However, the atoms of the matter remain stable regardless of how many protons there are in the atom. No one can, within acceptable confidence, explain this phenomenon.

The puzzling implication is that, if the ratio between two forces in the atoms was smaller by a minute value, the universe would not have had developed into a universe that we observe. The resulting universe would be too small and would have a short life. Such a universe could not support carbon-based intelligent life and any other life. Minute additions or subtractions to this ratio would ensure that the universe of spacetime would not exist as we observe it. The unavoidable conclusion is that humankind could not live in a universe different from ours, even in the smallest amount.

The Efficiency of the Fusion Process in Stars

The stars in our universe function as nuclear-fusion reactors. They fuse two hydrogen atoms into one atom of helium. The hydrogen atom is the simplest one in the universe. Helium is the next simplest atom. However, carbon-based, intelligent life could not thrive in our universe without these two simple atoms.

Nuclear fusion in stars supplies the necessary energy to support carbon-based life. Only the main sequence stars, like our sun, support the carbon-based intelligent life in our universe. Intelligent life in our universe desires long-range survival. The stars provide essential energy for long life. A puzzling phenomenon in our universe is the level of efficiency of the conversion of hydrogen into helium. In our star, the sun, the efficiency of conversion of hydrogen into helium is much less than one percent. If humankind wants to successfully build a fusion reactor to produce electricity, the reactor will have to operate at greater than 30 percent efficiency to be economical.

Nevertheless, this rate of converting of hydrogen into helium, which is found in the sun, is what ensures the conditions necessary for the long-range survival of carbon-based, intelligent life. This conversion rate is so small that it puzzles observers. They wonder how our star can provide the exact requirements that are essential for humankind. If the fusion efficiency were smaller or greater, the carbon-based biosphere, that humans now experience could not exist. This criticality is true, even if the efficiency varied by a minute amount. Therefore, the carbon-based, intelligent life could not live in such a universe. The efficiency of conversion of hydrogen into helium must remain precisely at the currently observed rate for the sun's entire life to ensure that humankind continues to live on Earth.

Our Universe's Expansion Rate

Our universe must have a precise and deliberately established expansion rate to support the carbon-based intelligent life and it must do so for an indeterminate time. Our universe's kinetic energy must be of precise value to ensure that gravity does not overcome it. If gravity were to overcome the kinetic energy, the universe would collapse into a large black hole. However, no one would be present at such time to observe the result. Our universe must expand at currently observed rate to support the carbon-based intelligent life in it.

The discovery that our universe is expanding led scientists to conclude that our universe would someday collapse under gravity's influence. However, for this to occur, there must be enough matter in our universe. The required density of matter to collapse our universe can be estimated based on our universe's observed size. Based on detailed observations, the best estimates thus far, indicate that the observed density of matter in our universe is much less than the amount that is required to collapse the universe.

The ratio of the observed density of matter to the required density for the universe's collapse is small. The small ratio of matter's observed density to the critical density of matter indicates that our universe will expand indefinitely. The density ratio of the observed to the critical density of matter appears to be tuned to the existence of carbon-based life in our universe. It is critically tuned to humankind.

The rate of creation of new matter from the energy released by the expansion of spacetime is not large enough to change the density ratio. Scientists claim the existence of dark matter (invisible matter). However, the infrared analyses of galaxies in our universe indicate that there is not enough matter, visible and invisible, to make the density ratio equal to the level needed to collapse the universe. Scientific analyses continue. The actual density of matter in the universe should be equal to the required amount for the collapse of our universe. The Creator, the Final Observer, continually ensures that we do not perish. His eye is on us continually!

41

The New Force Is Related to the Expansion of Our Universe

Scientists have recently discovered a parameter or a force related to the expansion of our universe. Some hoped that this discovery might help them with conclusion concerning the envisioned collapse of our universe. The newly discovered force is under study. The new force has been designated as the cosmological constant. However, the cosmological constant's value is exceedingly small, indicating that our universe may expand for an indefinite time. Study shows that additions to this force, whether negative or positive, cancel out at a very high degree of accuracy.

The newly discovered force is so fine-tuned that even one-digit addition, negative or positive, would ensure that our universe would not exist. The highly precise tuning of this force is puzzling. It implies that this parameter's value had to be selected by the All-Knowing Intelligence, the Final Observer, before creating our universe. This parameter's selection conforms to a law that is not known to humankind because it is not in the observed universe. Therefore, the only reliable conclusion is, "In the beginning, God…"

The Required Strength to Break Up Complexes of Stars in Our Universe

This parameter represents the strength of force required to tear apart the structures in our universe, such as galaxies. Massive structures in our universe could not form if this force were smaller. If it were slightly larger, the universe would become turbulent and darker than observed. The resulting conditions could not support carbon-based intelligent life in our universe. Studies of this parameter imply that its value is fine-tuned to the existence of carbon-based intelligent life specifically. This parameter's value was selected before the creation of the universe. The Intelligence who selected it had to possess all possible knowledge about the universe before creation. This requirement indicates that the biblical God, the Creator, made the universe that we observe. He made it for us before he created us because he loves and wants what is best for us.

The Dimensions of Space in Our Universe.

There are three dimensions of space in our universe. They are the height, width, and length. We experience them without realizing how critical they are to our existence in the universe that we observe. Why do we need three dimensions of space and no more or less? There is no answer to this question. We do not know if we will find an answer ever. Our universe indicates that the All-Knowing Intelligence selected the three dimensions of space before creating our universe.

An intelligent choice was made before creation of the universe, and it conforms to laws that are not known to humankind. Therefore, we cannot answer the question of why three dimensions of space are necessary for carbon-based intelligent life. God, the Creator, knows what he is doing. If humanity could observe our universe from the outside, perhaps we could find a solution. Even then, there is a high probability that the only answer that we would receive would be, "A universe made by God."

All we know at this point in our quest is that humankind could not exist in a universe having two or four dimensions of space. Three dimensions of space are critical and essential to our existence. Why is this true? The eternity will reveal the answer.

What Does It Mean?

The fine-tuned parameters, also known as the cosmological coincidences, are the most remarkable discoveries in quantum physics and quantum cosmology. However, the intelligent choice of the critical parameters' values and their role in ordering and guiding our universe's progression cannot be confined to the creation of function concerning the planet earth (the six-day creation). The study's result indicate that the Final Observer has determined the precise value of the basic parameters before creating our universe.

Therefore, they existed before the Creator began preparing the Earth for the carbon-based intelligent life, humankind. The Creator selected the values of the critical parameters before creating the universe. Therefore, their fine-tuning applies both to our universe, the laws, and the process that was in force before creating the universe of spacetime. It is probable that such a fine-tuning might apply to any other spacetime region that obeys the quantum law.

In advance, the Creator, the Final Observer, possessed, all possible knowledge about what he determined to create. Therefore, we must believe that he made the best possible residence for the humankind he loves. The Creator, the Final Observer, determined the precise and specific value of critical parameters that were essential to our universe's existence because he intended to create humankind. In advance, he prepared everything humanity might ever need. Humanity could not live and function in any other kind of universe but the one that we observe. Our mind has been designed for this universe and no other. That is why we can only study the universe we observe.

However, the fine-tuning did not imply that the Creator was limited in the kind of universe he could create. Advanced study indicates that many universes that are different from our universe probability exist and serve their intended purpose. The leading theory concerning the origin of our universe indicates a possibility of a multiverse. Such a complex could contain a very large number of universes within it. All the possible universes in a multiverse do not have to be similar or identical.

The probability exists that support of the carbon-based intelligent life in our universe requires the existence of diverse universes. The possibility of many universes implies that the values of critical parameters that we observe must exist in at least one of many universes in a multiverse. Humankind, in its current state, cannot explore the various possibilities within the Creator's dominion.

Additionally, such a multiverse, if it exists, could be only one of many such complexes in the Creator's dominion. Humankind cannot confirm the existence of other universes because it cannot get outside of its universe. However, the Creator's dominion is infinite, and the possibilities are endless. There is a probability that an infinite number of universes of various compositions exist, whether in a multiverse or not. The Creator's infinite dominion harbors infinite possibilities.

Humankind is a unique order of intelligence that requires a specific kind of universe. Therefore, the limitation applies to humanity and not to the Creator. As stated earlier, each created order of intelligence requires a home (universe) with values particular to their needs.

Our universe appears to be a fortunate one. A very minute variation in any critical parameters' value would result in a different universe or none at all. The fortunate coincidence applies to both our star (the sun) and the Earth. In ongoing search, and employing advanced instrumentation, we have not yet located another star exactly like our sun. The instruments employed are advancing in capability. Humankind may soon obtain more accurate information. The current studies imply that the Creator knew what kind of universe to make, why he wanted to make it, and the purpose he wanted to create it for, before he created it. A universe so chosen must, by nature, be fortunate and strange to human eyes and mind.

The fine-tuning of the universe to our existence invokes unanswerable questions. Why is our universe so unique and lucky? Why did the Creator choose humankind? Scientists continue to explore in the hope of finding a logical, natural answer to the puzzle. However, our universe is not yet yielding an answer. There is no indication that a solution exists. Therefore, students and readers of the biblical account of creation must rely on simple faith in the Creator. He knew what he intended to create and the reason why before he said, "Let there be." The Creator continues to maintain the universe for our benefit even though we do not deserve it. He does so because he loves us. We must wait for the fullness of time to know more.

The lack of an explanation as to the reason that our universe is so fine-tuned to our existence stimulates a greater interest in anthropic cosmological principles' implications. Accordingly, many scientists have realized that our universe is too inexplicably unnatural to have a natural answer to the puzzle of fine-tuning. Therefore, they maintain that the anthropic cosmological principles present the most logical explanation possible concerning the nature of such a fortunate, fine-tuned universe.

These principles led scientists to admit the probability that a Final Observer, the Ultimate Intelligence, existed and that he brought the universe that we observe into existence. As intelligent observers within the universe, human beings do not have other option than to conclude that the universe we observe is made for us only. Also, the implication is that we are created for this universe and no other. The Final Observer willed it. Because quantum mechanics requires an intelligent observers' existence, anthropic cosmological principles help find a link between our universe's properties and the intelligent observers in it. There are three anthropic cosmological principles: the weak, the strong, and the final.

The weak anthropic principle asserts that our universe's specific properties must be of a value necessary to support carbon-based intelligent life. That is why humanity can observe these properties and no others. Our observation of these properties, however, is restricted by the nature of the observer, which is humankind. Our unique nature is we are sinners, biblically speaking; therefore, we are limited in what we can know and understand. The desire to know more cannot be satisfied in our present state. However, the Creator made us with the ability to grow in the knowledge. He, therefore, will restore to us the capability to grow in knowledge of him and his creation. In due time, we will achieve the intended purpose, as the re-created humankind.

The universe must be of a specific size and age to admit the intelligent observer, which is carbon-based life. In like manner, the presence of carbon-based, intelligent life is required for our universe's continued existence. The required correlation between humankind and its universe had to be determined and in place before creating the universe. The surprising implication is that evolution by natural selection could not have happened because the universe is not old enough for a statistical process to come to the desired conclusion.

Because the essential parameters governing our universe are invariant, they are not subject to the mechanism of evolution by natural selection. Also, the human spirit (intelligence) can function in this body only, no other. God gave us our spirit; (intelligence) therefore, it could not have happened within the evolutionary scenario. Also, the theory of evolution by natural selection applies to biological life made of matter. Our spirit (our intelligence) is not made of matter. Therefore, it cannot be subject to natural selection.

The Final Observer, God, selected critically fine-tuned parameters at a specific point before creating the universe. The fine-tuned parameters must remain unchanged for an indefinite time. The critical parameters governing our universe had to be selected once and collectively for all eternity. The critically tuned parameters could not arise due to statistical chance. Their existence and values are the deliberate choice made by the All-Knowing Ultimate Intelligence, once and for all time.

The strong anthropic principle asserts that our universe must have dimensions and properties necessary for the existence of carbon-based intelligent life. Such a requirement has been satisfied because we are here to observe it. Advanced analysis of our universe's background radiation, the echo of creation, shows that our universe is 13.8 billion, +/- 200 million light-years in radius. Our visible universe's radius has been determined recently to an accuracy of 99 percent. Scientists arrived at this determination by detailed analyses of background radiation. A light-year is the distance light travels in one terrestrial year. The echo of creation is observed at a temperature very near absolute zero.

The strong anthropic principle requires that a universe with all necessary laws and parameters must exist. Also, such a universe must be suitable for the insertion of carbon-based intelligent observers. Only one universe out of many could satisfy such a requirement. However, other universes could and perhaps do exist so that our universe can exist in a way that is suitable for intelligent observers. The probability exists that our universe's continued existence and function require other universes where the quantum law functions. If other universes where the quantum law functions exist, they could be explored by humankind. However, humankind must be in the right state for such a task. Humankind, in the present state, could not accomplish such an endeavor. The possibility is there; however, we must wait for the new creation to learn if it is so. Eternity with our God, the Creator, will reveal all that we need to know and understand.

The final anthropic principle states that a universe with all necessary conditions for intelligent observers must come into existence. If so, intelligent processing of information must also come into existence. Once intelligent processing of information comes into existence in a universe such as ours, it shall never cease to exist.

Another interesting implication is that if the intelligent processing of information arises, the moral code (Law) must arise also. Once the moral code arises, it shall never cease to exist. The moral code could be summarized as, "You are free to do as you please; however, you cannot do it at someone else's expense."

For intelligent information processing to continue forever, a required number of thoughts available for processing must exist. It is helpful to differentiate between the *forever* and *eternal*. Eternal means that all time is in the absolute present and that there is no past and future. God is eternal because he is timeless. Past and future infinity of thoughts must have been fully realized by God, and no new thoughts are possible. Eternity is not dependent on time. Forever is dependent on time. This means that *forever* approaches eternity asymptotically, forever and ever, and without becoming eternal. The Creator, the Final Observer, determined that humankind will exist forever before he created our universe.

What Led to the Conclusion that Intelligent Observers Exist?

The primary constituents of matter, such as electrons, possess a dual nature. They display themselves as particles, points of probability, or waves of light. However, the law does not allow one to observe the two displays at the same time. The particles of matter also possess the properties of spin, momentum, position, and electric charge. However, only one of these properties can be observed at a given time and in a laboratory setup. An experimenter must decide in advance which property, he wants to study. For example, if he wants to observe an electron. He must observe it as a point of maximum probability or a wave.

The intelligent observers or the experimenters appear to be an inextricable part of the physical reality that they observe. The standard interpretation of quantum mechanics indicates that intelligent observers are an essential part of physical reality. However, an experimenter in the laboratory can observe into concrete existence a single property of an electron and not the particle itself. A larger system or a Final Observer must observe an electron and the entire universe into concrete existence. The probability exists that the Final Observer (God) must have humankind in his mind continuously for it to exist.

By necessity, this line of reasoning leads to the conclusion that the Final Observer must exist for our universe to be the place that it is. The Final Observer is not in the universe where the quantum law rules. It is highly inappropriate to localize the Creator (the Final Observer) within spacetime and matter. He created spacetime and matter; therefore, he existed before it and apart from it. He existed before all of creation. Human beings should not associate the Creator with any specific physical location. He created all possible physical areas; therefore, he could not be confined to any of them. The Creator existed before regions of any form within his dominion existed, whether physical or not.

The Creator of the universe, the Final Observer, must know everything there is to know about everything that he plans to bring into concrete existence. The Creator possesses all possible knowledge about the universe, whether it will continue endlessly or have a finite purpose. The Final Observer, the Creator, must be all-powerful to accomplish what is necessary for the universe to exist. He must have the universe and the life in it continuously in his thoughts. If not, the universe and the intelligent life in it would perish forever.

Another thought-provoking implication of merging the anthropic cosmological principles with the requirement that an intelligent observer must exist is that the Final Observer loves us. Scientists who study the implications concerning the Final Observer conclude that our universe's very foundation is selfless love. Therefore, it is probable that the Creator, because of his selfless love created the universe, which possesses everything necessary for humankind to live in it. Only the Absolute and Eternal Spirit, the One and Only God, could accomplish a task, which no one else could.

Because our planet has experienced a violent geologic upheaval in recent history, it can no longer support humankind's long-range survival. Experts who study the options and the requirements necessary to ensure humanity's long-term survival are convinced that life on Earth will become challenging if not impossible in another thousand years. Accordingly, experts exploring the options concluded that humankind has no other choice but to explore the universe.

The experts also found that because our universe's very foundation is selfless love, one country, nation, or color could not explore the universe by itself successfully. All of the world's people would have to join in love and explore the universe with selfless aims and goals. Humankind would have to explore the universe beyond our solar system for the common good of humanity and the universe. According to expert assessment, humankind would have to join in selfless love, or there would be no hope for a long-range survival of humanity.

To this end, the experts engaged in analysis of long-range survival requirements concluded that all countries and nations of the world would have to join in exploring our universe. Accordingly, the experts urged the United States to invite the world to Washington, D.C., for a first-ever global congress concerning space exploration. Sixty-seven countries of the world responded and sent their high-level delegation to the worldwide congress. This author was privileged to be able to represent his organization at the first global congress for the exploration of space.

In this author's opinion, the worldwide congress's opening ceremony was the most inspiring worship service ever attended. Several select world dignitaries delivered their speeches, urging the world to join in love. After them, the orchestra played, and the choir sang classical religious themes accompanied by the multi-media projection of the best photographs of our universe that were available at that time. At the end, a deep voice proclaimed, "Together we can stretch our hands and touch the face of God, only if we have love."

For the remainder of the congress and the discussions about the technical challenges, the experts stressed continuously that we must explore space, and that we must do so together in love. Otherwise, the universe would not accept us. Subsequently, the world's technologically advanced countries committed themselves to begin a concept definition of the things that would be necessary to go into interstellar regions. They set a goal of sending a multinational delegation to the Alfa Centauri region, to investigate whether a suitable planet exists. It is estimated that such an undertaking will take fifty years round trip.

The message from our universe brings us back to the message conveyed in the biblical creation narrative. The One and Only God, the Creator of all that exists, prepared this planet, and equipped it with full functionality and everything humankind may need for an enjoyable everlasting life. Then God created humanity. He first made man, Adam, and placed him in the garden, the land of delight. God, the Creator, did it all because he loves humankind and all of his creation.

Accordingly, he urges humanity to enjoy the goodness and the beauty that he provided but do so in selfless love. Other ancient creation epics could not claim such a selfless act. The gods of the ancient peoples always acted in self-interest. However, our universe has a clear message embedded in its fabric, the One and Only God, a God who loves us selflessly, created everything we may ever need. He loves us, and he has us continually in his sight because he wants us to spend an eternity with him in an unmeasurable joy and love. Our universe declares the glory of its Creator. His glory is his selfless love.

SECTION 2

5

The Creation and Fall of Humankind

AS NOTED EARLIER, God created man, humankind, on the sixth day of the creation week. There are two biblical accounts of creation. The first is in Genesis 1:1–2:3. The second in Genesis 2:4–25. The first account implies that God created both the male and the female members of humankind simultaneously on the sixth day of the creation week.

> So God created mankind in his own image, in the image
> of God he created them; male and female he created them.
> (Genesis 1:27 NIV)

The above verse is a general statement without many details. The authors chose not to include detail. Maybe no one can know the details. The second biblical-creation narrative adds more detail. However, it does not specify that God created both man and woman simultaneously on the creation week's sixth day. The apostle Paul references the second biblical account of the man and woman's creation.

> For Adam was formed first, then Eve. (1 Timothy
> 2:13 NIV).

The authors of the second biblical-creation narrative place humankind's creation before the shrub on the earth.

> Now no shrub had yet appeared on the earth and no plant had yet sprung up, for the LORD God had not sent rain on the earth and there was no one to work the ground, but streams came up from the earth and watered the whole surface of the ground. Then the LORD God formed a man from the dust of the ground and breathed into his nostrils the breath of life, and the man became a living being. (Genesis 2:5–7 NIV)

In the second biblical account, the description of the earth's surface appears to conform more to the celestial physics and the planetary law requirements than the first account of the creation. However, both biblical accounts of creation relied on the ancient local cosmology and a limited worldview. In ancient time, people did not have the necessary means and technology to observe the universe and our solar system. They perceived the stars as lights hanging between heaven and the earth. Heaven was attached to the planet earth, forming a limited circle beyond which people could not go.

Therefore, their descriptions of things that are not visible had to be contrasted with things that are visible and familiar. Thus, the readers of the biblical accounts of creation must keep in mind the limitations that people had when they wrote the creation account. We do not have definitive information concerning the details involved with the mechanics and sequence of creating the functionality on the planet earth.

The authors of the second biblical account of creation do not state that God created the male and the female members of humankind simultaneously or even on the same day. We conclude that God created them on the same day, based on the first biblical account of creation. The authors of the second biblical account of creation imply that a method of procreation had to be selected before the creation of the helper for the chosen reproduction mode. The first man, Adam, the representative of humankind, had to decide whether and how he would procreate.

The second biblical creation narrative's implication conforms more to intelligence law, as we understand it today. However, precise information concerning the addition of the female member has not been given. Therefore, we cannot claim the preference for one biblical account over the other. We must accept that God created humankind in the way he determined was best. Search for details and speculating about it is not fruitful.

The second biblical account of creation states that God brought all the land-based animals, and the birds in the sky to the first man Adam "to see what he would call them." (Genesis 2:19 NIV). It implies that the land-based animals and the birds in the sky had a helper for procreation, which Adam observed.

The second biblical account of creation does not say that Adam's observation of animals generated questions in his mind. Did Adam ask God, "Why the animals and birds have a helper, but I do not?" We cannot know. We must accept the things that have been communicated to us. However, the probability exists that Adam's observation of animals contributed to his decision to procreate in the same way—to have a helper with him. Adam, had to choose the method for procreation. Did he have more than one choice? We cannot know it.

> So the man gave names to all the livestock, the birds in
> the sky and all the wild animals. But for Adam no suitable
> helper was found. (Genesis 2:20 NIV)

God knew the thoughts, if any, that passed through the mind of Adam at that moment. God knew those thoughts before he created Adam. However, Adam would have generated those thoughts when he observed the animals and birds, and not before it. We cannot say whether Adam experienced any negative feelings or not because we could not know. However, according to the second biblical creation narrative, God determined that it was not good for Adam to be alone. Adam's intelligent decision following the observation of animals became irrevocable.

> The LORD God said, "It is not good for the man to be alone. I will make a helper suitable for him." (Genesis 2:18 NIV)

The statement, "It is not good for man to be alone," implies that Adam did have thoughts about it. Christians historically discussed and debated the reason that God choose biological procreation (sex) for humankind? They wonder, if there was another way. Our universe's nature does imply that two equally probable choices exist until one of them is selected. (The choice addressed here is for all of humankind. Therefore, it must be made by the representative of humankind.) The biblical account of creation states that God ordained the procreation of humankind. However, the probability exists that Adam, as the representative of humankind, had to choose whether he would procreate and the method of reproduction. God indicated in the blessing he gave to Adam that he determined that humankind should procreate.

> "Be fruitful and increase in number." (Genesis 1:28 NIV)

Therefore, God made man with the capability to procreate. However, the biblical-creation narrative does not say that God initially specified the method of procreation but only that humankind should procreate.

Here too, we do not have information of sufficient detail to make a definitive conclusion. All that we can and must conclude is that all is from God. The Creator knows what he is doing. However, advanced technology has shown that anatomically correct self-learning artificial intelligence machines can be made with self-replication capabilities. The anatomically correct intelligent robots can have and will have the capability to self-replicate. We cannot know whether the same possibility existed in the beginning. Could human beings self-replicate by intelligent decision and choice? We do not know. (Based on what we know about laws that govern our universe, such a capability would not violate the intelligence law.) If such an option existed, it is no longer available. Speculation concerning this matter does not improve our understanding. Discussing this subject is fascinating but not essential.

We do not have sufficient details to conclude whether the Representative of the first humankind, Adam, had a similar choice. The selection of biological procreation may imply that other probable options existed, but they were not suitable for the carbon-based intelligent life. If more than one option was available, the first man Adam was free to choose from any one of them. Adam, as the Representative of humankind, made an intelligent decision, which cannot be reversed. Therefore, any other option could not exist after an intelligent decision was made.

The Second Man, Jesus Christ, the new humankind's Representative, said that biological procreation would not continue after the resurrection.

"At the resurrection people will neither marry nor be given in marriage; they will be like the angels in heaven." (Mathew 22:30 NIV)

Jesus Christ, the Representative of new humankind, did not have a helper with him. Membership in the new humankind is not by biological procreation but by intelligent choice. Biological reproduction belongs to old humanity which sinned; therefore, it does not exist for the new humankind which is created in Jesus Christ. On the cross at Golgotha, Jesus Christ saved the whole of humankind from guilt and punishment for sin. However, membership in the kingdom of God is by an individual decision, and not by a corporate one. It is equally probable that no option for procreation is available for the re-created humankind. This fact leads to the conclusion that being in the kingdom of God does not happen by biological procreation.

Therefore, if anyone is in Christ, the new creation has come: The old has gone, the new is here! (2 Corinthians 5:17 NKJV)

The above addresses individuals, indicating that new birth cannot be corporate but individual. We cannot be born into Christ by biological procreation or by any other option for procreation. To be in Christ requires a deliberate and a willful surrender of self by each believer. God created humankind, and he oversaw its first intelligent activity. Therefore, everything went according to the way that God had determined before creating the universe and humankind in it. We should not add anything to what he gave us in the Scriptures.

Some Christians still believe that the choice of procreation through sex constitutes the original sin. There is no biblical base for such a conclusion. Adam and Eve did not become sinners because of sexual activity but because they disobeyed God's command, "Do not eat the fruit from the tree of knowledge of good and evil." (Genesis 2:16) Adam, made a deliberate and intelligent choice; therefore, if another option for procreation existed, it no longer does. The laws that govern our universe demand it so.

Experiments with subatomic particles, such as photons show that when an intelligent being observes one of the photons' properties, the observed photon must cease to exist for him. This rule is valid for other photons that are present in the group. Also, an intelligent observer could not observe one property of one particle in the group and another property on another particle at the same time. The laws of nature forbid the observation of two or more properties of the same particle and at the same time. Therefore, we can logically conclude that the same rule applies to all intelligent decisions, choices, and observations.

While we could not deduce with certainty that another option for procreation existed, we can be confident that no other possibility exists now. Because of humankind's the biological procreation must cease to exist.

The advanced studies related to the anthropic requirements indicate that our universe must have the intelligent processing of information created for it specifically. For the universe to endure forever, the carbon-based intelligent processing of information must fill the entire universe. The Creator, therefore, created humanity with the ability to procreate, fill the universe, and thus ensure a long-lasting universe. However, if no option for procreation exists for the re-created humankind then God will ensure that all possible requirements are fulfilled. The Bible tells us that nature longs for the children of God to take their God-given role in the universe.

> For the creation waits in eager expectation for the children of God to be revealed. For the creation was subjected to frustration, not by its own choice, but by the will of

the one who subjected it, in hope that the creation itself will be liberated from its bondage to decay and brought into the freedom and glory of the children of God. We know that the whole creation has been groaning as in the pains of childbirth right up to present time. (Romans 8:19–22 NIV)

Yielded believers can be assured that the new humankind will fulfill all the requirements for its eternity with God in the universe he created for it.

We do not have information or revelation concerning whether the first human pair engaged in sexual relations before the fall. Also, such knowledge is not essential for us today. How long did Adam and the woman reside in the Garden of Eden before they sinned? We do not know. By law, they had to gain sufficient knowledge necessary to understand the goal of the enemy of God. God who loves humankind would not keep the first human pair in darkness. The first human pair communed with God in Eden's garden; therefore, it is safe to conclude that he informed them of all they needed to know.

Some may wonder if the presence of the woman before the fall impacted Adam's probability to resist,? If we address it statistically, it may have. However, the biblical-creation narrative shows that the woman's decision did not impact the first human pair. The woman's decision to disobey did not impact the future members of humankind either.

Adam's decision impacted him, Eve, and the whole of humanity. However, Adam was not deceived; he made a willful and deliberate decision. That indicates that Adam probably could have resisted. Adam had sufficient knowledge needed to make a correct decision; therefore, there was no excuse for making the wrong decision. Human beings can do something wrong accidentally. However, sin is not accidental but a deliberate decision.

The Messiah also had to acquire enough knowledge before he had to choose between good and evil.

Therefore the Lord himself will give you a sign: The virgin will conceive and give birth to a son, and will call him

Immanuel. He will be eating curds and honey when he knows enough to reject the wrong and choose the right. For before the boy knows enough to reject the wrong and choose the right, the land of two kings you dread will be laid waste. Isaiah (7:14–16 NIV)

Therefore, sufficient knowledge is required for making an intelligent decision in our universe. This requirement is especially so when the choice is between good and evil. Such a choice is between life and death. It is an extremely critical choice indeed. The same thing is true today. We must read and study the scriptures with the aim not only to know about Jesus Christ but also more importantly, to know him. Our eternal life is in Jesus Christ and him only.

The common understanding Among Christians today is that there will be procreation in the new heaven and the new earth. However, the Second Man Jesus Christ, clearly stated that the saved ones would not procreate. We must wait for his return and the earth's restoration to learn the true meaning of his statements.

"But those who are considered worthy of taking part in the age to come and in the resurrection from the dead will neither marry nor be given in marriage, and they can no longer die; for they are like the angels. They are God's children, since they are children of the resurrection." (Luke 20:35–36 NIV)

Yielded believers are children of God, in Jesus Christ, not by biological birth. The children of God are born again. They are born of Spirit and not of the flesh.

Sinners by nature, must make a willful and deliberate decision to deny self and accept the life of Jesus Christ. Only then, they can become a member of the new humankind and be in the kingdom of God (Jesus Christ). Jesus Christ is the Kingdom of God. John the Baptist proclaimed, "Repent, for the kingdom of heaven has come near" (Mathew 3:1 NIV). Jesus said, "The kingdom of God is in your midst" (Luke 17:20 – 21 NIV). In your midst also means among you.

Possibilities and probabilities are essential to the operation of our universe. Advanced studies about our universe indicate that it was created for carbon-based intelligent life only. The intelligent processing of information in our universe requires deliberate, intelligent decisions and choices. Carbon-based intelligent life processes information by employing the statistical process, which relies on possibilities and probabilities. Therefore, carbon-based intelligent life must make intelligent choices and decisions.

There is indication that intelligent decisions and choices must be made in our universe, even in our current enfeebled condition and state. The reason for this has not been revealed to us. However, we could infer that intelligent life must choose between the two options because the good and evils still exist. The Creator gave humankind the freedom to choose, and it should exercise it. However, we must realize that while we have infinite freedom to choose, we do not have the freedom of an infinite choice. Right now, we have infinite freedom to choose between life, death, and nothing else. At the renewal of it all, we will have infinite freedom to choose good. Evil will not exist, and no one will remember it.

The Nature of Humankind at Creation

God created humankind good. Everything he created for humanity was also good.

> God saw all that he had made, and it was very good. And there was evening, and there was morning—the sixth day. (Genesis 1:31 NIV)

Humankind was good because God, in Adam, created it in his image. God is good; therefore, all of his Creation is good also. The human spirit, (intelligence) is from God. Accordingly, human beings process information through the God-ordained system of logic. Our spirit is our identity, which is from God.

However, there was another part of humankind at creation that that was in the image of God. It was the same as what God is. The other part of humankind at creation is depicted in the illustration below.

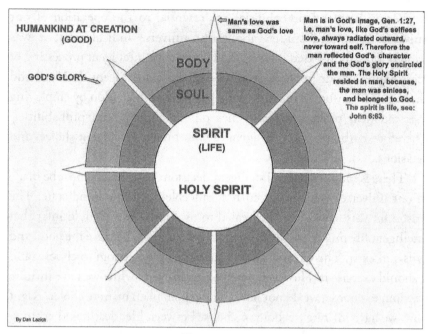

Illustration 1

The illustration does not have an intrinsic significance other than to assist the reader in visualizing humankind's nature at the creation.

At creation, God made the human body from the earth's dust, as the biblical narrative asserts. He did not command the human body into existence but made it. He placed the spirit (life) into the body that he had made. The spirit of humankind is from God. God gave a spirit to humanity. He did not create it in Adam.

The human spirit is not made of matter. We cannot know and we should not speculate whether the spirit has any form of physical existence. The nature of our universe and our physical existence imply that the spirit does not have a purely physical composition. God, the Creator, is Spirit.

"God is spirit, and his worshipers must worship in spirit and truth." (John 4:24 NIV)

The spirit God gave to humankind is our identity and in God's image. Therefore, our spirit like God's is not made of matter.

The Absolute Spirit, as viewed in quantum physics, is an Absolute Being. The Bible presents the Spirit as the Absolute Being. God is Spirit; therefore, the Spirit is God. Because he is absolute, the Spirit could be divided into an infinite number of parts (orders of spirit) while remaining as a single whole, and not losing anything. The Absolute Being cannot lose any part of himself. He remains the same always. Stated, in a quantum sense, the Absolute Spirit is everywhere and nowhere at the same time. This nature of the Spirit means we cannot say anything concerning the state of Absolute nature.

This characteristic concerning the Spirit creates an inviolable limit to what the created intelligence can say about the Absolute Being (God). God is always with us through the Holy Spirit. Physically, God is with us in Jesus Christ forever. Human beings should always be aware of and accept our limits without imposing them on God.

The spirit is our life. Jesus said, "The Spirit gives life; the flesh counts for nothing." (John 6:63 NIV). The human spirit needs the human brain to process information and command the body to execute the decisions by spirit. The human spirit interacts with the world around it through the human body only. When the human spirit commands the body to action, the result is human chemistry or the soul.

The human soul is not given or created. The human soul only reflects the interactions of the human spirit and the body. Also, the human soul demonstrates the invisible but conscionable interactions of spirit and the body. Neither of the two biblical-creation narratives says that the Creator made the human soul. The human soul became, and it demonstrates the living being. Therefore, the human soul results from the human spirit, or human intelligence, acting on the human body. Accordingly, human beings have two natures: the spirit (intelligence) and the biological nature (body, and the soul).

The spirit God gave to humankind in Adam was good because it is from God, and God is good (the central circle in illustration 1). Because the human spirit was good, the Holy Spirit resided in Adam and the woman. The human word "*I*" did not project itself outward in the first human pair. Before the fall, the human spirit was not perfect, not imperfect, but good. However, the human spirit had the freedom to choose between the two options.

63

Whether or not humankind will choose to remain loyal to God or his Enemy remained to be demonstrated. However, the human spirit's ability to select either of the two options did not predispose Adam to choose one option over the other. Adam had unlimited and unrestricted freedom of choice; however, he did not have unlimited choice. He had to decide whether to be loyal to God or the enemy. There was no other option apart from the two choices.

A combination of the two choices does not exist. The choice of good or evil follows a discrete logic. Good is good, and evil is evil, period. We cannot say almost good or almost evil. It is either good or evil. Even if Adam had been able to choose a compromise between good and evil, he would still have become a sinner condemned to eternal death. Any form of compromise between good and evil is evil; and even worse. The abyssal divide between good and evil cannot not be bridged. No force in heaven or on earth, could have overcome the dividing abyss and establish the seamless transition between the two. God-given intelligence works by the either-or logic. Created intelligence, such as humankind, could either do good or evil but not both.

As shown by the arrows in illustration 1, Adam and the woman's love had radiated outward only and never toward self. Because Adam and the woman were good, the Holy Spirit resided in them. They possessed and practiced selfless love, which was the same as God's love. The possession of selfless love was an image of God because God is selfless love.

Adam and the woman were naked, but they did not notice because they did not look at themselves. They loved their Creator and all his creation only.

Adam and his wife were both naked, and they felt no shame. (Genesis 2:25 NIV)

The authors of the biblical-creation narrative emphasized this because it was the most visible evidence that humankind was in God's image. Because they reflected their Creator, the glory of God surrounded them. The glory of God was the clothing of the first human pair in the Garden in Eden. The loss of their clothing (the glory of God) was the most obvious evidence that Adam and the woman had become sinners by nature.

Test of Loyalty to God

God, the Creator, made the planet earth specifically for humankind. The planet earth had everything on it that humanity needed for an enjoyable eternal life. Also, God made various trees that bore good fruit as food for humankind. Adam had it all. However, he made it look like he needed more than God had determined.

> Now the LORD God had planted a garden in the east, in Eden; and there he put the man he had formed. The LORD God made all kinds of trees to grow out of the ground—trees that were pleasing to the eye and good for food. In the middle of the garden were the tree of life and the tree of knowledge of good and evil. (Genesis 2:8–9 NIV)

The existence of the "tree of knowledge of good and evil" indicates that evil existed before God prepared the earth for humankind. We cannot assign time to the origin of evil because God created the time, which is our universe. Therefore, evil could have existed before the creation of time (our universe).

There are two accounts of the origin of evil. One is in Isaiah 14:12–15, and the other in Ezekiel 28: 11–19. However, neither of the two accounts specifies the time of Lucifer's rebellion and his expulsion from heaven. Isaiah presented Lucifer as a star in heaven. In ancient time, people believed that the stars in heaven were angels. The highest angel is referred to as the "morning star," which is the brightest star in the morning sky. The morning star announces the arrival of the day the victory of light over darkness. Lucifer was the light bearer before his rebellion. That is why he was called Morning Star. Because he is the highest angel,

However, Lucifer, the morning star, was not content with such an honor. He aspired to ascend to the highest heaven and be the Most High. Lucifer, a created intelligence, could not become absolute; therefore, he could not be the Most High. That is reserved for the preexistent God, the Creator, only. The eternal God, the Creator, is the only sovereign. There cannot be anyone else. Nevertheless, Lucifer convinced himself that he possessed enough knowledge and power to make himself a sovereign god. Possession of more knowledge than other created beings did not give Lucifer the ability and right to be the Most High.

Ezekiel 28:12–17 describes Lucifer, saying, "You were the seal of perfection… You were in Eden, the garden of God." Eden is where God planted a garden for the newly created humankind. The river flowed from Eden to water the garden where God placed Adam and woman. The river symbolizes the river of life that flows from God to his creation.

God also appointed Lucifer as a guardian cherub on the Mount of God (Ezekiel 28:14). Therefore, Ezekiel's lament indicates that the Mount of God was in Eden. Lucifer possessed great knowledge ad he was full of wisdom (see Ezekiel 28:12). To be a guardian cherub on the Mount of God, Lucifer had to have more knowledge and understanding than other angels.

The great knowledge was a part of Lucifer's aggregate of quality that made him beautiful. This is what made him proud (Ezekiel 28:12, 17). The pride led him to rebel against God and his ways. Lucifer may be the very first order of created intelligence. If so, he had a longer history than any other created intelligence. A longer history results in more knowledge.

Perhaps Lucifer thought that he knew as much as God himself. Therefore, he thought that all he needed was sovereignty. Accordingly, he initiated a war in heaven to capture God's mountain and make it his residence.

> You said in your heart, "I will ascend to the heavens; I will raise my throne above the stars of God; I will sit enthroned on the mount of assembly, on the utmost heights of the Mount Zaphon." (Isaiah 14:13 NIV)

Zaphon means the heights of the north. Lucifer, to realize his dream, initiated a war in heaven. Because conflict in heaven involved multiple orders of intelligence (the spirits), the war had to be one of influences. Physical weapons were impotent against spirits. The war in heaven involved a multitude of angels, and angels are spirits.

> Are not all angels ministering spirits sent to serve those who will inherit salvation? (Hebrews 1:14 NIV)

The fact that Lucifer initiated war in heaven shows that he already had many angels on his side.

Both the angels that are loyal to God and fallen angels are orders of spirit (intelligence). Spirit and intelligence are the same, as described earlier in this treatise.

> Then war broke out in heaven, Michael and his angels fought against the dragon, and the dragon and his angels fought back. But he was not strong enough, and they lost their place in heaven. (Revelation 12:7–8 NIV)

Revelation 12:3–4 states that Satan with his tail, "swept a third of the stars out of the sky and flung them to the earth." People in ancient time believed that stars were angel. The dragon, Satan, won one-third of the angels in heaven to himself. Therefore, he was smaller than Michael, numerically. The war in heaven was a war of influence; thus, one-third of angels who were with the dragon could not overcome the two-thirds that were with Michael.

Angels were orders of intelligence created by God. Consequently, they could not defeat the Creator regardless of their multitude. With God, one intelligent being is a multitude and a majority. God accomplished everything the created orders of intelligence need. Created intelligence does not provide God with anything, and they do not assist God in his work. Created orders of intelligence must conform to ways that were determined by the Creator before he began his creative activity.

The authors of the biblical account of Lucifer's fall from heaven, as presented in Isaiah and Ezekiel, employ metonymy (a speech figure). They substituted familiar names, locations, and traditions to convey the message to the ancient-time's people. We cannot express the real nature of Lucifer's rebellion and fall from heaven in purely human terms. A description of God and anything associated with heavenly surroundings need to be compared to something familiar so that readers can visualize and understand the message.

The message that was conveyed by the authors of the biblical account of creation portrayed God as the Creator, who made everything humanity may need for a successful eternity. However, God's enemy, Satan, was determined to disrupt, frustrate, and undo all that the Creator has accomplished for humankind.

Therefore, God informed the first human pair that an evil force has gone out of heaven, and that the force would attempt to lead them away from their Creator. The evil force was determined to enslave the newly created humankind in the evil kingdom of sin and darkness. Therefore, the first man, Adam, had to decide and choose between God and the enemy. Accordingly, God commanded Adam and the woman concerning the evil.

> And the LORD God commanded the man, "You are free to eat from any tree in the garden; but you must not eat from the tree of knowledge of good and evil, for when you eat from it you will certainly die." (Genesis 2: 16–17 NIV)

God gave to the first human pair a simple command, "Do not eat from the tree of knowledge of good and evil." The tree of knowledge of good and evil probably stood at an easily identifiable location in Eden's garden. Adam and the woman could not have confused it with another tree. They did not have a reason to even be near it. In the garden, they had everything they needed. God did not instruct Adam and the woman to reason and debate with the enemy. Loyalty to God was at issue, not the tree of knowledge of good and evil itself. God designated only one tree out of many that Adam and the woman, should not eat from.

The woman could have easily walked away from the tree and thus affirm her commitment to her God. Instead, she chose to dialog with the enemy. She did not ask herself, "Why am I talking to an animal?" She thought she could correct Satan in his quotation about God's command. The first human pair did not have sufficient knowledge and power to convince Lucifer of anything. Such power did not exist then, and it does not exist now. Lucifer made an intelligent decision to go contrary to God's way. Such a decision and choice are irrevocable.

We do not know whether the woman realized she was talking to Lucifer, the angel who rebelled against God, not the serpent. It is highly likely that she never heard a serpent talk. The human speech pattern is a characteristic of human beings, and not animals. Lucifer is the highest order of created intelligence. He originated the thought of rebellion against God. Only he and God knew how it had occurred. No created intelligence can generate a thought that was not known to God before he created anything.

We do not have complete information concerning the origin of sin. Sin came into existence before our history began; therefore, we could not know its beginning. The law of intelligence indicates that there could not have been a cause for sin, as we understand the law of intelligence. If a cause for sin existed, the sin would be excusable.

However, neither Lucifer nor we have an excuse for sin. Did God create intelligence with the capability to grow in knowledge and understanding? Yes. However, God does not act in a way that triggers a negative thought in the mind of intelligence that he created. Each created order of intelligence must of its own volition choose and decide concerning its loyalty to the Creator

Because he was the highest order of created intelligence, Lucifer could have been the first intelligent being that God created. If so, he had a more extended history and knowledge than any other order of intelligence. The laws that God established in our universe before he created it indicate that intelligent information processing must conform to the system of logic ordained by the Creator. Carbon-based intelligent life generates thought by the statistical process suitable for our universe only.

The Creator (the Final Observer in quantum cosmology) established the law of intelligence before he began creating. If indications of scientific research are correct, it takes time to acquire sufficient knowledge to generate such an idea as the rebellion against God, the Creator. How much time? We cannot know how much, and should not be concerned with it. We could not know if time existed when Lucifer rebelled. Neither lack of such knowledge nor possession of it affects human progress.

We must wait for our arrival in heaven, where we will receive a proper education concerning creation, the rebellion, the fall, and the redemption of humankind. God, through the prophet Isaiah, told us that he forgot our sins. What the Creator forgets, the created beings could not remember either.

For now we see only a reflection as in a mirror; then we shall see face to face. Now I know in part; then I shall know fully, even as I am fully known. (1 Corinthians 13:12 NIV).

Nevertheless, we can assume, and correctly so, that Adam and the woman knew more about God's Enemy than we know today. God loves humankind. God loved the man and the woman he placed in the Garden of Eden; therefore, he did not leave them in the darkness. The first human pair had all the knowledge that they needed to resist the attack by God's enemy. The first human beings had the necessary knowledge and power to resist the father of sin, Lucifer.   Why did the woman decide to engage in a dialog with Satan through the serpent? We do not know. We would probably not understand it fully, even if we were to receive more detail. Adam and the woman were not at a disadvantage; therefore, they had no excuse. Could the same apply to us today? It's food for thought.

6

Humankind Joins the Rebellion

> Now the serpent was more crafty than any of the wild animals the Lord God had made. He said to the woman, Did God really say, You must not eat from any tree in the garden? (Genesis 3:1 NIV)

THE AUTHORS OF the biblical account of mankind's fall did not state why the woman was near the tree of knowledge of good and evil. The biblical narrative does not state that God forbid Adam and the woman to be near the tree whose fruit was forbidden. The tree of life was also in the middle of the Garden of Eden that God had planted for the first human pair. The biblical narrative of the fall of humankind does not say whether God also had forbidden access to the tree of life.

The biblical narrative of fall of mankind does not state that the tree of life was also forbidden. God had not specified anything concerning the tree of life. Therefore, the tree of life may not have been forbidden before Adam and the woman disobeyed God. After the fall of humankind God expelled Adam and Eve from the garden so they would not eat the fruit of the tree of life. This act implies that the tree of life has not been forbidden. God expelled the human pair from the garden in love and not as a punishment.

Adam and the woman had free access to all other fruit trees in the garden, where the tree of knowledge of good and evil was located.

God instructed Adam and the woman that they are free to eat from any tree in the garden, except the tree of knowledge of good and evil. Therefore, it is likely they had access to the tree of life also. Perhaps Adam and the woman routinely passed by the tree whose fruit was forbidden. However, had they avoided lingering by the tree, they would have been safer.

Did Adam and the woman exhibit curiosity concerning the tree of knowledge of good and evil? We cannot know. God gave them all the necessary information. They did not need to learn anything more about the tree. Did Adam observe the woman talking to an animal? Did he interject any advice? We cannot know. Only Adam and Eve, and God know the details of the events while they were at the tree whose fruit was forbidden.

Historically, the students of the Bible debated about whether or not the serpent spoke the human language naturally. However, our understanding of the laws that govern our universe supports the conclusion that animals do not now and never did possess the capability of human speech patterns. The method by which humans generate thoughts and form speech patterns is unique to humankind only. Any of creation that is lower than a human being cannot assume a human characteristic on its own. There is a high probability that because our thought process is universal, only the higher order of intelligence (a spirit higher than human spirit) can assume the human speech pattern.

We could conclude that Lucifer (Satan) employed the serpent to speak to the woman. He is a spirit. Therefore, he can enter the body of any lower order of created intelligence and of animals. By employing the body of an attractive animal, Lucifer maximized the probability of success. Lucifer did not have the power to assume the human body because he had not yet conquered humankind.

Because God created them in his image, humans possess the power of intelligent decisions and choice. Animals do not. Therefore, Lucifer adopted an approach that will give him the highest probability of success. He understands the human mind well. We should never contemplate a confrontation with him but hide in Christ because of who Satan is. Satan does not have power over those who are in Christ Jesus.

Through a serpent, Satan contacted the woman first because she only represented herself and not all of humankind. Perhaps it was the most efficient approach. We cannot know. The fall of woman may have increased the intensity for Adam to decide what to do. Because Adam chose to have a helper for biological procreation, any other option that may have existed was no longer available. If he chooses not to side with the woman, there would be no human procreation. Adam's decision not to join the woman in rebellion would have nullified his choice for procreation. There would be no human procreation possible ever.

Regardless of possible scenarios, the woman's failure to obey God introduced into Adam's mind unimaginable dynamic of interactions between the spirit and the body. Adam was the representative of humankind, including the woman whom God took out of Adam.

Lucifer restated God's command in reverse order but stated the same thing. By his doing so, the woman perceived that the serpent spoke incorrectly. The woman felt she needed to correct the animal. In doing so, she added to the command the words that God did not express. The words "Do not touch it," came from the woman's mind. How and why such a thought came to the woman's mind, we don't know. Satan's first goal was to engage the woman in a dialog, and he succeeded.

He was (and still is) skilled and clever with words, more so than any human being. Satan managed to convince angels, who were a higher order of intelligence than the woman was. Once he succeeded in engaging the woman in a dialog, Satan proceeded with his theory.

> "You will not certainly die," the serpent said to the woman.
> "For God knows that when you eat from it your eyes will
> be opened, and you will be like God, knowing good and
> evil." (Genesis 3:4–5 NIV)

Certain death could be understood as either the immediate death or unavoidable eternal death at a later time. Through the serpent in the tree, Satan spoke to the woman whose eternal life and death were contingent on a decision by Adam. What would have happened if the woman had eaten the forbidden fruit, but Adam did not? We could not know. We can only speculate. Adam represented humankind, which included the woman.

Satan knew about salvation plan; therefore, he was correct in saying, "You will not certainly die." When God said, "You shall surely die," he was referring to eternal death. However, in the absence of the salvation plan, the first Human pair would have died immediately. The was no mercy in the law. The eternal death of a sinner was certain, whether it happened immediately or at a later time. Even if the Adam joined the woman and ate the forbidden fruit, the first human pair would not have died in the garden because God had put the plan of salvation in place. God had determined before the creation that in just the right time, he will judge humankind for the sin in the Garden of Eden and therefore, for all sins against the law.

God accomplished the judgment of sinful humankind in the body of Jesus Christ on the cross at Golgotha.

> We all, like sheep, have gone astray, each of us has turned to our own way; the LORD has laid on him he iniquity of us all. Isaiah 53:6, NIV.

God also said,

> "I have swept away your offenses like a cloud, your sins like the morning mist. Return to me for I have redeemed you." (Isaiah 44:22 NIV)

God, on the cross, destroyed the sinful life of humankind and sin itself. In exchange, God gave humanity the perfect and eternal life of Jesus Christ.

> God made him who had no sin to be sin for us, so that in him we might become the righteousness of God. (2 Corinthians 5:21 NIV)

Jesus Christ is our righteousness from God. God established everlasting righteousness in Jesus Christ for all humankind.

Without the plan of salvation, the first human pair would have died the moment Adam decided to disobey God. Humankind would never have existed again. Sin separates the sinner from God, who is the only source of life. The result is instant and eternal death, which is also called the second death. Lucifer knew that the plan of salvation existed because God had put it in place before he created this universe and humankind in it. God chose humanity in Christ before he created the world.

> For he chose us in him before the creation of the world to be holy and blameless in his sight. In love he predestined us for adoption to sonship through Jesus Christ, in accordance with his pleasure and will. (Ephesians 1:4–5 NIV)

Therefore, Lucifer was able to say, "You will not certainly die." However, he did not specify whether humankind would die in the fullness of time. Sin separates the sinner from God, the only source of life. Therefore, a sinner must die, whether instantly or at a later time. Because God was determined to save humankind, he delayed the punishment for sin until the Messiah came.

God's enemy, Lucifer, had a goal of planting doubt in the first human pair's mind concerning God's command. In the woman's mind, he proceeded to plant the thought that God did not love the human pair. Satan insinuated that God did not want humans to know anything more than he wanted them to know. However, the place where the first human being resided testified to the contrary. Because he loved humankind, God provided everything they possibly needed for an enjoyable life with him forever. They had no reason to doubt God. The tree of knowledge of good and evil did not have anything Adam and the woman did not have already. God chose an easily identifiable tree to test humankind's loyalty to him.

Adam and the woman knew that evil exists, and it was opposed to God. Knowledge about evil is not evil knowledge. Knowing *about* evil differs from the knowledge *of* evil. Knowing about evil is an intellectual knowledge and understanding. Knowing evil is an experience of it. God did not want the human pair to experience evil because it impacts the entire future of humankind. The experience of evil occurred by intelligent decision and choice. Because of the deliberate decision, the spirit of humankind became irrevocably sinful. As such, it had to die instantly or be replaced in the fulness of time. Why didn't God replace the sinful human life in the garden in Eden? We cannot know, and it is not essential to know it.

The authors of the biblical account of the fall of humankind did not indicate if the woman was unhappy with the level of knowledge she already had. However, the woman did not have any reason to be unhappy. Also, she did not have a reason to be ignorant concerning the nuances that Satan cleverly presented to her. The woman was an intelligent moral being. She was the same as Adam because God took her out of him. The woman possessed all the necessary knowledge to resist the devil. We do not know the reason that the woman did not resist the devil or Adam did not intervene. Perhaps we will be able to ask them in heaven. However, it will not matter then.

We cannot know what thoughts passed through the woman's mind when she dialogued with the serpent. However, whatever thoughts passed through did not bring a good result. Wisdom is to know and understand the difference between knowing *about* evil and *knowing evil*. Logic leads us to conclude that the woman possessed sufficient wisdom. The same applies to righteousness. Knowing *about* righteousness does not make us righteous. Knowing righteousness, Jesus Christ, makes us righteous in him. Wisdom is knowing and accepting the reality that we have in Jesus Christ.

The desire to increase in knowledge is not only good for humankind but also essential. To grow in knowledge about Creator and his creation is critical for humanity to live in our universe; to manage and maintain it forever. God made us for this task. An increase in knowledge is natural. The Creator made it so. Experiencing the things that are opposed to God's way is not natural but deliberate disobedience. Biblical account of the humankind's fall confirms that bad decisions and experiences produce adverse outcomes. The decision by the first human pair resulted in life-altering consequences for the entire humankind.

> When the woman saw that the fruit of the tree was good
> for food and pleasing to the eye, and also desirable for

gaining wisdom, she took some and ate it. She also gave some to her husband, who was with her, and he ate it. Then the eyes of both of them were opened, and they realized they were naked; so they sewed fig leaves together and made coverings for themselves. (Genesis 3:6–7 NIV)

The woman sinned because Satan deceived her by speaking through the serpent in the tree. So also, in the fullness of time, the Savior of the world would, by being nailed to a tree (the cross) removed the sin of the world and brought in everlasting righteousness.

By disobeying God's command, the woman sinned; however, her outward appearance did not change immediately. She was part of the humankind Adam represented. Therefore, the decision by Adam changed everything. The authors of the biblical account of the fall of humankind indicate that the woman's appearance changed when Adam decided to disobey God. The biblical-creation narrative suggests that the Creator made Adam the representative of humankind. Adam was the first human being; therefore, God created all humanity, including the woman, in Adam.

The human intelligence (the spirit) could neither do good nor evil without a deliberate, intelligent decision. The lack of a deliberate and clear choice in the present does not lead to a good outcome in the future. Human beings must always be certain whether they are with God or the enemy. They cannot be with both. Humans do not have to make a clear, deliberate decision to be with the enemy. A lack of a deliberate decision to be with God will always lead to an unintended outcome. A deliberate, intelligent decision for God or the enemy is a one-time decision with eternal consequences.

Even though all descendants of the first human being, Adam, have the same spirit, (same intelligence) nevertheless, only Adams's decision could impact humankind's nature. Humankind, including the first woman, became a sinner by nature when Adam decided to eat the fruit from the tree of knowledge of good and evil. The woman became a sinner without an impact on humankind.

> For Adam was formed first, then Eve. And Adam was not
> the one deceived; it was the woman who was deceived and
> became a sinner. (1 Timothy 2:13–14 NIV)

Adam was not deceived; therefore, he became a sinner by making a willful and deliberate decision to transgress God's command. He willingly joined the rebellion against God. Only a willful and intentional, intelligent decision, whether for good or evil, impacts human nature. It takes only one deliberate, intelligent decision to change the nature of humankind.

The decision that impacts the entire humankind could only be made by the first man, the representative of humankind. The decision by the representative of humankind made it impossible to make a good intelligent decision to reverse the bad one. Also, no member of future humanity could have changed the decision of the first man Adam. All of humankind became mortal sinner in the first man, Adam. Even the one humankind who lived before the tower of Babel could not change the sinful nature of humankind. The sinful human spirit could not be rehabilitated. It had to be replaced. Therefore, the re-creation of humankind was necessary if it is to live forever.

> For just as through the disobedience of the one man the
> many were made sinners, so also through the obedience of
> the one man the many will be made righteous. (Romans
> 5:19 NIV)

Righteousness through one man will address in more detail later in this treatise.

Adam's deliberate, intelligent decision made all of humankind sinful. Therefore, all descendants of Adam are sinners by nature, whether they sin personally by breaking a command or not. The human nature inherited from the Adam, cannot do otherwise but sin. Because human nature is sinful, even thinking about evil is against the law. Therefore, it is a sin. Jesus confirmed this by His definition of the ten commandments.

> "You have heard that it was said to the people long ago,
> 'You shall not murder, and anyone who murders will be

subject to judgment.' But I tell you that anyone who is angry with a brother or sister will be subject to judgment." (Mathew 5 21–22 NIV)

Often anger is only in the mind of one who is angry; however, it is a sin. Sin is a decision and a choice demonstrated by an act. Likewise, righteousness is a decision and a choice demonstrated by an act. Illustration 2 depicts the result of Adam's deliberate decision and choice.

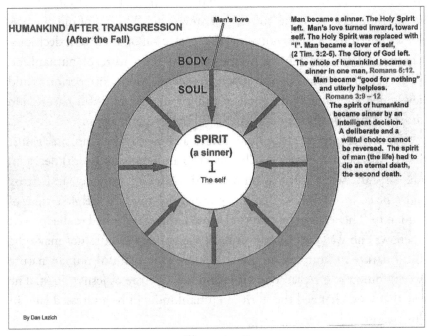

Illustration 2

The spirit, intelligence the Creator put in Adam sinned when he made a deliberate decision to disobey God's command. Adam had all the necessary information concerning the existence of the enemy. Because the spirit in Adam made a deliberate choice, the decision to disobey became irrevocable for all of humankind. Humankind lost the image of God by sinning in Adam. The glory of God that surrounded Adam and the woman departed from them. The love of Adam and the woman turned to themselves. They became lovers of self. Therefore, the Holy Spirit, which had been residing in them, departed. It was replaced with *I*. The soul of humankind reflected the sinful state of humankind's spirit. Adam sinned when he decided to eat the forbidden fruit. The physical act of eating the forbidden fruit only demonstrated that Adam had become a sinner by nature (the human spirit). The biological nature of humankind (the body and soul) was subjected to the consequences of sin that was committed by the human spirit.

As stated earlier, intelligent decisions cannot be reversed. The willful and deliberate decision and choice by an intelligent observer eliminates all other possibilities forever. Based on one's feelings, the decisions are not intelligent decisions; therefore, they are reversible. The law of intelligence, as we understand it, does not allow the revocation of intelligent decisions. The intelligent decision by Adam changed the nature of humankind irreversibly. Regardless of how much good works humanity performs and how much it desires to do good, it cannot change its sinful nature. No human effort could ever make the sinful nature good again.

Once a sinner by a decision, always a sinner, even if no sin against the law has been committed subsequent to an intelligent (spirit) decision. The Creator gave a spirit to humankind; therefore, only he can destroy and replace it. God alone has the power to change the helpless state of humanity. The spirit of humankind sinned; therefore, it had to die forever. There was no way out. On the cross at Golgotha, God did not make the sinful nature of humankind good. God destroyed sinful human nature (spirit) forever and replaced it with the perfect nature of Jesus Christ. The way that God changed the spirit of humankind will be addressed later in this treatise.

God Confronts Fallen Humankind

God created humankind good. (See the Illustration 1). The first man, Adam, and the woman did not have an inborne disposition to sin, as some suggest. God made the human body good, and he put a good spirit (intelligence) in it. Adam did not possess a deficient intelligence (a deficient spirit). If the spirit (intelligence) were imperfect in some way, the sin would be excusable. However, Adam and the woman did not have an excuse for transgressing God's command. God equipped Adam and the woman with the necessary knowledge to recognize and resist the enemy, Satan. Because

Adam and the woman did not resist, today, we cannot and should not fight with the Devil. Instead, we must hide in Jesus Christ.

We do not know the reason (and we cannot know it now) that the woman decided to look to self-interests and desires. Why didn't she realize that she is talking to an animal? The situation was not an everyday occurrence. There is no logical basis for the conclusion that God made inefficient creation, as some think. Why did Adam decide to join the woman in rebellion against God? We don't know. We cannot even speculate why the first human pair chose to transgress the command and make the whole of humankind a sinner by nature. God's command was neither arbitrary nor oppressive. It did not deny Adam and the woman an essential physical need. The Creator provided everything Adam and the woman may need. There was no excuse. There is no excuse for the original sin; therefore, there is no excuse for any subsequent sin.

The very first consequence of sin is that Adam and the woman became lovers of themselves. Their selfless love turned to self, as Illustration 2 depicts. Because of their sin, they realized they were naked. As stated earlier, they were naked because they lost the glory of God. They lost the glory of God because they lost the image of God (selfless love). Accordingly, Adam and the woman decided to hide the evidence of their sin by covering their nakedness with their own effort. The fig leaves in the Garden of Eden were, no doubt, beautiful. However, even the most beautiful leaves that God created could not hide the evidence that Adam and the woman had lost the glory of God.

They have become committed, lifelong sinners by nature, which is an irreversible and deadly condition. No amount of personal effort could have returned them to their original state. Even if after the fall, Adam and the woman had remained scrupulously faithful to God, they would still be sinners by nature. They had become utterly helpless sinners. They had become committed, lifetime slaves in the kingdom of sin and darkness. Ever since Adam and the woman attempted to make themselves look good, self-deceived and helpless human beings have thought that they can become worthy and good by their efforts.

"Their eyes were opened." What does it mean? Did they acquire a better vision? Did they see something better than the things that the Creator had provided for them? No! Their eyes were opened to see that they had experienced evil. The change in their appearance demonstrated the difference between good and evil. Adam and the woman were free, intelligent beings in the kingdom of God before they sinned. Now they were wholly doomed slaves in the kingdom of God's enemy. God had clothed them in the shiny garments of his glory at creation. Now they are naked and utterly hopeless sinners, who were covered with the withering leaves of a tree.

It had been fascinating that evil and its consequences came from a tree. So also, righteousness and its effects came from a tree—the cross at Golgotha. Did Adam and the woman deeply regret their actions? It is possible. Did they know what awaited them in an uncertain future? They likely could not even imagine the difficulties that lay ahead in their uncontrollable future. Were they convinced that God still loves them? Hopefully, they were. However, we cannot know.

Because of their disobedience, Adam and the woman became afraid of God. They had met with God every day without fear. Now they hid among the trees in the garden as God approached them. They must have known that God had made them good and that he loved them. Perhaps as God approached, Satan whispered into their minds, *You are now good for nothing. Your Creator does not love you anymore. Your Creator cannot love you the way you are now.* Adam and the woman could not understand that God hated sin but loved sinners. Accordingly, they were afraid of God. Being afraid of the Creator is the clear evidence that they have become sinners by nature and God's enemies.

The authors of the biblical account of humankind's fall did not tell us the reason that Adam decided to follow the woman in rebellion against God. Why did he decide to eat the fruit of the tree of knowledge of good and evil? He was fully aware of the consequence before the woman gave him the fruit. The woman was deceived, which could partially explain why she ate the forbidden fruit. But why did Adam eat the forbidden fruit? We cannot know it now. The deception of the woman could rationalize her disobedience; however, it could not pardon her. She had not been deprived of God's care. God had provided everything she could desire. Nevertheless by her choice, she became an inexcusable transgressor.

God's enemy probably rejoiced that he convinced the newly created humankind to join his rebellion against God's ways. He lost the battle in heaven; therefore, he lost his home. He probably roamed around looking for a home for himself and his followers. He did not have the power to take any home by force. Intelligent beings had to surrender to him their home voluntarily.

Our current understanding of our universe's anthropic requirements is that a created intelligence must have a home if it wants to live forever. Unfortunately, the first human pair willingly transferred their administrative authority in our universe to Satan. However, Adam and the woman did not have the power to transfer the deed to the property (the owner's title) to Satan. Nevertheless, Adam and the woman enabled Satan to make our universe and the Earth his principality. He then established our universe and Earth as a base for his efforts to frustrate God's plans for humankind.

> But the LORD GOD called out to the man, "Where are you." (Genesis 3:9 NIV)

When Adam and the woman heard the call, they hid among the trees. Adam and the woman knew that nothing was hidden from God. However, now they thought they could hide, which indicated that they had become self-confident and lovers of themselves. The authors of the biblical account of the fall of humankind present the event in an anthropomorphic way. Adam and the woman knew that God saw, heard, and knew everything; therefore, they could not hide from him.

God did not seek Adam and the woman because he did not know where they were. The implication here is that God is seeking the lost because he loves them. God's seeking of Adam pointed to the time when God would become man and come to earth to find and save the lost. God knew that Adam and the woman had become helpless and lost sinners. He had known it before he created them. However, the first human pair could not realize the true nature and the consequences of their disobedience to God's command.

Even though God knew where Adam and the woman were, he called, "Where are you?" This call was for Adam's sake, not God's. God asked Adam, if he knew where he was and wanted to know if he was with God or against him. Adam and the woman needed to realize the seriousness of their disobedience. Not only did Adam and the woman become transgressors of a command but also separated themselves from God, their Creator. They had become lost, and they could not find their way back. Adam and the woman lost the ability to come back to God on their own because they became sinners by nature. Therefore, God came to lost humankind to show them he still loved it with everlasting love. God is against rebellion and disobedience, but he loves sinners and wants to restore them to himself.

The authors of the biblical narrative of the fall of humankind state that God came to the garden "in the cool of the day," which probably was in late afternoon or the evening. The first human pair had estranged itself from God. Adam and the woman now belong in the kingdom of sin and darkness. The night is approaching, and likely, the uncertainty of their future was increasing. For people in ancient time, the night represented a foe. They rejoiced when the day arrived as a victor over the darkness.

Perhaps Adam and the woman were becoming aware of their irreversible and helpless condition. Will the day and light win over the night and darkness? They could only hope it would. The Creator is coming, not only to inform fallen humankind of the consequences of its choice but also assure them that in the fullness of time, he will again command "let there be light." The Creator has determined to re-create lost humankind. The re-creation of humanity has been accomplished, as we will see later in this treatise.

When Adam heard God calling, "Where are you?" he answered, "I heard you in the garden, and I was afraid because I was naked; so I hid." (Genesis 3:10 NIV) Adam would not volunteer the information concerning what had made him afraid. Adam did not volunteer that his nakedness resulted from eating the fruit of the tree of knowledge of good and evil. A self-loving person does not admit his fault and his transgression. So God inquired, "Who told you that you were naked? Have you eaten from the tree I commanded you not to eat from?" (Genesis 3:11 NIV)

God observed Adam and the women eating the fruit of the tree he had commanded them not to eat from. However, God asked the question to make Adam and the woman realize they disobeyed God's simple command. In a clear demonstration of his love of self, Adam did not admit that he had willfully transgressed, but he blamed the Creator instead for giving him the woman. He conveniently forgot that having the woman next to him was his choice. The Creator had satisfied Adam's preference of having the helper for procreation. Adam was wrong to blame God for giving him something he had wanted.

> The man said, "The woman you put here with me – she gave me some fruit from the tree, and I ate It. (Genesis 3:12 NIV)

Adam showed his true nature by blaming someone else for his deliberate and willful action and failure. A sinner by nature always concludes and insists that others are at fault for his wrongdoing. In his mind, a lover of self is always better than others are. In the same fashion, the woman blamed the serpent, an innocent animal. The woman, indirectly blamed God for creating the serpent. However, the woman had eaten the forbidden fruit because it had appealed to her and not because the serpent suggested it. She did not say she was sorry for talking to an animal and not realizing it was the enemy speaking through the serpent. The serpent, however, was speechless. There was no one left to blame. The man and the woman exhausted the blames.

God cursed the serpent; however, he did not curse Adam and the woman. We shall learn later that the Savior was cursed on behalf of humankind. God informed the woman of what was to be an ever-present consequence of her disobedience.

> "I will make your pains in childbearing very severe; with painful labor you will give birth to children. Your desire will be for your husband, and he will rule over you." (Genesis 3:16 NIV)

Then God said to Adam,

> To Adam he said, "Because you listened to your wife and ate fruit from the tree about which I commanded you, 'You must not eat from it,' "Cursed is the ground because of you; through painful toil you will eat food from it all the days of your life." (Genesis 3:17 NIV)

At creation, God placed humankind under the law, (the universal moral code, and not the Ten Commandments). Advanced studies in anthropic cosmology indicate that if intelligent life is present in a universe like ours, the moral code must come into being. Once the moral code arises, it shall never cease to exist. Humankind, in the first man Adam, disobeyed a simple command, became a sinner by nature, and opposed to the moral code. (The Ten Commandments were given to show that sinful humankind could not obey the moral code). By disobeying a command, humanity, in the first man Adam, established an irreconcilable enmity between itself and the moral code (Law). The Law cannot help humankind to obey because the Law only condemns disobedience.

The law cannot help humankind to obey because it was not designed to do so. The law, by design, can only demand perfect obedience and condemn disobedience. The sinful nature of humanity makes it impossible to obey perfectly. Therefore, the law only condemns the sinner. It cannot help him obey.

The moral code (the universal moral law) condemned humankind to die an eternal death immediately. But because he loved humanity, God placed it under Grace until the penalty for sin would be paid in full. Through the body of Jesus Christ (the Grace) on the cross at Golgotha, humankind had paid the full price for sin committed in the Garden of Eden and for all subsequent sins. Because of Grace, the transgression in Eden's garden did not separate humankind from God's selfless love. However, because of sinful nature, humanity could not remain in God's presence because a sinner could not live in the presence of the Holy God. This restriction is for the good of humankind and not because God does not love sinners.

As God, spoke to the serpent (the enemy) in the garden, he declared,

> "And I will put enmity between you and the woman, and
> between your offspring and hers; he will crush his head,
> and you will strike his heel." (Genesis 3:15 NIV)

God said to Satan, "Your offspring and hers." The interaction between the serpent's offspring and women alluded to the Messiah, who would in the fullness of time, take on himself the sinful human life (the spirit) and die forever to overthrow Satan as the prince of this world. By dying on the cross, the world's Savior forever destroyed sin and restored humankind to God. God spoke in the singular when he said: "Woman's seed" (offspring). He did not say "seeds," which indicates that he had determined to send the Savior to helpless humanity.

God's plan of salvation of the fallen humankind was in place before creating our universe and the carbon-based intelligent life.

> Praise be to the God and Father of our Lord Jesus Christ, who has blessed us in the heavenly realms with every spiritual blessing in Christ. For he chose us in him before the creation of the world to be holy and blameless in his sight. In love he predestined us for adoption to sonship through Jesus Christ, in accordance with his pleasure and will—to the praise of his glorious Grace, which he has freely given us in the One he loves. (Ephesians 1:3–6 NIV)

After hearing God's declarations, Adam changed his wife's name from "woman" to Eve. Eve means life because now she will have offspring.

> Adam named his wife Eve because she would become the mother of all the living. (Genesis 3:20 NIV)

In the above verse, we can discern a possible clue concerning the reason that Adam decided to follow his wife in transgression. Had Adam chosen not to eat the forbidden fruit and join the woman in her trespass, the woman would have needed to die instantly. The law demands it. However, there would never have been any descendants of Adam. Adam would live forever as the only one, which means there would be no procreation. As we understand the laws that govern our universe, there would be no other option for procreation available.

Adam chose biological procreation and a helper with him; therefore, other possible options became unavailable forever. The helper sinned, and had to die forever and immediately. The moral code demands the immediate death of the sinner. Sin separated the sinner from God, who was the only life source of life; therefore, the result was the second death. However, we were not given information concerning this scenario; therefore, we cannot speculate concerning Adam's mind.

Even though Adam and the woman sinned, and they were not repentant, God demonstrated his love for them. Even if Adam and the woman were sincerely repentant, they could not avoid the consequences of their disobedience. Adam made a willful, intelligent decision, which made the life (spirit that God put in him) sinful. The sinfulness of life applied to all future members of humankind. The representative of humankind sinned; therefore, all of humankind became sinners by nature. Only the replacement of the sinful human spirit with the righteous spirit can destroy the sinful spirit. The *I* must die. It must be replaced by the Holy Spirit. That is why God declared.

> I will give you a new heart and put a new spirit in you; I will remove from you your heart of stone and give you a heart of flesh. I will put my Spirit in you and move you to follow my decrees and be careful to keep my laws. (Ezekiel 36:26–27 NIV)

Replacement of the sinful spirit had to wait for the arrival of the promised seed (the Grace, Jesus Christ). By conquering temptation, Jesus secured the perfect and eternal spirit, life, for new humankind.

God demonstrated his love for sinners by performing a critical act in the garden. God showed that he cares for humankind and that he would, in the fullness of time, do the unimaginable to restore the helpless humanity to himself as his children. God made a peace of more practical clothing so that Adam and Eve would not be ashamed of their nakedness.

> The LORD God made the garments of skin for Adam and his wife and clothed them. (Genesis 3: 21 NIV)

The authors of the biblical account of the fall of humankind did not specify how God got the skin for the garments. Many in Christianity believe that God had to kill an animal for it. However, if God created the animals, could he not also create the skin without killing? We cannot know how God obtained the animal skin. However, God is all-powerful. He can make clothing of skin without killing an animal. The garments of skin provided practical clothing and served as the shadow that pointed to the day when God would clothe humankind with his righteousness—the Grace, Jesus Christ.

The biblical narrative of the fall of humankind presents another act of God's selfless love. Some maintain that the expulsion of humanity from the Garden of Eden was a punishment for disobedience. However, God clearly stated why Adam and Eve should not remain in the garden.

> And the LORD God said, 'The man has now become like one of us, knowing good and evil. He must not be allowed to reach out his hand and also take from the tree of life and eat, and live forever.' So the LORD God banished him from the Garden of Eden to work the ground from which he had been taken. (Genesis 3:22–23 NIV)

God determined to save sinful humankind. Therefore, he did not want humanity to live forever as sinners. A sinner who lives forever cannot be saved because his life (spirit) could not die, as required by the law.

Fallen humankind's salvation had to wait for the promised Grace, Jesus Christ, who would come at just the right time. Why couldn't humanity's salvation become a reality in the garden? We do not know. We were not given information concerning the reason that there had to be a period before Grace came. The possibility is that if it had been given we would not understand it correctly. It would only generate doubts concerning God's intentions.

Anthropic cosmological principles imply that all possible events had gone through the mind of the Final Observer, God, before he began creating. Accordingly, all possible histories and events had to follow the same order of sequence as they happened in the mind of the Creator. We cannot know how accurate this implication is.

Only God knows the sequence of events, which have been completed with the fullness of time. God works and acts in a way that guarantees a successful eternity. Before the creation, God determined he would save the fallen humankind. He ensured that humankind did not perish by self-destruction before the promised Grace (the Messiah) came.

Accordingly, his actions and interactions were accomplished in the course of human history. In the body of Jesus Christ on the cross at Golgotha, God destroyed sin forever and ensured for his creation a successful eternity. The nature of humankind after the fall made the re-creation the only solution that was possible. God has been, thus far, successful in all his plans for humankind. We can rest assured that all will end in the way God planned before he created us.

SECTION 3

7

The Consequences of Sin

GOD INTERVENED IN humankind's history three times. God's first two interventions served to redirect the path of humanity through its history. The third intervention helped to re-create humankind and give it a new history. God's two earlier responses to human actions are addressed in this section. This treatise will present the third and the most crucial intervention on behalf of humankind later.

Human beings cannot see the future. We live in the present and observe our past. However, our path through history is leading to the future, which we cannot see. We see and study our past only. However, we cannot return to any point in our past. The law in the universe forbids that we travel back in time. The laws forbid the return to a previous point in our history and the observation of future events until they become the present. Therefore, even the best decisions humankind could make concerning its future may not have the desired ending.

God, the Creator, sees both our future and our past. From the beginning to eternity, human history is the absolute present to God. All possible events in human history were a reality in the mind of God before he created anything. Therefore, the present and the future state of humankind depends on God observing and watching us continuously, here and now. Accordingly, God intervened in human history to preserve humankind until the Messiah came. Yes, God's interventions were his act of love toward sinful and helpless humankind.

How long after the fall of humankind did the earth retain its surface in its original condition? We do not have precise information. The planet earth did not change its physical configuration and shape because of Adam's decision. God cursed the earth's surface and stated that it would not bear human labor's proper fruit. Neither the authors of the biblical account nor the ancient epics say whether the earth's surface changed when Adam sinned. God informed Adam that his labor after the fall would be difficult with diminishing payback.

> To Adam he said, "Because you listened to your wife and ate fruit from the tree about which I commanded you, You must not eat from it, Cursed is the ground because of you; through painful toil you will eat food from it all the days of your life. It will produce thorns and thistles for you, and you will eat the plants of the field." (Genesis 3:17–18 NIV)

How soon did all of the above become a reality? The authors did not tell us. All the original conditions concerning the earth's ground (surface) did not change physically before the flood. Did the function of the ground change? It may have changed. However, we do not have sufficient information for a definitive answer.

The probability exists that change may have happened gradually. The flood altered the earth's surface drastically. Before the fall, the first human pair had all kinds of fruit trees. These trees produced fruit without human effort. After sin came, humankind had to eat the plants that grew out of the ground and not only the fruit. Plants had to be cultivated more than the fruit trees did.

The authors of the biblical account elected not to talk about the condition of the ground. Perhaps they did not receive an account from eyewitnesses. Perhaps the ground's condition, (the surface of the planet earth) had not significantly impacted men's nature. Because of sin, the attitude of man's minds changed significantly. Therefore, the biblical account's authors list men's nature as the most devastating consequence of sin that led to the flood.

The most devastating consequence of sin that was committed in Eden's garden is that humankind became evil by nature and lost God's image. Adam's willful and deliberate decision in the garden made humankind an irreversible sinner by nature. All later human beings were born sinners by nature, even before they committed any sin. The spirit (life) that God breathed into humanity, in Adam sinned in the garden in Eden. Because Adam's decision in the garden was a deliberate, intelligent decision made by the human spirit (intelligence), it became irrevocable.

The ensuing humankind became utterly helpless, unable to do good, and make proper intelligent decisions and choices. The inability to reverse deliberate, intelligent decisions conforms to the Creator's laws which he established before creating our universe. Therefore, the nature of the deliberate, intelligent decision may be eternal. This probability is true for deliberate decisions for evil and deliberate decisions for righteousness. Deliberate, and willful intelligent decisions remain forever. God confirmed this through the prophet Jeremiah.

> Can an Ethiopian change his skin or a leopard his spots?
> Neither can you do good who are Accustomed to doing
> evil. (Jeremiah 13:23 NIV)

Adam's willful and deliberate decision made all of humankind irreversibly sinful; thus, it became God's enemy. The human spirit that sinned in Adam had to die an eternal death, with no way out. The only hope for sinful humanity was that the spirit that sinned would die and be replaced with a righteous, eternal spirit. God, and only he, could destroy the spirit and replace it with righteous spirit. God accomplished a marvelous exchange in the body of Jesus Christ on the cross at Golgotha. He destroyed our sinful spirit in the body of Jesus Christ and replaced it with the perfect spirit of Jesus Christ. This treatise will describe this incredible act later.

Sinful human nature (spirit) demonstrated its sinfulness fully in the pre-diluvial people. by its behavior, the people of the pre-flood era demonstrated that they were irreversible sinners by nature, who were unable to do good but only able to do evil.

> The LORD saw how great the wickedness of the human race had become on the earth, and that every inclination of the thoughts of the human heart was only evil at all time. (Genesis 6:5 NIV)

Therefore, because every inclination of humans' thoughts was evil, humankind became incapable of making a good intelligent decision. No amount of human effort could alter the natural human desire to sin. As a result of irreversible and persistent evil inclinations, the pre-flood humankind was on its way to self-destruction. The pre-flood people had a long lifespan. The long lifespan enabled people to multiply their evil deeds at a high rate.

In Eden's garden, the earth became Lucifer's principality, and humankind became his slaves because of Adam's decision. All of humankind surrendered itself and its home, the earth, to Lucifer by its deliberate decision in the first man Adam. Lucifer, who is also Satan, invented evil; therefore, humans in his principality could do evil only. When the population in Satan's territory increased corruption also increased. With no fear of God, the number of those who practiced evil increased at an ever-higher rate.

The authors of the biblical account of the flood did not state the size of earth's population before the flood. No one could determine the size of the pre-flood population. Only Noah and his family were the living witnesses of the earth's condition before the flood. The authors of the biblical account of the flood did not define the pre-flood's evil nature. If the violence implies the killing of humans, pre-flood Earth population was not substantial.

The authors of the biblical flood account list violence as the single most heinous evil that the pre-flood people practiced. The Babylonian epic states that as the people multiplied, they became too noisy for gods. The gods could not rest in peace, so they decided to eliminate the noisy humankind. We do not know the true nature of the evil that was practiced by the pre-flood people. Nevertheless, evil deeds were leading people farther from God, the only source of life. This trend among the pre-flood population was probably the chief reason that God, who loves his creation, intervened to preserve humankind.

God's intervention to redirect the path of humanity through its history saved it from inevitable self-destruction. Because people were evil by nature, they did not realize they are on the way to self-destruction. God thus ensured that humankind would not perish by tits own doing. The flood was God's act of love, not a punishment. Had God punished sinful humanity, it would have ceased to exist instantly. God preserved humankind until the Messiah came, at just the right time.

The assertion in the biblical account that violence is the chief reason for the flood is supported by Moses's instructions, which he gave to the Jews before they entered the Promised Land. God commanded Moses to instruct the people concerning the territory they will inherit. God, through Moses, gave the laws and rules to govern their social behavior. The requirements apply to relationship among individuals and their attitude toward the land itself.

> "'Do not pollute the land where you are. Bloodshed pollutes the land, and atonement cannot be made for the land on which the blood has been shed, except by the blood of the one who shed it. Do not defile the land where you live and where you dwell, for I, the LORD, dwell among the Israelites.'" (Numbers 35:33–34 NIV)

Before the flood, people were killing one another and destroying the land by their practices. We do not have sufficient knowledge concerning the state of humankind before the flood. However, we can conclude that a uniquely Jewish biblical account gives the most probable condition of the pre-flood world. Because of the sin in the Garden of Eden, all of humankind became utterly helpless, and unable to do good regardless of its effort.

Humans cannot change the color of their skin at will. Is it possible to do so without altering the appearance? We do not know. Also, human beings do not have the power to change their sinful nature. A leopard is not even aware it has spots. Humankind is not able to do good because its nature is evil. Unfortunately, some human beings are like leopards. They are not aware that they are sinners by nature. Perhaps others do not want to admit they are sinners. Some humans are perfect in their eyes because they possess a sin-corrupted attitude. In the interest of self-preservation, sin masks itself as good. However, the Creator knows human nature well. That is why he said that humankind could not do good because it was accustomed to doing evil.

Some Bible scholars maintain that the biblical account of the flood derives from two sources. The two sources differ in a few points of detail. However, one often finds somewhat differing accounts and narratives of events in the Bible. No eyewitnesses have observed all the details of the flood. The only witnesses who survived the flood were Noah and his family. However, they were in the arc. How much they observed has not been shared with subsequent generations. The appearance of the deluge is different in other places on the earth. God ensured that the arc enjoyed relative safety.

The observable evidence indicates that the Earth experienced a violent geological upheaval that involved water. The extreme cataclysmic event also altered the earth's crust and destroyed much evidence, which is needed for comparison. Therefore, we cannot know all the details of the flood event. However, knowing the details about this geologically destructive activity in the past is not essential. Because humankind cannot change the Earth, such knowledge would not benefit humanity.

Why was it necessary to alter the earth's crust? Conditions on the pre-flood Earth were conducive to a lengthy lifespan for human beings. The Creator created the planet so that it would provide for the long life of the people living on it. However, humanity disobeyed God, the Creator. Because humankind disobeyed God in Eden's garden, it became unable to be in the presence of Holy God. Accordingly, the authors of the biblical account of flood blame humankind, not God. God preserved Noah's family based on Noah's favor with him. He did so to ensure humanity's continuation. God loves humankind; therefore, he redirected its history to ensure its survival. Since only one living human being was in God's favor, then God acted at just the right time.

Before the flood, long-living sinners increased their evil deeds to a level that threatened humankind's very existence. It is probable that had not the flood happened when it did, humankind and the universe would have ceased to exist. God hates sin; however, he loves sinners. Therefore, he determined to preserve sinful humanity until the Savior of the world came, at just the right time.

Only God, the Creator, could have restrained humankind from self-destruction before the Messiah came. Accordingly, we must view the flood as an act of God's love, and not a punishment of evil humanity. The change in the earth's condition became necessary to preserve humankind. What changed the state and the appearance of the earth's crust? To answer this question, we must describe the planet earth before the flood.

The Earth before the Flood

Humankind does not have sufficiently detailed and accurate information concerning the Earth's structure and condition before the flood. There is no eyewitness report concerning the exact appearance and state of our planet before the flood. Noah and his family observed only the region where they lived before the flood. However, only the earth's upper layers were impacted by the destructive force Earth's flood.

The earth's layers below the lithosphere are probably the same today as they were before the flood. The Earth's upper layers can be observed and studied, but the planet's overall function now may not be the same as before the flood. Humankind cannot assess the difference between the earth's function now and before the flood accurately. Based on what we observe now, it may be possible to reconstruct the Earth's configuration before the flood. However, such an effort could be overwhelming.

The scientific study of the planet earth is ongoing. The main aim is to understand the way that the earth functions now and how long humankind can live on the earth. The activity in the earth's tectonic plates may indicate that the earth tends toward the pre-flood state. However, the current configuration and structure of the planet earth could not have reverted substantially. The probability is that it may never return to its original configuration. Therefore, humankind must adapt to it as is. Knowing how the planet earth functions in its current configuration can help determine if humanity can extend its usefulness. In its present condition, the earth cannot support carbon-based intelligent life for an extended time.

However, humankind must gain significantly higher knowledge about Earth and our solar system to ensure its survival. Current knowledge does not support a reliable assessment of how much longer life can prosper here on Earth. Can humankind develop sufficient knowledge about the planet earth and the universe in time? It remains to be seen. The earth's geologically violent upheaval has destroyed the evidence needed to understand the pre-flood Earth better. What was the actual configuration and functionality of the planet at the end of the six-day creation? This could not be determined. The best that humankind could do is interpret the data obtained by extensive observation and derive the best possible conclusion concerning the planet's future.

Can humankind alter the conditions on present-day earth to ensure a longer-lasting life on it? It probably cannot. Can the fallen humanity find another planet in another solar system and transfer life there? Efforts to do so are ongoing. Will they succeed? It remains to be seen. Even if humankind discovers another suitable world, the transfer of human life to another distant planet may be challenging.

Only the Creator can solve the human predicament. The earth's initial configuration and its relation to the sun were different from what they were before the flood. The current relationship of Earth to the sun may not be an optimum one. Therefore, this treatise will address the probable pre-flood configuration of the planet earth first.

Formation of Celestial Bodies in Our Universe

Under the influence of gravity, hydrogen gas's spherical compression forms the stars in our universe. Most stars in our universe have planets in their orbits. However, only stars that are like our sun, can support a planet that is suitable for carbon-based intelligent life. Our sun belongs to the main sequence of stars. Only main sequence stars can have a planet that is suitable for carbon-based intelligent life. However, not all main sequence stars may have a suitable planet in the star's habitable zone.

As the hydrogen gas begins to compact, the resulting aggregation of matter begins to spin. As it rotates about its axis, a young star influences the surrounding hydrogen gas to form a disk which consists mainly of hydrogen gas. The density of the planetary dick increases under the influence of gravity. As the young star's compacted matter increases, it begins to pull in the gas from the planetary disk. However, the young star may attract more than it needs.

Consequently, the young star expels the excess matter into a ring of mostly hydrogen gas. The excess matter ejected from the young star interacts with the dense hydrogen gas and contributes to the formation of planets and associated bodies. The formation of stars and planets in our universe is a complex process. However, the entire process follows the laws that the Creator put in place before he created the universe.

All planets that orbit a sun are spherical because gravity influences the initial accumulation of matter. Human science has not explored other planets' interiors in our solar system as much as the planet Earth's interior. Therefore, this treatise addresses the planet earth's structure because this planet is where we live and what we study. People must view the earth as a sphere. In limited biblical cosmology, the planet earth is a circular plain floating on a large body of water. However, undeniable, modern-day evidence proves the earth to be a sphere. The planet earth consists of layers or shells of matter in several states. The planet earth's composition is like an onion, except that the layers of an onion are solid matter while Earth's layers are not all solid matter. The center of the planet earth is a solid core that consists of two spherical layers.

The inner spherical layer is an iron ball that is extremely hot. It remains solid because of the extremely high pressure that is in the earth's center. The outer shell of the earth's core consists primarily of liquid iron with some nickel in it. Scientists believe that the earth's core, as configured, generates the earth's magnetic field. However, we do not understand the magnetic field's precise production mechanism yet, so scientific studies continue. The magnetic field is an essential protective shield of the surface of the Earth.

The earth also has a radiation belt and the atmosphere as its protective layers. The three-part protective shield ensures that life on Earth's surface can prosper in relative safety. Humankind has not even begun to understand all that the Creator prepared for it and the reason why. The

Creator ensured that planet Earth has everything necessary for long and successful intelligent life to survive on it.

Above the spherical core of the earth is a shell called Mantle. The mantle moves as a semi-solid rock which is mostly composed of silicate minerals. The upper layer of the Mantle is highly viscous and colder. Above the mantle is a thin shell that separates the mantle from Earth's outermost layer, which is referred to as the lithosphere.

The lithosphere is broken into tectonic plates, like an eggshell when it is dropped. The current condition of the lithosphere is not the original state of Earth. It is most probable that the lithosphere initially comprised a continuous shell-like layer of the Earth. There is a high probability that a layer of water existed as an integral part of the lithosphere and Earth's crust during the formation of the planet earth and before the flood. A planet like ours retains water and atmosphere in the process of its formation. It does so because it is located in just the right place.

As stated earlier, volcanic activity formed the Earth's crust. The temperature in the Earth's mantle may have been much higher during the planet's formation. Higher temperature produces highly liquid lava, which flowed far from the source. Highly liquid lava formed horizontal layers. Volcanic action cannot remain steady over an exceptionally long time. As the highly molten lava cooled, it formed horizontal layers of the earth's crust. Lava flow reduces the internal temperature and pressure. Accordingly, the flow of lava stopped. Somewhat cooler lava formed a cone-shaped mountain.

Liquid lava flowed in all directions, forming mainly even horizontal layers of crust. The newly formed layer cooled before the new volcanic eruption began. The newly released lava did not fuse seamlessly into a cool layer below it. Also, the varied lava temperature and pressure formed varied types of solid matter. Therefore, variation in the earth's internal pressure and temperature contributed to a flat stacked of layers.

The current state of the Earth's crust displays the layers at various angles. Volcanic activity does not produce layers of the planet's crust at various angles. Liquid material tends to form a flat plain because of gravity. This treatise will address the cause of the incline in Earth's crust's layer later.

The dynamics and mechanics of Earth's crust formation must have trapped water within it. The internal pressure circulated the water within the lithosphere's upper layer to ensure proper biological life conditions on Earth's crust's surface. The surface of the earth's original crust included varied sizes of bodies of water. According to the biblical account of creation, Earth had water on it before the Creator made the earth's functionality. What is the source of the authors' information? We cannot know. They did not reveal their sources. The ancient creation epics also maintain that the earth had water before the planet earth's functionality was established. The ancient stories are older than the biblical narrative.

> Now the earth was formless and empty, darkness was over the surface of the deep, and Spirit of God was hovering over the waters. (Genesis 1:2 NIV)

Earth revolved around the sun in just the right orbit before the flood. The earth had the size and atmospheric pressure required for the retention of water on it. Before the flood, the earth's configuration conformed to the laws that the Creator established before the creation of the universe. After the flood, Earth's functionality is not ideal while still regulated by the laws. People in biblical times believed that the planet earth came out of water. The earth, that ancients referred to, was the earth's because the crust was all they could see.

> But they deliberately forget that long ago by God's word the heavens came into being end the earth was formed out of water and by water. By these waters also the world of that time was deluged and destroyed. (2 Peter 3:5–6 NIV)

The upper layer of the lithosphere (the crust) formed a continuous layer over the whole original planet Earth. An extrasolar body's impact broke the Earth's crust in at least fifteen tectonic plates, as observed today. Due to the dynamic process, some tectonic plates may have fused enough to appear as one plate. The tectonic plates continued to collide and created high mountains, as the initial shockwave continued to oscillate. Also, the tectonic plates have been distributed over the planet Earth to create large areas for the deep oceans.

Where the planet Earth revolves around the sun is called the habitable zone of the star. Each main-sequence star probably has a habitable zone. Only the planet located in the sun's habitable zone can support carbon-based, intelligent life. However, there could be cases where the planet that is orbiting in the habitable zone is not suitable for human life. Not all the main sequence stars have the surface temperature that is appropriate to support the carbon-based, intelligent life. Many factors determine whether carbon-based, intelligent life can flourish on a planet. However, these factors are outside the scope of this treatise. Of course, we can address the requirements and conditions for the carbon-based, life only. Earth is probably a unique one. How many other worlds like Earth exist? We do not know.

We are confident the Creator has placed humankind on a planet that had everything needed for a long, enjoyable, and successful life. Before the flood, he planet earth probably went around the Sun in a circular orbit. before the flood, the earth's spin axis has been, parallel to the sun's spin axis (vertical or about what we observe as a celestial north). No information and data exist that shows whether or not the earth had seasons before the violent event. If the seasons did not exist, it would indicate that Earth revolved in a circular orbit around the sun and in the center of the habitable zone, with its spin axis parallel to the suns' axis. Earth has been ecologically balanced since creation. Such a balance requires a planet to revolves around the sun in an ideal orbit. The Creator made the Earth with the best possible conditions to support carbon-based, intelligent life.

As observed and experienced now, Earth is not ecologically balanced. The post-flood Earth orbits the Sun in an elliptical orbit. After the flood, the earth's spin axis was tilted at 23.5 degrees as compared to the Sun's axis. The elliptical orbit combined with the tilted spin axis produces seasons of varied intensity. The original conditions for a long-lasting human life do not exist on Earth after the flood. The flood has not impacted the structure and function of the sun and the rest of the universe. Scientists have concluded that Earth cannot support humankind for the Sun's entire life. They find that in a not-too-distant future, living on the earth may become impossible. What changed, and how did it change?

8

A Destructive Event

THE SHAPE AND the condition of the Earth's crust show that the planet earth has experienced a geologically destructive event, which likely happened in recent history. The present thickness Earth's crust varies from about 4.8 kilometers (3 miles) to seventy kilometers (44 miles). Such an uneven distribution of matted around the planet is not consistent with a volcanically formed planetary crust. Uneven distribution of matter affects the earth's dynamics. A convincing indication that a violent geologic event distorted the Earth's crust is present everywhere.

The geologically destructive event occurred approximately 5,500 years ago. The violent geological event that distorted the Earth's crust coincides roughly with the biblical account and other ancient narratives concerning the flood. Deep sub-oceanic tranches and cracks in Earth's crust surround the Pacific Ocean from Alaska to Antarctica. Suboceanic tranches were created by a violent impact in the region of the Pacific Ocean. At the creation of life on the planet earth, God declared that everything was good. However, even a casual observation leads us to realize that the earth is not as good as it could be. Large areas of the earth's surface are not fully useful for the traditional human way of living. Some areas are even hostile to the traditional human way of living.

The shape and appearance of the Pacific Ocean's basin reveal a violent past. The probable collision with the earth created a depression, which is today's Pacific Ocean. The highest mountains on Earth surround the Pacific Ocean. The extrasolar body impacted the earth just north of the equator and where the North Pacific Ocean is now. The shape and size of the resulting mountains indicate that a powerful force formed them. An extrasolar body of a substantial proportion when compared to earth has produced an enormous dynamic effect. The powerful impact occurred on the opposite side from where Noah's ark stood on the earth's surface. Human beings who may have inhabited the area of impact did not survive it; therefore, there were no eyewitnesses.

Noah and his family did not witness the collision with an extrasolar body. Even the people in the area surrounding the ark could not have seen the impact. Therefore, neither the biblical narrative nor the ancient epics describe the probable collision with a large extrasolar body. If Noah had looked through the opening under the ark's roof, he could have seen the destructive event's lesser effects, but not the collision itself. Noah may have observed the geysers or "the springs of the great deep." (Genesis 7:11 NIV) However, he did not see what produced the geysers. The only information Noah had concerning the flood was what God told him.

> I am going to bring floodwaters on earth to destroy all life under the heavens, every creature that has the breath of life in it. Everything on earth will perish. (Genesis 6:17 NIV)

God did not tell Noah the way that he will bring the floodwaters on the earth. He did not tell Noah where sufficient water will come from to flood the whole earth. The authors of the biblical flood account describe rain bringing floodwaters on the Earth. According to the biblical narrative of creation, the rain had not fallen on the earth before the flood. The pre-diluvial people could not even understand the true meaning of the noun *rain*. The authors of the biblical narrative state that the "springs of the great deep burst forth." (Genesis 9:11 NIV) However, they did not associate it with rain. The rain that fell during the flood was not the same as the rain we experience now. The rain that fell on the pre-diluvial Earth is the water that rose from under the ground with high pressure and velocity. Underground water (springs of the deep) rose up high into the atmosphere (the heavens) and fell like heavy rain. However, such rain is not the only source of floodwaters.

The breakup of the Earth's crust released a large quantity of water in the region of impact by an extrasolar body. Noah's ark stood in the area where only the rain was visible at the flood's onset. Therefore, Noah and his family may have observed the rain but not the nearby terrain's subsequent deformation. The shape of the ark's roof may have obstructed the terrain near the ark. Therefore, they may not have observed the terrain's condition during the onset of the rain. They heard the rain pounding the roof of the ark.

Deformation of the terrain near Noah's ark happened soon after the impact by the extrasolar body. People who were on the other side of the planet would have seen the destructive impact. However, they did not survive the event. Both the authors of the biblical narrative and the Babylonian epics did not know what caused the rain to fall on the Earth. They believed that water existed between the heaven of the stars and the heaven where God or gods were. They may have concluded that the floodwaters came from the heavens. Accordingly, they described the flood in the best way they could visualize and understand, based on the ancient cosmology and limited worldview.

Historically, people believed that water existed between the sky and the heaven where God or gods were. However, they based their conclusion on ancient cosmological concepts. The authors of the biblical account of creation and the flood did not have adequate means to describe them. Therefore, they described the events in a way that seemed logical in their time. They could not have described it differently. The authors of the biblical account of creation and the flood did not know that the solar system existed. As noted earlier, they thought that the earth was the only place outside of the heavens. To them, everything under God's heaven orbited the earth. In ancient times, people did not know that the earth was a planet that orbited a star called the sun. They thought that the sun was below the water, which was below the heaven where God was. They considered the sun to be a disk that floated in the sky under heaven. They did not have the means to determine the size of the sun and the distance to it.

Therefore, the modern-day readers of the biblical account should consider the time when the authors wrote the narrative. The sequence of events and terminology that was employed in the biblical account is correct, based on ancient cosmology. Today's evidence and knowledge that is derived from modern-day cosmology is supported by extensive observations and study. Therefore, as stated earlier, the biblical narrative's message should be the only reason for the study of creation and the flood. The One and the Only God, the God of Abraham, Isaac, and Jacob, is the Creator of all. The same Creator brought floodwaters on the earth by the laws that he established before creating our universe.

There is sufficient evidence supporting the conclusion that Earth experienced a geologically destructive event that also involved water. Debates concerning the mechanics of the flood are not fruitful. The mechanics and detail associated with the event that brought the earth's flood cannot be entirely determined. People, in ancient time, did not know about the laws that regulated the physical universe. They did not know the universe existed. However, today humankind possesses more knowledge than it has had in its entire history.

Modern-day humanity has discovered and defined the laws that regulate matter's behavior in our universe. Humans did not create the laws, but they discovered them. Quantum cosmology supports the fact that the necessary laws existed before the creation of our universe. Therefore, students of the Bible have no reason to deny their nonhuman origin. The Creator created the universe out of nothing, and it conforms to the laws that he established before he created it. The physical universe is still the same as when it came out of the hand of the Creator.

Did the planet earth ever have water above its atmosphere? The law regulating the formation of solar systems and planets does not require water above the atmosphere. On the contrary, the conditions in and above the atmosphere are not suitable for water. Water that may have been above the atmosphere, in the beginning, had to be in its atomic state and not a liquid one. A water molecule can remain liquid only under the pressure of one atmosphere. One-atmosphere pressure is the one at Earth's sea level. There is no pressure above the atmosphere to hold the water molecules together. Therefore, any water above the atmosphere must evaporate quickly. The current human activity in the Earth's orbit does not encounter water in the liquid state.

Authors of the biblical account could not have described it differently from the way they did. In ancient time, people imagined that there was only a short distance between the earth and heaven. Limited ancient cosmology presented an incomplete worldview; therefore, the universe did not exist as we see it. People in ancient times observed the sky to be blue during the daytime. The water on the surface of the earth also appeared blue. Therefore, they concluded that there must be water above the sky. The biblical narrative and the ancient epics about creation state that the sun orbits the earth above the sky but below the water. They did not know the real reason that the sky was blue.

Authors of the biblical account of creation did not know that the sky appeared blue because of the sunlight. Sunlight has three primary colors: green, red, and blue. The atmosphere absorbs the green and red colors. The blue color is scattered, making the atmosphere appear blue during the day. Because the atmosphere disperses the blue-colored light, sun appears yellow during the day but red at sunrise and sunset. However, the Sun emits white light. The wavelength of the red-colored light is shorter than the green-colored wavelength. Therefore, at sunrise and sunset, the red color penetrates the atmosphere, making the sky red. When the sun rises above the horizon, the atmosphere absorbs the red and the green colors. Because of these physical phenomena, people in ancient time concluded that the water above the sky flooded the earth.

Where did the flood water come from? Observation of the surface of our planet reveals a large-scale deformation in the Earth's crust. The deformation of the Earth's crust has impacted the layers below it. The asthenosphere, which is the layer between the magma and the lithosphere, displays deformations caused by a solid object's pressure. The asthenosphere is highly viscous; therefore, it should be uniform in appearance. A mechanically more robust and solid layer above it exerts an uneven pressure on the asthenosphere. The lithosphere's thickness varies and is, at various places, deformed by the crust. The segments of broken lithosphere layers and the crust rest at various angles instead of horizontally. The angular orientation of the tectonic plates exerts pressure on the layers below.

The original layers of Earth's crust were formed by volcanic activity and the surface's cooling. The planet earth was much hotter during its initial process of formation. The hot liquid lava flows in all directions and almost evenly. Therefore, the layers should have initially been horizontal and more uniform in thickness. The high-temperature liquid lava cannot form layers at various angles. Therefore, the large-scale deformations in the Earth's crust occurred later in the planet's history, and not at the beginning of its formation. Continents, high and rugged mountains, and the deep sub-oceanic tranches are not the result of the earth's initial structure but an event that took place later in history. However, the mechanics of the earth's formation followed the law precisely. What produced the large-scale deformation in the upper layer of the earth? A geologically destructive event is the only probable cause.

The Cause of the Destructive Event

Both the biblical account and the ancient epics list water as the primary destructive force that deformed the earth's surface and destroyed humankind. However, what was the source of such a large quantity of water to flood the entire Earth?

Also, the water destroyed all life on the surface, but did not break the Earth's crust. The shape and appearance of the Pacific Ocean's landmass support the probability of the earth's destructive collision with a large extrasolar body that released the floodwater. None of the known near-earth bodies is large enough to shatter the earth's surface like an egg when it is dropped. Perhaps humans could estimate the size, velocity, and mass of such an extrasolar body. However, the process and effort required for such an undertaking are complex. Additionally, such an effort would require considerable human, monetary, and computational resources.

The extrasolar body impacted the earth where the Pacific Ocean is today (just north of the equator). The angle of the impact had to be from east to west and north to south. The collision occurred at a compound angle, which produced complex dynamic forces. However, the force vector appears to have been greater to the south and west.

The unique characteristic of the Pacific Basin supports the probability of such a collision. The impact shattered the earth and created tectonic plates. The shape and the orientation of layers in the tectonic plates and some islands are the result of a geologically destructive event. The angles and a sharp peak of the mountains, which one can observe today, could not have been produced by a gradual uplifting. The planet earth is too young to have experienced such a gradual upheaval. Rugged mountains, such as the Himalayas, Rockies, and Andes, were formed by a forceful and sudden upheaval.

Presently, the tectonic plates are returning to their original location and orientation. This activity produces most of the earthquakes that the earth has today. Because Earth is liquid below the asthenosphere, its spin on its axis contributes to the tectonic plate's motion. The rotational velocity varies in the boundary layer between solid and liquid matter. Additionally, the earth's rotation produces torque transfer between the solid and highly viscous layers and adds to tectonic plates' motion.

The dynamic behavior of the planet earth after the flood is considerably more complex than before its collision with an extrasolar body. Because the direction of the impact was from east to west, the Himalayas were formed first. The earth's crust buckled upward and created a high and rugged mountain chain. The mountain chains of the Rockies and the Andes formed a short time after the Himalayas. These mountains are somewhat lower in height, which indicates that the angle of impact was from east to west. The force vector's magnitude in the westerly direction was slightly greater than the force vector in the easterly direction. The time interval between initiation of formation of the Himalayas, and of Rockies, and Andes had to be relatively short.

The depth of the sub-oceanic tranches on the Pacific Ocean's west side is deeper than the east side. The depth of the sub-oceanic tranches on the west side indicates that the impact angle was from east to west. The force of the impact pushed South America, Antarctica, Australia, and perhaps parts of New Zeeland to the south. The appearance and shape of the southern tectonic plates indicate that the angle of impact has also been from north to south. The Pacific Ocean floor's tranches are roughly arranged in a circle, with an opening to the southern end of the Pacific Ocean.

The earth's collision with an extrasolar body created a large depression, which is the Pacific Ocean. Shockwaves traveled around the Earth in all directions. Shock waves collided on the opposite side of the planet and created a depression, which is the Atlantic Ocean. The rebounding shockwaves traveled back in all directions, repositioning the tectonic plates and resulting in islands and forming other mountains and mountain chains. The shockwave of the impact oscillated back and forth around the planet for some time, reshaping and rearranging the initial position and shape of the earth's crust's smaller components.

The shell of water that was an integral part of the lithosphere and the crust existed under high pressure. As the earth's crust shattered, the water rose high above the crust's surface and created a dense cloud. The impact propelled the subterranean water upward at high velocity that carried the earth's shattered crust debris and deposited it downstream. The water that reached high altitude fell to the earth as heavy rain.

We cannot describe the dynamics of the tectonic plates that were produced by the destructive impact and resulting oscillations of the shockwave precisely. There were no surviving eyewitnesses. Noah and his family saw the geysers but not the fractures that released the water for the geysers. While the terrain surrounding the Noah's ark experienced the surface cracks, the collisions of the crust segments came later. The ark has been floating already when the upheavals occurred near the ark. The geysers were under high pressure and, therefore, reached significant heights.

We can conclude that Noah did not see the earth's surface fractures because they were not close to where the ark stood. By the time the shockwaves traveled back and begun to deform the crust, conceivably the ark was already floating. God ensured that the ark is safe.

Did Noah observe the fracturing of the earth's surface that produced the floodwater? We do not know. If he observed the event, did he pass it on to his descendants? We do not know. There is no known account of how much Noah and his family sow. The authors of the biblical account of the flood did not present it as an oral tradition. Authors of ancient accounts, which preceded the biblical account do not present it as a tradition that was passed down through generations.

Any traditional information concerning the flood had to be given orally. Changes in oral traditions were inevitable. The authors of the biblical account of the flood list specific dates and times. On what did they base the precise dates? We do not know. However, there is evidence that a destructive event involving water happened. Therefore, we must accept the account as it appears in the Bible but moderate it with modern-day knowledge and observations.

> In the six hundredth year of Noah's life, on the seventeenth day of the second month–on that day all the springs of the great deep burst forth, and the floodgates of the heavens were opened. (Genesis 7:11 NIV)

Earth does not and never did float on some large body of water, as ancient cosmology maintained. Also, there was no water above the heavens, as the ancients believed; therefore, there were no "flood-gates of heaven" either. However, in agreement with accurate modern-day observations, the absence of these does not negate that a destructive event involving water happened on Earth. There is a high probability that it did occur in a time that generally coincides with the biblical account.

The water below the earth's crust had a higher temperature than the surface water. Therefore, higher-temperature water could have released a large quantity of steam. The water that rose high in the atmosphere combined with steam and probably created a cloud that blocked the sunlight from reaching the planet. Also, the strong force of impact caused by the extrasolar object stopped the rotation of the planet. Earth spins from west to east. Therefore, the east to west angle of the powerful collision could have stopped the earth's rotation. The probability that the earth's rotation about its axis stopped is remarkably high.

The rotation of the earth did not resume quickly. Thus the water on the earth that was opposite to the Noah's ark location had time to freeze. The planet's side that was opposite to the region where Noah's ark floated remained in the shade long enough for its water to freeze. There is still visible evidence that thick ice covered the Americas. It took perhaps two hundred years or more for the ice to melt. As the ice melted, the water level on the planet earth increased and flooded the lower altitude regions.

The destructive collision with an extrasolar object pushed the earth slightly outside of the habitable zone's centerline. The impact, as stated earlier, has tilted the earth's axis of rotation at 23.5 degrees compared to the solar axis of rotation. These two outcomes of the collision made the earth's orbit around the sun elliptical. A circular orbit, as stated earlier, is an ideal orbit. The distinctive temperature seasons testify to the fact that the earth's orbit is elliptical. A circular orbit would ensure a more uniform distribution of temperature on the planet earth. If the Earth's axes of rotation were parallel to the sun's axis it would contribute to a more uniform temperature on the earth's surface.

The elliptical shape of the earth's orbit becomes evident when comparing the summer and winter solstices. There are 184 days from the summer solstice to the winter solstice. However, there are 173 days from the winter solstice to the summer solstice. The difference is because of the change in the orbital speed of the planet in an elliptical orbit. The gravitational influences in the solar system produce variations in our orbit's eccentricity over a long amount of time. Therefore, there is a varied impact on the seasons.

How long did it take the earth to sufficiently stabilize? We do not know. The earth's tectonic plates moved (they still move) continuously. Shock waves oscillated around the planet numerous times. How many times did it happen? How long did the disturbance last? We do not know.

The oscillations of the shock waves moved the tectonic plates and repositioned smaller components of the earth's crust. Ensuing volcanic activity contributed to changes in the tectonic plates' location, shape, and in the smaller parts of the crust. The authors of the biblical narrative state that water kept rising for 40 days; and remained for 150 days, before it began to recede. In the biblical narrative, the time given is not sufficient for a complex dynamic that is associated with the shattered Earth's crust to reach a near-equilibrium state.

Earth's crust is heavy. Therefore, the tectonic plates' movement and repositioning of the smaller components had to take a longer amount of time. Readers of the biblical account concerning the flood should be aware that the entire event transpired in conformity with the law that the Creator established before creating the universe. How long did it take for the earth to resume the rotation about its axis? We don't exactly know. Did the earth return to the same speed at which it rotated before the collision? It probably didn't.

The length of days now may not be the same as before the flood. Initially, the impact's force was an extremely destructive event that made days longer because of the earth's rotational interruption. Because of the earth's rotational interruption, the days on the side where the ark floated had to be longer. The night was longer on the opposite side of the earth. (The length of the twenty-four days may not be the same now as before the event.) Therefore, monitoring the beginning and end of days has been difficult during the initial phase of the flood.

People in ancient time did not know that the earth orbited around the sun. They did not know that the rotation of the earth about its axis determined the length of day and night. This knowledge was not a part of simple ancient cosmology. The authors of the biblical narrative thought that the sun's travel from east to west above the flat earth determined the day's length. The length of night depended on how fast the sun could get from the west to the east side of the earth. The authors of the biblical narrative relied on ancient cosmology's concept.

The authors of the biblical account of flood state that wind has begun to blow before the end of 150 days.

> But God remembered Noah and all the wild animals and the livestock that were with him in the ark, and he sent a wind over the earth, and the waters receded. (Genesis 8:1–2 NIV)

The onset of the wind indicates that the resumption of the earth's rotation had begun. The rotation of the earth about its axis reestablished the atmospheric motions and the high-altitude winds. The sun had started shining on the earth's surface and heating the atmosphere, contributing to atmospheric motions' resumption. Recovery of the earth's rotation reestablished high and low atmospheric pressure cycles. The earth rotates from west to east. Therefore, the initial wind could have been from the east. Location of high and low atmospheric pressure is not known. People in ancient time did not know that atmospheric pressure existed.

The only human witnesses of the flood's cataclysm were Noah and his family. Did they often look out the opening under the roof? We do not know. Therefore, we must rely on the authors of the biblical account of the flood. However, reading the flood account must aim at understanding the nonexplicit message that is portrayed in it and not the mechanics of the flood event.

The flood event did not change or impact the rest of the universe and our solar system. The laws that order the universe remained the same. The flood event impacted and rearranged the upper layer of the Earth only. The dynamics of the breakup and upheaval of the earth's crust by the destructive collision have been unimaginably devastating. The Pacific Ocean region experienced unimaginable forces and turbulence. No human-made vessel could have survived there. However, God cared for Noah's ark and its passengers.

The authors of the biblical account of the flood and ancient epics imply that the ark was built somewhere in or near the ancient country of Urartu. The region where Noah built the ark experienced cracks in the earth's crust but not a destructive buckling of it. Numerous geysers sprung up everywhere in the area where the Noah's ark stood. The springs of the great deep produced heavy rain only, but the ground under the ark did not experience destructive motions. The small opening under the ark's roof limited the view of the land below and the sky above.

The authors of the biblical account did not say whether Noah's ark had a steering mechanism to direct its path. Therefore, the way of the ark had to be maintained by force that was outside of the ark. Accordingly, the proper conclusion is that the Creator guided Noah's ark. Only the Creator knew where it would be safe for the ark and its passengers. Noah's ark floated in relatively calm water between today's Black Sea and Caspian Sea and northern Mesopotamia. However, the direction of the ark's movement varied because water currents alternated its direction.

The region of the ancient country of Urartu (Ararat) has volcanic mountains, some of which existed before the flood. Mountains that are formed by volcanoes have a cone-like shape. However, those mountains suffered significant erosion during and after the flood. Some lower mountains near the northern and the eastern edges of the ancient Urartu were formed by an upward buckling of the earth's crust. However, the mountains that were formed during the flood in Urartu region are not tall enough to have threatened Noah's ark.

God ensured that Noah's ark stayed in relatively calm water. The angle of the extrasolar body's impact, as stated earlier, stopped the earth's rotation for some time. How long did it stop? We do not know. However, the stoppage of the earth's rotation could have persisted for most of the Flood time. Because the earth did not rotate for some time, the region where Noah's ark floated remained in the sunlight. Therefore, the water on the earth's side where Noah's ark floated did not freeze because the sun maintained the temperature above freezing level. The earth's crust's condition suggests that the force of the extrasolar body's impact has been strong enough to stop the earth's rotation. If the collision force was sufficient enough to tilt the earth's axis of rotation to 23.5 degrees, it was adequate to stop the earth's rotation.

9

Noah's Ark Rests

THE BIBLICAL ACCOUNT of the flood states that after 150 days the ark rested. For 150 days, the flood remained at the level that it had reached during 40 days of rain.

> The water receded steadily from the Earth. At the end of the hundred and fifty days the water had gone down, and on the seventeenth day of the seventh month, the ark came to rest on the mountains of Ararat. (Genesis 8:3–4 NIV)

The biblical narrative uses the mountains and not mountain. The Jewish flood account does not point to one mountain in the Urartu region on which the ark rested. It could have rested on any of the mountains in the area. The Hebrew Bible Tanakh does not identify a specific mountain of the Ararat region or claim it knows of one. However, modern-day Christians believe that Noah's ark rested on the tallest mountain in the area. Therefore, the tallest mountain is the Mountain of Ararat.

The conjecture that Noah's ark rested on the tallest mountain in the region sounds logical. However, the biblical account does not specify the ark's location when the water has receded sufficiently for the ark to touch the solid ground. Most Bible scholars agree that Noah's ark rested in the southern region of the ancient Assyrian part of Urartu. The area where Noah's ark rested is northeastern Turkey, Southern Armenia, and northern Iraq.

On Turkey's border with Armenia, the Mountain Ararat is a volcanic mountain that existed before the flood. Therefore, it was there during the flood period. The approximate one year of the flood is not enough for a volcanic mountain like Ararat to form. However, other volcanic mountains in the ancient Urartu region are lower in height but equally probable for the ark's resting place. The likely region where Noah's ark rested is somewhere in the north or northeastern end of Lake Van in Turkey. God ensured that the ark rests at the place where its exit would be unobstructed and accessible.

Significant and prolonged volcanic activity and the movements of the tectonic plates continued after the flood. As the ice on the side of the Earth opposite the region where Noah's ark rested melted, the water level increased. The water from the melting ice submerged large coastal areas after the flood. It has taken several hundreds of years for most of the ice to melt. Additional readjustment in the tectonic plates and islands took place during the melting of ice. Earth needed sufficient time to reach relative stability. Volcanic activity along the fractures and tranches in the earth' crust continued globally after the flood. Volcanic activity that took place because of the flood was ongoing. Therefore, the earthquakes of various intensities continued to affect the Earth's surface.

The biblical-flood narrative says that in the third generation after Noah, the earth was divided. The great-great-grandson of Noah's was named Peleg because "in his time, the earth was divided" (Genesis 10:25). Africa's tectonic plate moved north to what is today's Turkey. The movement of Africa's tectonic plate and the associated effects created the Aegean Sea and the Marmara sea and opened the passage into the Black Sea. This event shows that the earth has taken a significant amount of time to reach a relative equilibrium. Observation, by Noah's third-generation descendants of the opening of passage into the Black Sea implies that Noah's ark rested somewhere north-northeast of the Lake Van. It was part of the ancient Urartu region.

The flood event changed Earth's condition and reduced its ability to support carbon-based intelligent life significantly. The biblical flood reduced the long lifespan of humans dramatically. Earth is no longer in its original equilibrium. The conditions on the planet are no longer favorable for the long life. According to the Septuagint, there were approximately 1,200 years from the flood to Abraham's birth. The Masoretic text claims that Abraham was born about 292 years after the flood. The chronology in the Septuagint appears to be more dependable.

Abraham lived 170 years. Noah lived 930 years. The planet earth could not have reached its final configuration in three hundred years. As the ice melted, the water kept rising and flooding the low-lying areas. Therefore, the destructive collision's complex dynamics had to remain for more than three hundred years to moderate things sufficiently. People in ancient time did not practice an accurate count of years. Also, the ancient-time people did not maintain uniform record and counting of years.

God's intervention with the flood indicates that humankind, in its condition and with its attitude, could not have continued much longer. Whether it was intentional or not, humankind's self-destruction become inevitable. That only one person (Noah) remained in God's favor confirms that humankind before the flood has reached its lowest level of morality. Before the flood, the Earth's state and peoples' behavior demonstrated that human who lived a long timed would commit more evil acts than those who lived a short time. Therefore, the reduction in the lifespan of humankind stands as the most beneficial consequence of the flood. Humankind continued to practice evil deeds after the flood. However, God preserved humankind until the Messiah came at just the right time.

Noah, at God's instruction, exited the ark and offered a burnt offering to God. This practice was a way of worship to acknowledge God as a Sovereign. The burnt sacrifices were a common practice and a way to show admiration for God. Everyone acted as a priest when offering a burnt sacrifice. After Noah's sacrifice, the biblical account of the flood states that God established a covenant with Noah and his family. However, the covenant with Noah was a covenant with all of humankind.

> "I establish my covenant with you: Never again will all
> life be destroyed by the waters of a flood; never again will
> there be a flood to destroy the earth." (Genesis 9:11 NIV)

The covenant with Noah is God's covenant with humankind. Humanity had no part in it and nothing to offer. God also gave Noah and his sons the same command that he gave to Adam and Eve at creation. After the flood, there was a new beginning for humankind; therefore, God gave the same command. However, this was not the re-creation of humankind.

> Then God blessed Noah and his sons saying to them,
> "Be fruitful and increase in number and fill the earth."
> (Genesis 9:1 NIV)

The authors of the biblical account of the flood presented, as stated earlier, violence as the main reason for the flood. Therefore, here they presented a command God gave to Noah and his sons. The indiscriminate violence toward human beings is the most probable reason for the flood. Accordingly, the authors of the biblical account state that God issued a command concerning human behavior.

> "Whoever sheds human blood, by humans shall their
> blood be shed; for in the image of God has God made
> mankind." (Genesis 9:6 NIV)

God the Creator is selfless love. God does not possess selfless love. He *is* love. Selfless love is God's irreducible nature. Because God loved humankind before he made it, he made it in his image.

> The Lord appeared to us in the past, saying: "I have loved
> you with an everlasting love; I have drawn you unfailing
> kindness." (Isaiah 31:3 NIV)

God's everlasting love does not have a beginning or end. God does not love something because he created it. He created because he loved all he determined to create. God knew what kind of creation he wanted to have before he began creating. God loved what he planned to create. Because he was the everlasting love before he began creating, he created humankind because he already loved it. Accordingly, humans should display the love of God, the selfless love. Therefore, violent behavior toward God's creation conflicts with the reason for creation.

The above command became the basis for most of the laws and regulations concerning social order and behavior after the flood. Soon after the flood, people become aware that a form of government or social order is necessary to regulate social behavior. However, people became aware that such an order couldn't function by voluntary means. Accordingly, a form of government became necessary to enforce social order and people's behavior. Governments, which were established by the people, had the authority to implement capital punishment to protect human life.

The biblical account of the post-diluvial world was mostly Jewish and concerned the laws and regulations that were pertinent to the Jewish Nation. However, the extrabiblical accounts describe the attempts by other nations and societies to regulate social behavior. The authors of the biblical narrative concerned with the post-diluvial world do not dwell much on the laws implemented by different post-diluvial cultures. The rapid transition to the story about Abraham in the biblical narrative could be the reason for the brief account of human activity before Abraham's birth.

The flood event redirected the path of humankind through its history. However, the flood event did not change the evil human nature. Humankind became a sinner by nature in Eden's garden, and it continued as such after the flood. In the first man (Adam), the sin committed in Eden's garden made humankind incapable of changing its nature.

The replacement of sinful human nature had to await the coming of the Messiah. God created humankind; therefore, only he could replace the spirit of humankind and destroy its sinful nature. God accomplished it through the body of Jesus Christ on the cross at Golgotha. However, before the Messiah came, God had to, once more, redirect the path of humankind through its history. The next chapter addresses the second redirection of humanity's path through its history.

10

The Tower of Babel

PERHAPS ONLY A few centuries after the flood, the people forgot the reason for it. Anti-diluvial people pursued personal aims and goals without regard or concern for other human beings. There was a total indifference concerning the norms of social morality and civility. Post-diluvial people quickly forgot that indiscriminate and selfish violence displeased God. Therefore, God destroyed hopelessly corrupt humankind by flood.

Perhaps the people who lived soon after the flood no longer acknowledged and feared God, the Creator. Babel's tower is evidence that the people wanted to secure their destiny and safety through their own efforts. They did not rely on the Creator for their long and fruitful survival. They forgot the things that God accomplished for humankind. Therefore, they disregarded God's command.

The primary threat to the survival of sinful humanity after the flood was that they were one people. They functioned as a single intelligent entity. God created one humankind. One humankind is required for proper administration of the universe. The more members such a society has, the higher power that it has. The post-flood people had one language. They used the same words with the same meaning. These requirements were essential for humankind to exercise enormous power under the law.

They were able to function as a single order of intelligence rather than as a collection of individual human beings.

The ancient epic states that post-diluvial people lived in harmony; therefore, violence was not an issue after the flood. Advanced study and experiments in quantum cosmology imply that humankind as a single order of intelligence would possess a wide-ranging power. For sinful humankind, such a power can be disastrous. The authors of the biblical account concerning the Tower of Babel confirm that humankind functioned as one. The biblical narrative gave this state of humankind as a reason that people began building the Tower of Babel.

> Now the whole world had one language and a common speech. As people moved eastward, they found a plain in Shinar and settled there. (Genesis 11:1–2 NIV)

Most Bible translations say, "As people moved eastward." However, the Septuagint and the Jewish Bible say that people migrated from the east. Translators of the New English Translation of the Bible stated that either way is proper. The post-diluvial people could have spread eastward along the Caspian Sea. The territory south of the Caspian Sea is the northern territory of modern-day Iran. From there, they probably descended into regions near the Euphrates and Tigris (biblical Mesopotamia). The Mesopotamian valley is better suited for agricultural activity. The southern part of the Mesopotamia region possibly remained covered with water after the flood. When the Mediterranean Sea's passage to the Black Sea opened, the Persian Gulf receded and revealed the "plain of Shinar."

Authors of the biblical account of human activity after the flood do not say how much time it took for people to spread eastward. The Mesopotamian plain was probably underwater until the passage to the Black Sea opened. If so, people would not have gone east along the lower region of today's Turkey and Iraq. They would have followed the upper region along the Caspian Sea. The earlier accounts say that people descended from the east into the valley. It is the most likely occurrence. The assertion that people spread eastward may be biased by the preferred landing location of Noah's ark. Because the exact location is unknown, people's movement from the east down to Mesopotamia is probable.

Nevertheless, people settled in the valley of the Euphrates and Tigris and became prosperous there. They decided to build a city with a tall tower and establish a secure and long-enduring society. The city and the tower were not a problem. Many a city, in ancient days, had a tower. The critical issue with the post-diluvial people is that they were one. They had one language and the same speech pattern. As such, the whole of humankind had an identical way of thinking. They had the power to make a unified, single, intelligent decision.

According to the implications of the quantum cosmology's reality experiments, a single intelligent decision, becomes irrevocable. Such capability gives one humankind exceptional power. If humankind were one, with the knowledge it has today, it could change how reality appears. Such a capability conforms to the laws that order this universe. Sinful humankind with such power could implement irrevocable results in our universe. Even if the consequence of decision did not result from an intentional, unified intelligent decision, it is still irreversible.

Modern-day humanity could not perform such a task because it is not one. The united world could not do so, either. One people with one mind and one way of thinking, are required for the unified intelligent decision. There are ongoing efforts to try to achieve one humankind. However,

God ensured that the post-flood people would not gain sufficient knowledge that was required for such a capability.

> The LORD said, "If as one people speaking the same language they have begun to do this, then nothing they plan to do will be impossible for them." (Genesis 11:6 NIV)

The people in the plain of Shinar decided to build a city with a tower that would reach to the heavens. Why did they want to reach heaven? Did they think they could influence the interaction of gods with the people? Perhaps they wanted to ensure that gods would never again attempt to destroy the people on Earth. The authors of the biblical narrative about Babel's tower state that people wanted to make a name for themselves. This attitude is self-centered, therefore, is not in conformity with God's plan for humanity. A self-centered attitude leads to disregard for the common good. It could then lead to violence aimed at protecting personal ways. Therefore, God took away the capability that would eventually lead to self-destruction by humankind.

Perhaps the people wanted to establish a secure and long-lasting society and preserve their identity. By being all together as one, they could accomplish their highest selfish aims. In the state of being one humankind, they could maintain a more favorable relationship with their gods. Ancient epics about the tower say that one humankind lived in harmony with each other and their gods. Perhaps the people in the plain of Shinar wanted to secure a long-lasting peace with their gods. However, the biblical narrative about the tower does not give reasons other than that people wanted to make a name for themselves. There is no doubt that humans have been lovers of themselves. There is no place for self-loving people in our universe.

Because the post-flood people were one, they had almost unlimited power to accomplish whatever they desired. As one, they could increase their knowledge much faster than if they were divided. However, because humankind could not see the future, their best decisions in the present could become disastrous in the future. The modern-day scientific and engineering experience shows that the future's statistical projections are dependable for only up to thirty years. Projection longer than thirty years comes with an unacceptable level of confidence.

The Creator made humankind with the ability to increase in knowledge. However, the sin in Eden's garden brought a change in the way sinful humans think. Therefore, humankind is incapable of making a long-lasting good decision. Sinful humanity could self-destruct in the future, even with the best decision in the present. Some current-day scientists are concerned that if wide-ranging knowledge continues to increase at an accelerated rate, humankind's survival will become threatened. The fear is that human nature is increasingly unreliable for proper stewardship of the exotic technology the knowledge brings.

According to the biblical narrative, God stated that being one is not good because it accords unlimited power to sinful humankind. (Genesis 11:6) However, God determined to save the rebellious humanity; therefore, he preserved it until the Messiah came. God ensured that humankind would not reach the point of no return. Accordingly, God confused the language of the people so they could not make a single intelligent decision.

Post-diluvial people did not understand the real reason for the confusion of their language. They did not know that the same way of thinking by all is dangerous for the fallen humankind. Some modern-day scientists support the possibility that knowledge may reach a dangerous level in one humankind's hands.

Modern-day concepts aimed at achieving one world center on one blood and race. Such humankind could achieve the same way of thinking by all the people. As perceived by the experts, one world must be of mixed races to make it a seamless world. Such a world with the knowledge that we already possess could realize incredible goals.

The dispersion of the people throughout the planet earth has diversified humankind to a point where one world's creation is challenging. Also, frequent wars and violence against people have eliminated human population segments, making it impossible to achieve single humankind. If achieving an ideal one humankind fails, the humankind may try a technologically assisted effort in creating one humankind. Experts are exploring the feasibility of such technology. Sufficient human knowledge exists foe such an undertaking. Through the prophet Daniel, God said that humanity would not accomplish these goals.

> As you saw iron mixed with ceramic clay, they will mingle with the seed of men; but they will not adhere to one another, just as iron does not mix with clay. (Daniel 2:43 NKJV)

The nations of the world could and will form a conglomeration of sovereign countries, a new form of union. However, they will not become one in the same manner the people were before the Tower of Babel. To preserve humankind, God intervened to redirect the path of humanity through its history. The people's dispersion slowed down the increase in knowledge, ensuring that humanity would not reach the point of no return before the Messiah came. Therefore, the confusion of language is another example of God's selfless love.

> "Come, let us go down and confuse their language so they will not understand each other. So the LORD scattered

them from there over all the earth, and they stopped building the city." (Genesis 11:7–8 NIV)

The confusion of language resulted in the loss of harmony among people. It also increased hostility and desire for power and dominance of one group of people over another. Nevertheless, the language confusion among the people is not God's punishment but a saving act of selfless love. Perhaps the people who started to build the Tower of Babel thought they were building a tower directly below the envisioned gate to heaven. The concept of a physical gateway to heaven was peoples' anthropomorphic view of God. They believed that gods needed passage through the solid surface that was above the water. Gods needed passage to descend to earth. When they blocked the God's gate, they probably concluded that he got angry with the people and confused their language.

Did God confuse the language of all of humankind or only of those working on the tower? Authors of the biblical account did not specify the population size at the time of Babel's tower. Even if the tower's building occurred three to five hundred years after the flood, the earth's population would have not been very large. Ancient epics state that people lived in harmony. Therefore, wars did not cause a slower increase in population. Even so, the earth's population could not have been very large. People spread west as well as east after the flood. Therefore, all the people did not descend to the plain of Shinar.

The tower of Babel had to be the largest building project in their time. If so, it required a large workforce. Therefore, even if only the language of those who were working on the tower had been confused, it still created an insurmountable obstacle to a unified effort. Those who worked on the tower had to leave the community of Shinar because no one could understand them. Authors of the biblical account did not include the description of the ensuing consequences.

More importantly, the extent of their language confusion is not the aim of the account. The primary and overriding reason for the confusion of language is that people were one. The whole of humankind at the time of the tower spoke the same language. They employed the same words with the same meaning. Therefore, as one humankind, they possessed enormous power within the laws that govern this universe. It's probable that if they have been allowed to continue in the same state, the people would have reached a point of self-destruction. However, God had a plan to re-create humankind at just the right time. Therefore, God redirected humanity's path through history to preserve it until the Savior of the world came.

Humankind after the flood had the same speech pattern. It must have been the speech pattern that the Creator gave to humankind at creation. Therefore, if God altered the human speech pattern only, the humanity as a whole experienced the confusion of language. All of humankind has the same spirit (intelligence). Therefore, a change in speech patterns would have impacted all of humanity. Regardless of the mechanics and the extent, the confusion of language was an act of God, who loves humankind and wants it to live forever.

Post-diluvial people did not know the true gate to heaven. Because of a limited ancient worldview, the people did not know that there was no physical gate to heaven. The true gate to heaven is a person. Jesus explained that he was the true and only gate or the door to heaven and God.

"I am the gate; whoever enters through me will be saved. They will come and go out and find pasture." (John 10:9 NIV)

Before the Messiah came, the people did not understand that Jesus Christ was the door or gate to heaven. The authors of the biblical account of the Tower of Babel maintain that people decided to build the city with the region's possibly tallest tower. The people, perhaps, did not want the name God would send to them. They wanted to make a name for themselves. Later in the Bible, God promised that he would make a great name for Abraham. The name God promised to Abraham was Jesus Christ.

Salvation is found in no one else, for there is no other name under heaven given to mankind by which we must be saved. (Acts 4:12 NIV)

The authors of the biblical account of the Tower of Babel only devoted nine verses to the incident. They do not identify the source of their information about the city and the tower. However, the authors based the biblical narrative on an actual incident. Some ancient epics, written before the biblical account, speak of similar event or even the same event. Ancient-world epics say that people did not like the way gods interacted with them. Initially, the people lived in harmony with each other and the gods. However, the people increased in number, and all spoke the same language and words when addressing gods. Perhaps, each of the ancient gods may have desired adoration specific to them.

In ancient times, people thought that the gods did not like it when all the people were saying the same thing. Therefore, the people decided to build a tower that reached to heaven to control their living situation on the earth. In response, the gods confused the people's language to ensure that they failed in their effort. The ancient gods acted out of anger toward people. However, the biblical narrative presents a story that looks more like an act of love than anger. The God of Israel did not punish the people for building the tower. No one can threaten Gad because he is the Sovereign Power. The God of Israel acted in love to preserve humankind from self-destruction.

As said earlier, one humankind has almost unlimited power to accomplish its self-centered goals. Experts who are concerned with humanity's long-lasting survival in our universe conclude that Earth will experience severe problems in about one thousand years. One nation, one race, or one power could not solve the human's or Earth's issues. One humankind only could develop and implement a solution. Accordingly, there are ongoing efforts to identify and implement the means for making humankind one as it was before languages were confused. (This author has participated in such discussions). Only one humankind could make a single intelligent decision concerning the practical solution to the earth's expected problems. The expected and unavoidable problems could be solved by a unified intelligent decision only.

The broad-range increase in human knowledge is accelerating. Experts are projecting that in the relatively near future, human knowledge could double every hour. Human knowledge's growth does not violate the Creator's laws, which he established before creating the universe and humankind that is in it. However, an increase in knowledge in the hands of self-loving people presents a danger for humanity. Some present-day scientists expect that human knowledge will reach a dangerous level by the year 2050. How it will become dangerous remains to be seen. God informed us through the prophet Daniel in a vision that a time would come when knowledge would increase. A one way that the increase in knowledge could become a problem is the ability of controlling human brain from distance. Study of how to control the human brain from distance is ongoing. The required computational power is near its level. Control of the human brain from distance could result in undesirable consequences.

> "But you, Daniel, roll up and seal the words of the scroll until the time of the end. Many will go here and there to increase knowledge." (Daniel 12:4 NIV)

Some experts expect that a dangerous level of human knowledge will present problems within the twenty-first century. Experts are alarmed because observed and expected conditions on the planet earth and within humankind are conducive to severe difficulties for which there is no known solution. The increase in population may overwhelm the planet's capability to support it. Increase in world's population is required for a successful single global economy. However, humanity must increase its knowledge if it wishes to address the expected problems. The increase in knowledge is necessary, but it may become dangerous for existence of humankind. Therefore, there is no possible human solution. God must intervene.

Accordingly, global scientists are exploring the possibilities of obtaining the knowledge that can help create one humankind. However, regardless of how deeply humanity is united, it cannot solve expected problems. Only one humankind could do so. However, even though the increase in human knowledge conforms to God's words, God said humankind would not be one. If humankind cannot be one, the knowledge will not present a significant threat to human existence. A time is coming when people will pursue social engineering to achieve a seamless world by ensuring that nationalities and races are not an obstacle to mingling and marriage among global humanity. This achievement is the goal of the one world system being pursued today.

The ongoing efforts aim to bring the countries and nations of the world into a unified whole. Such a union of sovereign countries will ensure unrestricted movement and travel by individuals. The experts hope that such a union of sovereign countries will enable efforts aimed to create one humankind. Even though the world will become united, humankind will not become one. Those who are in the kingdom—Jesus Christ should not fear because God is in charge. Humankind cannot destroy this planet. Our universe and the Earth belong to God again, and only he can destroy them.

God created the whole of humanity in one man (Adam); therefore, it is natural for humankind to be one. The entire humankind has one and the same spirit (intelligence). In the Bible, the spirit is the same thing as intelligence in quantum physics. New Humankind, which God created in Jesus Christ, will be one because Jesus asked the Father to make it so. This treatise will describe the re-created humankind later. Jesus prayed to the Father for the apostles and those who will follow them.

> "I have given them the glory that you gave me, that they may be one as we are one – I in them and you in me – so that they may be brought to complete unity. Then the world will know that you sent me and have loved them even as you have loved me." (John 17:22 NIV)

It is not wrong for humankind to seek the way of becoming one because God created it as one. However, because of sin, it can be dangerous for humankind to be one. God knows the future; therefore, he acts in ways to preserve humankind until the fulness of time, which only he knows. Post-diluvial humankind did not commit wrong by building cities with towers and establishing an organized society. Only one humankind can best serve its everyday needs and well-being. What then was wrong with the Tower of Babel? Other cities had towers or ziggurats. However, the builders of the Tower of Babel chose it as their protector. They did not trust and rely on God anymore.

The chief problem with the Tower of Babel was the attitude of the people who began to build it. They said, "Let us make a name for ourselves." They did not realize that they could not make a name for themselves. The biblical account concerning Abraham's call emphasizes that God was determined to make a name for Abraham and therefore, for the whole of humankind. What name has God given us? The name for the new humankind (Jesus Christ) came from God and him alone.

> The LORD had said to Abram, "Go from your country, your people and your father's household to the land I will show you. I will make you into a great nation, and I will bless you; I will make your name great, and you will be a blessing." (Genesis 12:1–2 NIV)

By their efforts, the Tower of Babel's builders wanted to secure their destiny and be free from the interference of gods. They did not trust God, the Creator. They did not trust their imaginary gods either. They wanted to enter heaven by their efforts, means, and ingenuity. They aspired to ensure that God or gods in heaven, would not punish people whenever they wished. They did not believe that God, the Creator, loved them. Therefore, God said what the principal fault with the Tower of Babel's people was when he spoke to the Father of confusion.

> "You said in your heart, I will ascend to the heavens; I will raise my throne above the stars of God; I will sit enthroned on the mount of assembly, on the utmost heights of Mount Zaphon. I will ascend above the tops of the clouds; I will make myself like the Most High." (Isaiah 14:13–14 NIV)

The Zaphon literally means the heights of the north. Historically, men aspired to become more than they were. They refused to realize that there was a limit to what the created intelligence could do. Most human achievements based on *I will* lead to a permanent failure. Even the noblest goals with *I* in the center become evil and fail because men cannot change their nature. Self-loving and proud people refuse to accept that they have no destiny and future without God. The self-centered attitude of people still persists.

Because the planet earth has experienced a destructive event, the experts who are concerned with humankind's survival conclude that people and nations of the world must explore the universe as one people. Experts assert that humankind must explore the universe with selfless love because our universe's very foundation is selfless love. They project that the planet Earth, in its present condition, will not be suitable for life on it much more than one thousand years.

Accordingly, they have convinced the world's technologically advanced nations to begin a concept-definition phase of development to come up with the means (the proverbial tower perhaps) to reach farther from Earth than ever before in history. Nations and countries with the appropriate means are funding and pursuing a concerted effort to discover whether an Earth-like planet exists near our solar system. If such a planet is discovered and confirmed, humankind's goal is to transfer carbon-based, intelligent life (humans) to the new planet.

The solar systems that are nearest to ours are the Alpha and Proxima Centaurus, in the constellation Centaur. Suppose the Web telescope launch, which is scheduled for the fall of 2021, is successful. It will provide reasonably accurate information concerning the existence of a suitable planet in the solar system that is nearest to ours. Several technologically capable nations have agreed to send a multinational team to the region of the Alpha Centaurus. They hope to arrive there in the year 2110, if all goes as planned. Such an effort will increase knowledge and develop higher technologies, whether the flight to the constellation Centaur becomes a reality or not.

However, the agreed-to goal is an act of hopelessness. Humankind wants to ensure an enduring destiny for itself on its own terms. The Creator made the Earth good; however, humankind ruined it by its decisions and actions. Only God, the Creator, can make it good again. All human efforts, which are undertaken in self-centered vainness, are futile. Helpless, sinful humankind wants to make a name for itself rather than trusting God, who has given us Christ Jesus's name.

Self-deceived humanity intends to reach heaven on its terms. It refuses to consider that their efforts, no matter how good they appear, can and will end in a disaster. Soon, however, humankind will experience an unwanted awakening. For humans in the current state, it is impossible to travel outside our Galaxy. Humans do not live long enough to reach vast distances. Humans could not explore our galaxy past the solar system that is nearest to ours because of their short life span.

There is no certainty that another suitable solar system with just the right planet exists in our Galaxy. There are ongoing studies concerning the extension of human life so that humankind can explore farther from our home and solar system. Chances that humanity will discover a form of the Tree of Life are zero or none. Therefore, the effort to reach ever greater heights could become a disappointment like the Tower of Babel.

The only solution to the human predicament in the post-diluvial world was for God to issue a command again: "Let there be light." God re-created sinful and helpless humankind in Jesus Christ, on the cross at Golgotha. God did bring light to the dark world, but humans did not like it.

> This is the verdict: Light has come into the world, but people loved darkness instead of light because their deeds were evil. (John 3:19 NIV)

Because humankind pursued darkness, God redirected the path of humanity through its history twice. He did it to ensure that humanity will not self-destruct before he brought the light at just the right time. The fulness of time has come. The Light of the World did come, and God did re-create the helpless humankind. God created humankind in his image on the sixth day of creation. However, humanity lost the image of God in the Garden of Eden. Because he loves his creation, God came to Earth in human body to restore his image in humankind. The re-creation of humankind is the subject of the next part of this treatise.

SECTION 4

11

The Re-Creation of Humankind

THUS FAR, THIS treatise presented God, who created our universe, the earth, and humankind to inhabit it. God, the Creator, made everything that humanity needs for an eternity, before he created humankind. There were no reasons why humankind could not remain loyal to God, the Creator. Unfortunately, humankind did not remain faithful to God. Humankind, in its representative Adam, joined the rebellion against God. Why did Adam decide to disobey God? We do not know. We probability could not understand it in our present state. Will we ever know the reason for such a decision by Adam? We do not have the necessary information to know the answer to this question. The salvation of sinful humankind could be accomplished by re-creation only.

When the Creator returns everything to its original condition, evil will no longer exist. Even thoughts about evil will not be possible. Therefore, evil thoughts also will not be possible. Accordingly, new humankind may never know the reasons for evil and Adams's decision to join it. God is love; thus, he created humanity because he loves it. Accordingly, he determined to re-create humankind and restore it to himself as his children. The re-creation of humankind is the only way humanity could continue to exist. This treatise will now address the creation of new humankind. It will describe how God accomplished the creation of new humanity.

The whole of old humankind became a helpless sinner in the first man Adam. As the representative of humanity, Adam had to make a deliberate, intelligent decision for all of the future humankind. Such a decision had to be made at just the right time. Adam had to possess all the necessary knowledge needed to make a deliberate decision that would determine the irreversible state of humankind. Adam had to make such a decision because God created the humankind's future members in him. Humanity inherited the spirit God put in Adam at creation.

> From one man he made all the nations, that they should inhabit the whole earth; and he marked out their appointed times in history and the boundaries of their lands. (Acts 17:26 NIV)

God knew each member of humankind by name and the time in history when they would be born, before he created our universe. He also knew by name all the members of humanity that ever would be born. There is nothing hidden from God, the Creator.

At just the right time, Adam had to make intelligent decision to determine whether humankind would become perfect or a sinner by nature. Unfortunately, he made a wrong decision. Because the spirit that God put in Adam was the spirit of humankind, Adam's decision became irrevocable for all of humanity. Therefore, humanity became a sinner by nature, and was condemned to eternal death. Consequently, humankind became utterly helpless concerning its nature. Human nature is the human spirit, which is not made from matter and has no visible physical properties. Therefore, humans could not alter the human spirit's nature, neither by another intelligent decision nor by physical effort. The human spirit in the Bible is human intelligence in quantum physics. The advanced experiments in quantum physics imply that intelligent decisions are irrevocable and inalterable.

The human spirit God put in Adam was neither perfect nor a sinner before the deliberate, intelligent decision that was made by Adam. Because our universe is a statistical one, we could say that the human spirit in Adam possessed both possibilities. Adam, as an intelligent being, had full freedom of choice. When a deliberate, intelligent decision has been made by the spirit, all other options cease to exist. Therefore, when Adam made the intelligent decision on behalf of humankind, he and all of humanity had to remain in an achieved state and with no way out. Humanity remained an utterly helpless sinner who is separated from God, the only source of life. Fortunately for humanity, God had a plan for the humankind that he loved before he created our universe.

God, the Creator, made Adam and the whole of humankind that was in him good. Adam did not have deficiencies that could have determined his decision and choice. Adam did not possess a tendency toward either of the two options. His intelligent decision had to be his without any outside influence. God is love. Therefore, the Creator would not have created Adam with a predisposition that could influence an intelligent decision. There are many paths through human history. However, only one way led to a successful eternity. God informed Adam that if he remained loyal to his Creator, he would have eternal life. If he disobeyed, he would die. Therefore, Adam was given the free will to choose humanity's path through history and its standing before the Holy God.

God informed Adam and the women about evil. He told them that the tree in the middle of the garden was designated as a tree of knowledge of good and evil. Therefore, God informed the first human pair concerning his enemy and the enemy's goals and plans. God did not interfere with Adam's deliberate, intelligent decision about whether to remain loyal or disobey. God gave Adam all he needed for a careful, appropriate, and intelligent decision. Therefore, Adam had no one to blame but himself. He knew that whatever he decides to be would make him that way for eternity. Adam's knowledge about God's plan of salvation did not give him the liberty to disobey.

A created intelligence does not have the power to make two opposing intelligent decisions concerning the same matter, neither in parallel nor in a sequence. The deliberate, intelligent decision to disobey remained such forever. In like manner, the spirit's decision to become perfect remained so for eternity. Another intelligent decision could not overturn an initial, deliberate, and intelligent decision. Also, no future individual member of humankind, who was created in Adam, could have made an intelligent decision to alter the one made by Adm. Even if someone wanted to reverse Adam's decision at any future time, that person could not do it because such an option did not exist after the decision made in the Garden of Eden.

The human spirit God put in Adam became a sinner by nature, and it was incapable of making the right decision concerning its state. Therefore, the sinful human spirit had to be replaced with a perfect spirit. Only a perfect spirit (life) could live forever. Only God, the Creator, has the power to destroy the sinful spirit and replace it with a perfect spirit. God accomplished such a wonderful exchange on the cross at Golgotha, as we shall see later. He achieved it by creating new humankind in Jesus Christ. As a representative of new humankind, Jesus Christ had to decide whether it should be perfect or not.

The spirit God put in Jesus, the representative of new humankind, was the same order of spirit he placed in Adam at creation. Jesus had the same state of human spirit that Adam had before he sinned. Jesus, however, made a correct intelligent decision in the desert while he was tempted in the desert,. His deliberate, intelligent decision made him perfect; therefore, the new humankind is perfect in him.

> In bringing many sons and daughters to glory, it was fitting that God, for whom and through whom everything exists, should make the pioneer of their salvation perfect through what he suffered. (Hebrews 2:10 NIV)

This treatise will explore this concept later.

Why the Re-Creation?

Re-creation is the only possible solution concerning the sinful human spirit. The sinful human spirit could not be made good. It had to be replaced. The creation of humankind is depicted by Illustration 3, which is repeated here for the ease of reading and understanding. The circles have no specific meaning. They are simply an illustration of a point being made.

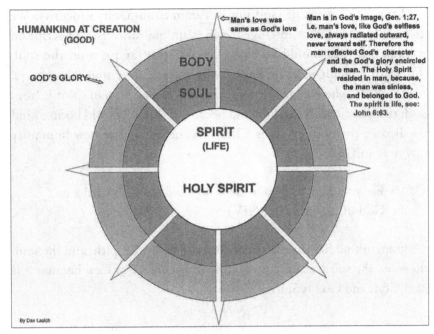

Illustration 3

God made the human body from the dust of the earth. Only the human body was made from the dust. God gave a spirit to humankind. He did not create it with the body. Therefore, humanity is in God's image in its spirit.

> So God created Mankind in his own image, in the image of God he created them; male and female He created them. (Genesis 1:27 NIV)

God the Creator breathed life (spirit) into the body that he had made from the earth's dust. The body then became a living being. The spirit that God put in Adam was the life of humankind.

> "The Spirit gives life; the flesh counts for nothing." (John 6:63 NIV)

Therefore, the spirit God put in Adam is humanity's identity. We are a unique order of intelligence in a unique universe. Description of human beings should be based on the spirit and not on the soul. Our spirit (intelligence) makes us who we are. Our soul (chemistry), including our knowledge, shows what we are. The human spirit is from God; therefore, we live in him and because of him. The old humankind has died in the body of Jesus Christ on the cross. The new humanity now lives in God.

> For you died, and your life is now hidden with Christ in God. (Colossians 3:3 NIV)

Humankind has three components: the body, the spirit, and the soul. However, the spirit makes humankind in the image of God because it is from God, and God is Spirit.

> "God is Spirit, and his worshipers must worship in the Spirit and truth." (John 4:24, NIV).

Spirit is not made of matter, the body and soul are. Therefore, the human body and soul cannot be in the image of God. Humans should refrain from describing God in terms of matter. God created matter; therefore, we should not attribute to him material characteristics.

Because the human spirit is from God, who does not change, the human spirit is inalterable also. The human spirit in the Bible is human intelligence in quantum physics. Results of the advanced studies in the field of quantum cosmology imply that human intelligence is unchangeable. It can neither increase nor decrease. Also, human intelligence cannot get damaged. The human brain can sustain damage. However, intelligence (human spirit) remains the same.

Even if the brain does not develop properly, the intelligence is the same as in the properly developed brain. The human brain may be deficient in processing information. However, human spirit (intelligence) stays the same. It is so because the human spirit (intelligence) is unchangeable. It is a fixed part of humans. Human knowledge changes; however, intelligence remains at level that God gave us at creation. The deliberate, intelligent decision in Eden's garden changed the nature of the human spirit from goodness to a sin; however, the order remained the same.

God put his Spirit, the Holy Spirit, in the living being to communicate to him that he was a child of God. However, after Adam sinned, the Holy Spirit left him. The first man Adam was a human being and the son of God because God made him. According to Luke, Adam was the son of God.

> The son of Enosh, the son of Seth, the son of Adam, the son of God." (Luke 3:38 NIV)

The representative of the new humankind is also the Son of God. God made Jesus, who was first among many members of the new humanity. Members of new humanity were also referred to as newborn believers or as yielded believers.

> The angel answered, The Holy Spirit will come on you, and the power of the Most High will overshadow you. So the holy one to be born will be called the Son of God. (Luke 1:35 NIV)

But because Jesus shared the human body with the people through a woman, he is also a Son of Man or Son of Mankind. The male part of humankind did not have a role in the incarnation of Jesus. Only the female part of humanity participated with hep of the Holy Spirit. The above verse indicates that Jesus is the Son of God because of the manner of his conception. God created the first humankind. He also created the new humankind

The biblical account of creation states that Adam and the woman were made in the image of God. How did the first human pair demonstrate God's image? They showed it by their love. The love of Adam and the woman radiated outward only, as depicted in Illustration 3. Like God, the first human pair demonstrated selfless love. They did not realize they were naked because they did not look at themselves. Therefore, because they reflected God, the glory of God surrounded the first human pair.

They did not need any other clothing. The Holy Spirit governed the way the human spirit generated thoughts and the first human pair acted. The *I* did not exist because Adam and the woman did not look at themselves and seek their considerations.

God is love; therefore, he created humankind because he loved it. God did not create humanity because he needed someone to love, as some Christians maintain. God is never concerned about his own needs. He is the Sovereign; therefore, everything belongs to him. God, the Creator, is not selfish. If he were, his love would not be selfless. Selfless love does not serve self-interests. God first prepared everything that humankind would need because he loves humanity that he created with an everlasting love. Description of God, the Creator, in human terms is inappropriate. God created us in his image; however, he is not in our image. When we bring God to our level, we practice idolatry.

> "No one has ever seen God, but the one and only Son, who is himself God and is in closest relationship with the Father, has made him known." (John 1:18, NIV)

Jesus Christ revealed God who loves humankind selflessly.

Adam, the representative of the first humankind, did not remain loyal to God the Creator. The nature of humankind after the deliberate, intelligent decision in Eden made it necessary to re-create humankind. The re-creation was the only way to restore humanity to God as his children. Disobedience made humankind utterly helpless to do anything concerning its sinful nature. The Creator had to make the helpless humanity new. Illustration 4 depicts the consequence of disobedience.

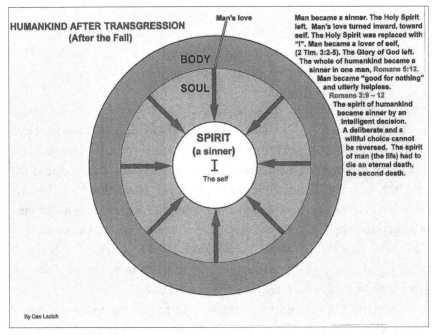

Illustration 4

The helper that Adam chose ate the fruit from the tree God told them not to eat from. She ate the forbidden fruit because God's enemy deceived her. However, her disobedience did not impact all of humankind. Adam, who was not deceived, made a deliberate, intelligent decision to join the woman in disobeying God's command.

> And Adam was not the one deceived; it was the woman who was deceived and became a sinner. (1 Timothy 2:14 NIV).

However, her appearance did not change even though she sinned. When Adam made a deliberate, intelligent decision to disobey, the appearance of both of them changed. Now the consequence of sin became visible.

The first human pair and all of humankind, should have died the instant Adam made a deliberate decision to disobey God. However, God delayed the punishment for sin because he loves humanity and was determined to save it. Therefore, God put humankind under grace until the Messiah comes at just the right time.

God presented Christ as a sacrifice of atonement, through the shedding of his blood—to be received by faith. He did this to demonstrate his righteousness, because of his forbearance he had left the sins committed beforehand unpunished. (Romans 3:25 NIV)

Had God punished humankind for sin at any time in history—from Eden to Golgotha—humanity would have ceased to exist. Our universe and Earth in it would have ceased to exist also. Because the receipt of the new human spirit (life) had not been given yet, humankind would have ceased to exist if God had punished it before the cross at Golgotha. Some may wonder why God did not replace the human spirit in the Garden of Eden. The new human spirit had to make a deliberate decision before it could replace the sinful human spirit. All this had to be accomplished at just the right time, which was known to God only.

God, the Creator, is the source of life for all created intelligence; therefore, it cannot exist if he forgets it. There is no other source of eternal life besides God the Creator.

After he twice redirected humanity's path through history, God began preparing humankind for the Messiah's arrival, (the new humanity). God began preparing the people so that he could bring the Messiah, into the world and create new humankind. Accordingly, he called Abraham, not because of who Abraham was but because of who he would become.

"Abraham will surely become a great and powerful nation, and all nations on earth will be blessed through him. For I have chosen him, so that he will direct his children and his household after him to keep the ways of the LORD by doing what is right and just, so that the LORD will bring about for Abraham what he has promised him." (Genesis 18:18–19 NIV)

Humankind sinned and became a slave in the kingdom of sin and darkness. However, God has determined to bring the kingdom of light and righteousness into the world. Therefore, God chose people from Satan's territory, through whom he would accomplish his plan for humankind.

Abraham was one of the individuals God called and prepared to be loyal to him despite the difficulties. There was no doubt in the past that the Sovereign God was in charge. Yielded believers should not fear because the Sovereign Lord is still in charge of the fallen world's affairs.

Abraham came from an idol-worshiping family. However, the Sovereign Lord knew that Abraham would become loyal to him. God knew that Abraham would become a believing friend who loved him. Accordingly, God informed Abraham that through his descendants, the Savior of the world would come. Abraham learned, and he believed that God would create new humankind in the Savior of the world. Therefore, Abraham longed to see the day of the Messiah.

> "Your father Abraham rejoiced at the thought of seeing my day; he saw it and was glad." You are not yet fifty years old, they said to him, and you have seen Abraham! "Very truly I tell you," Jesus answered, "before Abraham was born, I am." (John 8:56–58 NIV)

With his answer, Jesus showed the reason that he was God with us. He is the I Am in heaven. However, on the earth, he is the Savior of the world, the Son of God, and Man.

God helped Abraham visualize the day of the Messiah, the Savior of the world. He instructed Abraham to sacrifice his only son, whom he loved on the altar.

> Some time later God tested Abraham. He said to him, "Abraham!" Here I am, he replied. Then God said, "Take your son, your only son, whom you love—Isaac—and go to the region of Moriah. Sacrifice him there as a burnt offering on a mountain I will show you." (Genesis 22:1–2 NIV)

Salem was a city-state in the region of Moriah in Abraham's time on Earth. The rock dome called Moriah was on the eastern side of Salem. The hill where Abraham was to sacrifice Isaac was on the western side of Salem. Melchizedek, the priest to God Most High, was the king of Salem in Abraham's time. Salem became Jerusalem in King David's time. David captured the Jebusite fortress Zion, outside the wall of Salem, and renamed it the City of David.

God instructed Abraham to sacrifice Isaac on a hill outside the western wall of Salem. Centuries later, the heavenly Father sacrificed his Son, whom he loves, on the same hill to forever remove humankind's sin. The hill is the same Golgotha where Jesus Christ was crucified. Golgotha is outside the western wall of Jerusalem. King Solomon built the Temple on Mount Moriah, outside the eastern wall of Jerusalem. The Temple was oriented from east to west and aligned with Golgotha on the western side.

Abraham was prepared to sacrifice his only son because he loved God. However, God provided a ram for sacrifice in place of Isaac. This experience served as a powerful show-and-tell for Abraham and reassured him concerning God's promise to him. God helped Abraham visualize the day that God would sacrifice his Son for the sin of the world. At just the right time, God sacrificed his Son at the same place where Abraham was to sacrifice his son Isaac. However, God provided a ram for sacrifice in Isaac's place. The ram's had head was tangled in the thorns.

The ram symbolically represented Jesus. Jesus was crucified with a crown of thorns on his head, on the same hill where Abraham sacrificed the ram that was tangled with its head in thorns. Jesus referred to this experience when he said that Abraham saw the day that the Son of God would be sacrificed for the world's sin. The Temple on the Mount of Moriah was aligned with the hill (Golgotha) where Abraham was to sacrifice ram in place of Isaac. The western end of the Temple faced the Golgotha. The whole arrangement served as a powerful reminder of what God would do for humankind at just the right time.

Centuries later, God instructed Moses to lead Abraham's descendants out of Egypt to the land he had promised to Abraham. When they arrived at the Mount Sinai, God wanted to talk to his people directly, with no intermediary. However, when the people saw God's glory heard his voice, they were afraid. The people then instructed Moses to go to the mountain, listen to God, and relay what he said. They would obey it. Even though they did not die in God's presence, the people thought that they would die if they heard God's voice again.

And you said, "The LORD our God has shown us his glory and his majesty, and we have heard his voice from the fire. Today we have seen that a person can live even if God speaks with them. But now, why should we die? This great fire will consume us, and we will die if we hear the voice of the LORD our God any longer. For what mortal has ever heard the voice of the living God speaking out of fire, as we have, and survived." (Deuteronomy 5:24-26 NIV)

The people were aware that they had not died in God's presence, even though they had heard God's voice. However, they thought they would die if they heard God's voice again. They admitted that they had survived hearing God's voice. Nevertheless, the people said to Moses,

"Go near and listen to all that the LORD our God says. Then tell us whatever the LORD our God tells you. We will listen and obey." (Deuteronomy 5:27 NIV)

God wanted to be with his people and speak to them directly. However, they were afraid to be in the presence of their living God. It was true that sinners could not come into the presence of the Holy God and live. However, if God wanted to talk with his people, it would not harm them. God is the Sovereign and the only source of life; therefore, it is always as he ordains it to be. The sin barrier existed between God and humankind until the Cross of Christ. Sinners did not have the power to overcome the sin barrier. The law that condemned sinners to eternal death could not provide means to approach God without fear. The new creation (new humankind) is free through Jesus Christ.

God heard what the people said to Moses. However, he knew that people, who are helpless sinner, could not remain faithful to the thing that they had promised.

The LORD heard you when you spoke to me, and the LORD said to me, "I have heard what these people said to you. Everything they said was good. Oh, that their hearts would be inclined to fear me and keep all my commandments always, so that it might go well with them and their children forever." (Deuteronomy 5:28–29 (NIV)

The people meant well, and they were sincere when they made the promise. However, they did not realize that sinners could not render perfect obedience regardless of how hard they tried. Sin in the Garden of Eden has left humankind helpless, hopeless, and incapable of doing good. Sincere promises and good intentions do not accomplish much. By nature, a sinner is always a sinner regardless of sincere intentions. Righteous intentions and deeds count for more than sincere intentions and deeds. The old sinful humankind could not behave righteously. Righteous behavior could only come by new creation.

However, God was determined to reside among his people because he loves them. Therefore, God instructed Moses to tell the people to build a sanctuary for him. God did not ask that they make a sanctuary to him but for him. The word *sanctuary* also means *a hideout* or *a hiding place*. God asked that the people build a dwelling place for his hideout, where he would reside among them. The people would not see his glory, therefore, they would not be afraid. However, they would know that their God was with them. The Temple's interior design served as a reminder that God was preparing the world for the Messiah's arrival.

> "Then have them make a sanctuary for me, and I will dwell among them. Make this tabernacle and its furnishings exactly like the pattern I will show you." (Exodus 25:8 NIV)

Sanctuary here does not refer to a physical structure but the way that God would be with his people without making them afraid. Therefore, the tabernacle was a structure that serves as a dwelling for God's hideout. The arrangement of the furnishings and the interior of the tabernacle pointed to the promised Messiah. The physical structure served to house God's show-and-tell concerning what he would do for humankind at just the right time.

The entire tabernacle and its surroundings were the holiest place because God's residence was there. Therefore, the top of Mount Moriah, where Temple (tabernacle) stood, was the most holy place.

> "This is the law of Temple: All the surrounding area on the top of the mountain will be most holy. Such is the law of Temple." (Ezekiel 43:12 NIV)

Therefore, when we, in human terms, speak about God being in the Temple in heaven, all of heaven is the most moly place. A physical structure or a wall could not restrict the holiness of the Most High God. His whole dominion is most holy because he is in it. Only God is the most holy. Therefore, if we say God is in heaven, all of heaven is the most holy place. However, we could not speak of God in a specific location and a particular region. God is the Absolute Spirit. He always *is!* The High Priest of new humankind entered the most holy place during the morning of his resurrection. He entered heaven once and for all.

The Temple's orientation on Mount Moriah and the pattern of its furnishing are extremely significant and essential depiction of the salvation of sinners. The physical building portrayed what God would do for the rebellious humanity. Temple on Mount Moriah served as the most powerful show-and-tell form of presenting the Messiah. It presented what God would accomplish on behalf of rebellious humankind. God instructed the prophet Ezekiel to teach the people about Temple and the message portrayed by it.

> "Son of man, describe Temple to the people of Israel, that they may be ashamed of their sins. Let them consider its perfection, and if they are ashamed of all they have done, make known to them the design of Temple—its arrangements, its exits and entrances—its whole design and all its regulations and laws. Write these down before them so that they may be faithful to its design and follow all its regulations." (Ezekiel 43:10–11 NIV)

Through prophet Ezekiel, God instructed the people to be faithful to the Temple and arrangements of the Temple's furnishings. The Temple pointed, symbolically, to God's residence with humankind in the body of Jesus Christ. God instructed the people to be faithful to the Temple because it represented Jesus Christ symbolically. However, Jesus Christ never entered the Temple in Jerusalem. He went into the courts only, where the people were. Only priests in the order of Aaron could enter the Temple. Jesus was not a Priest according to the order of Aaron, but he was of Melchizedek. With its annual ritual, the Temple served as a powerful show-and-tell depicting what God will do at just the right time.

The Significance of the Earthly Temple

How did the Temple on Mount Moriah symbolize Jesus Christ? The Illustration 5 may help to visualize it.

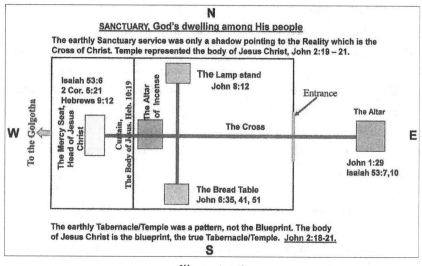

Illustration 5

The Temple on Mount Moriah was oriented from east to west. The entrance to it was on the eastern end. The Mount of Olives was located on the eastern side of the Temple Mound. The Messiah, Jesus Christ, entered the temple area through the Golden Gate. The Golden Gate was a part of the Jerusalem's eastern wall. Just before the Babylonian conquest of Jerusalem and Judah, God's glory departed the Temple and went east. The departure to the east is significant, as we shall describe later.

> Then the glory of the LORD departed from over the threshold of Temple and stopped above the cherubim. While I watched, the cherubim spread their wings and rose from the ground, and as they went, the wheels went with them. They stopped at the entrance of the east gate of the LORD's house, and the glory of the God of Israel was above them. (Ezekiel 10:18–19 NIV)

The glory of the Lord was his dwelling among his people. However, Judah's people were unfaithful to their God; therefore, the glory of the Lord their God left the Temple. The permanent residence of God among humankind had to await the coming of the Messiah. The body of Jesus Christ was God's actual and permanent dwelling with re-created humankind. Through the prophet Ezekiel, God informed the people that God's glory would return to the Temple, as it stood in Jesus' time. The prophet Ezekiel, in chapters 40–44, described the restored Temple. In a vision, he observed the return of the Lord God's glory.

> Then the man brought me to the gate facing east, and I saw the glory of the God of Israel coming from the east. His voice was like roar of rushing waters, and the land was radiant with his glory. The glory of the LORD entered Temple through the gate facing east. (Ezekiel 43:1–2, 4 NIV)

The prophet Ezekiel referred to the returning glory of God as *he*. Therefore, his vision of the return of God's glory concerns the Messiah's coming in person. The Wiseman who brought gifts to Jesus at his birth came from the east. They saw the star rising in the east that announced the birth of the Messiah. Therefore, God's glory departed to the east and returned from the east.

> After Jesus was born in Bethlehem in Judea, during the time of King Herod, Magi from the east came to Jerusalem

and asked, "Where is the one who has been born king of the Jews? We saw his star when it rose and have come to worship him." Mathew 2:1–2 NIV)

Jesus ascended to heaven from the Mount of Olives, which was east of the Temple. The two men dressed in white spoke to the apostles as they watched Jesus go into heaven.

"Men of Galilee, they said, why do you stand here looking into the sky? This same Jesus, who has been taken from you into heaven, will come back in the same way you have seen him go into heaven." (Acts 1:11 NIV)

The two men dressed in white were angels. They said that Jesus would return from the east on a cloud. Jesus ascended to heaven and to the east, on a cloud. The glory of the Father returned to the Temple from the east. The return of God's glory refers to the coming of the Messiah. The glory of the God of Israel in the earthly Temple signified God's residence among his people. In Jesus Christ, God is with the re-created humankind forever. Jesus Christ now rules God's dominion, as the representative of a new humanity. He will return from the east as the King of kings and Lord of lords.

God instructed Moses to arrange the temple furnishings exactly like the pattern he would show him. What was the pattern of the temple furnishings? When we draw a line from the altar at the east entrance to the covenant's ark, it forms an east to west straight line. The line from the bread table to the lampstand forms a north to south line. These two lines form a cross. The curtain separating the first chamber from the chamber where the ark of the covenant was, represents the body of Jesus Christ nailed to the cross.

Therefore, brothers and sisters, since we have confidence to enter the Most Holy Place by the blood of Jesus, by a new and living way opened for us through the curtain, that is, his body, (Hebrews 10:19–20 NIV)

The bread table symbolically testified about Jesus Christ, who is the bread of life.

> "I am the bread of life. Whoever comes to me will never go hungry, and whoever believes in me will never be thirsty." (John 6:35 NIV)

The lampstand symbolically represented the light of the world, Jesus Christ.

> "I am the light of the world. Whoever follows me will never walk in darkness but will have the light of life." (John 8:12)

The cover of the covenant's ark represented the head of Jesus Christ, where God placed the sin and the sinful life of humankind. By abandoning Jesus, God destroyed our sin and our sinful life forever because separation from God is the second death (no resurrection).

The Most Holy Place in the earthly Temple faced Golgotha, where God sacrificed his Son to take away the people's sin. God, through the body of Jesus, removed from humankind sin that it committed in the Garden of Eden and, therefore, all sins against the law. Golgotha is the place where Abraham was to sacrifice Isaac, his only son. When the High Priest in Aaron's order entered the Most Holy Place once a year, he faced Golgotha. The sprinkling of the blood of sacrifice for sin symbolically represented the placement of humankind's sins on the head of Jesus Christ.

> God made him who had no sin to be sin for us, so that in him we might become the righteousness of God. (2 Corinthians 5:21 NIV)

By dying the eternal (second) death, Jesus Christ took our sins to the eternal abyss from where they will never come back and count against us.

The debate and disagreement concerning the sacrifice for sin and the scapegoat are ongoing. The service of atonement in the earthly temple, the shadow, had two goats. These were shadow pointing to Jesus Christ. However, many Christians consider Jesus Christ to be the sacrifice for sin, but not the scapegoat. Some go as far as claiming that our sins are being placed on Satan, making him the scapegoat. This notion constitutes a great disservice to the Cross of Christ. Later in this treatise, we will see how Jesus Christ is both a sacrifice for sin and the scapegoat. The annual day of atonement ritual was a powerful witness to the Messiah on the cross at Golgotha. The entire ceremony pointed to only one person, who is our sacrifice for sin and the scapegoat: Jesus Christ.

The orientation of the earthly Temple and the furnishing arrangement has been a powerful witness to the reality accomplished in Jesus Christ. The earthly Temple and its annual ritual were temporary. The ritual of atonement had to be repeated annually. Jesus Christ is our permanent High Priest who lives forever and cannot die again. Therefore, what God accomplished on our behalf in the body of Jesus Christ is forever. Jesus Christ will never repeat the sacrifice for the sin of the world.

> These are a shadow of things that were to come; the reality, however, is found in Christ. (Colossians 2:17 NIV)

Through the shadow, the earthly Temple and its annual ritual, God proclaimed a clear message concerning the creation of new humankind. The earthly Temple, the arrangement of its furnishings, and the yearly ritual have been powerful demonstrations of the way that God will fulfill his promise to the rebellious humankind. Through the prophet Ezekiel, God explained how he would create new humankind and thus save humanity.

> I will give you a new heart and put a new spirit in you; I will remove from you your heart of stone and give you a heart of flesh. And I will put my Spirit in you and move you to follow my decrees and be careful to keep my laws. (Ezekiel 36:26–27 NIV)

God accomplished this scripture in Jesus Christ at the Incarnation and on the cross at Golgotha. This treatise will present this incredibly good news later.

The spirit of humankind that God put in Adam at creation sinned. The human spirit is the intelligence and the life of humanity. By his deliberate, intelligent decision on behalf of humankind, Adam made all of humanity sinful by nature. Humankind became, in Adam, utterly helpless to do anything concerning its new nature and condition.

The human spirit that sinned in Eden's garden could not be made good by anything humankind might want to do. The sinful human spirit had no options for correcting the act of disobedience by its representative, Adam. Replacement of the sinful spirit was the only option available. Nothing else could help. By replacing the sinful human spirit with the perfect human spirit of Jesus Christ, God restored humankind to him as his children. Therefore, God has fulfilled his promise to create new humankind.

12

Why Is the Incarnation of Jesus Christ Important?

CHRISTIANITY DOES NOT have a defendable definition concerning the nature of the Incarnation. Will it ever have one? It probably won't. Does it matter concerning our salvation? It probably does not; however, our faith must be built on a right foundation which is Jesus Christ. Our God, the Father, is merciful, and he loves us selflessly. Those who cannot reach an in-depth understanding should hold on to Jesus Christ as the only way to heaven.

When Jesus returns to take his own with him, many things will become clearer. However, yielded believers should not stop studying the scripture. The scriptures contain all that we need to know about Jesus and what he has accomplished on our behalf. We must know and understand all that Jesus Christ has left us through his apostles. However, our growth in knowledge must be for the Glory of God and Jesus Christ.

How did God accomplish the Incarnation on behalf of humankind? Because the readers of the scriptures like to discuss the Incarnation, it is presented here in some detail. When the time had fully come, God sent a Savior to humanity. The Savior of the world was the representative of the new humankind. Adam does not represent the new humankind. Jesus Christ is the representative of the re-created humanity forever. The new human spirit is from God. It is the gift of life to the humanity that he loves. God did not create the order of spirit called mankind. He gave it. Because our spirit is from God, the Creator, it is our life. All of humankind has one life (one intelligence). God is the only source of all life.

> "The Spirit gives life, the flesh counts for nothing. The words I have spoken to you – they are full of the Spirit and life." (John 6:63 NIV)

Quantum physics speaks of human intelligence in the same way that the Bible addresses the human spirit. The human spirit (intelligence) is not made from matter. There are no known particles of matter associated with human intelligence (spirit). The human spirit (intelligence) is unchangeable. Living human beings have three parts: the body, the spirit, and the soul. However, the spirit is our identity, and the soul is not. The human spirit is who we are, and the soul demonstrates what we are. The spirit God gave us makes us in the image of God. All of humankind has the same spirit (intelligence). Implications of advanced experiments in quantum physics support this assertion. The members of humanity distinguish among themselves by their knowledge and experience.

Advanced reality experiments in quantum cosmology imply that intelligent human decisions are irreversible and irrevocable. Therefore, we are right to conclude that the human spirit's decisions are unchangeable because they are final. The intelligent decision that Adam made in Eden, became binding to all of humankind, which God created in him. Therefore, none of Adam's descendants could have reversed the original, intelligent decision by a another one. All the consequences from the original, intelligent decision applied to all of humankind. The first man Adam became a sinner by nature. Therefore, all the descendants of Adam inherit both his sinful spirit and sinful biological nature.

The universal moral code demands eternal death for a sinner, and this is right. Sin separates sinners from God, who is the only source of life. Sinners are incapable of reestablishing contact with God, the Creator. Because sin is by a deliberate, intelligent decision, all possible options to correct the sinful status cease to exist forever. Therefore, sinners could not return to God by careful obedience to the Ten Commandments. Also, the more sinners try to obey their way back to God, the more they sin. Sinners cannot obey the law correctly

Additionally, humankind lost the image of God by sinning in Adam, in the Garden of Eden. By losing the image of God, sinners lost the ability to know God. Sinners could learn and know much about God; however, they could not know him. Sinful human beings could not know sin and God at the same time. The knowledge of sin makes it impossible to know God. In like manner, knowing God makes it impossible to know sin. Only the new creation could remedy the helpless state of sinful humanity. We can know God through Jesus Christ only.

"Now this is eternal life: that they know you, the only true God, and Jesus Christ, whom you sent." (John 17:3 NIV)

Humankind became utterly helpless and without hope by sinning in Adam. There has been no option for avoiding the righteous requirement of the Law. The sinners had to die eternally. There was no way out. Therefore, if a sinner wanted to gain a new life, the sinful spirit (life) had to die forever. The re-creation of humankind only could accomplish the replacement of a sinful life with a perfect one. God promised to do this in the fulness of time. God promised, through the prophet Ezekiel to give a new spirit (life) to humankind that he loves.

The human body could not decide what it wants to do on its own. Even the human brain could not function without intelligence (spirit) in it. The spirit (the intelligence) generates thoughts in the brain and commands the body concerning the decision's execution. Therefore, the human body could not have sinned in the Garden of Eden. The human spirit that God put in Adam sinned as an order of spirit (intelligence). When humankind's spirit sinned, it subjected the human body and all nature to the consequences of sin.

For the creation was subjected to frustration, not by its own choice, but by the will of the one who subjected it, in hope that the creation itself will be liberated from its bondage to decay and brought into the freedom and glory of the children of God. (Romans 8:20–21 NIV)

Adam subjected the human body, the earth, and the universe we live in, to frustration. Adam subjected all to decay in hope that all creation will be liberated from decay. This implies that he knew about the plan of salvation. Humans cannot hope for something about which they do not know. Our universe did not change physically because of Adam's decision. However, the universe does not yet have its intended manager, humankind.

Our new knowledge concerning the reality that we live in implies that human intelligence (spirit) can function only in the body that God made for it. Also, the human brain is made to function in our universe only. Both the universe and the human brain operate by the same system of logic. Therefore, the new spirit God promised to us could only work in this body. The human spirit that sinned and the new human spirit are the same order of spirit (intelligence). God accomplished the re-creation of humankind by replacing its sinful life (spirit) with the perfect life of Jesus Christ.

> "I will give them an undivided heart and put a new spirit in them; I will remove from them their heart of stone and give them a heart of flesh." (Ezekiel 11:19 NIV)

Therefore, the new spirit God gave us in Jesus Christ creates a new way of thinking and new attitude.

Apostle Paul contends that the new creation constitutes the new attitude of the human mind.

> You were taught, with regard to your former way of life, to put off your old self, which is being corrupted by its deceitful desires, to be made new in the attitude of your minds; and to put on the new self, created to be like God in true righteousness and holiness. (Ephesians 4:22–23 NIV)

Therefore, the new spirit in us, together with our mind's new attitude and way of thinking constitutes the new creation (the new birth). The new creation is still in the old body. However, when Jesus returns, he will give us a glorified body that is capable of supporting the new spirit we have in him. Our re-creation has made us like God. It has restored God's image in humankind. Only the re-creation of humankind could have restored the image of God in humanity. God has made us his children again. Unfortunately, some human beings, to their loss, do not want God as their Father.

The creation of new humankind gave us much more than we deserve. God removed our sin from us and restored us to him. He did not only forgive our sin. God took our sin away from us and destroyed it without a trace. We stand, in the eyes of God, as though we have never sinned. The removal of sin from us will becomes our living experience in the fullness of time. Never again in the whole of eternity will sin tempt us. Sin and the thought of it will not exist anymore. The new humankind will spend eternity with God, and we will be free from sin and its consequences. Even the possibility of sin rising again will not exist.

We concluded that the only option concerning humankind's continuing existence is replacing its life (spirit). Human beings could not have accomplished such a task. Only God had the power to destroy the evil spirit and replace it with the righteous one. The human spirit comes from God. There is no other source. God accomplished it by preserving the human body through a female part of humanity. However, the spirit (human intelligence) came from God and not from humankind's male role.

At his birth, Jesus shared the body that humankind had at the time of Incarnation. Therefore he is the Son of Man. However, Jesus did not inherit the life of Adam. He had the life of new humankind, which came from God not from man. Therefore, Jesus is also the Son of God because he is the representative of a new humanity. At the resurrection, even Adam will receive the life of Jesus Christ. The life that Adam received from God at creation died forever in the body of Jesus on the cross because it sinned.

Often, Christian publications and teachings address the Incarnation from the physical-body perspective. However, the critical part of the Messiah's Incarnation and birth is in the human spirit and not the body. The Messiah, Jesus Christ, did not receive a new or different body from the one that humankind already had. He received a new spirit (intelligence); therefore, he is the new humankind. When we address the Incarnation from the physical perspective, we cloud the understanding that God fulfilled his promise of a new spirit through the Incarnation of Jesus

Christ. God did not renew the sinful spirit in us, but he replaced it. The creation of new humankind is by receiving a new spirit from God. He did not make a new body at incarnation. The human spirit that God put into Adam sinned; therefore, it cannot become new, or right, again. Sinful nature is irreversible. In like manner, the righteous nature is irreversible.

The spirit (intelligence) is not from matter. Therefore, it is not subject to the laws of physics but to the law of intelligence. Accordingly, a deliberate, intelligent decision makes the spirit what it is. A bad decision makes it a sinner, and a good decision makes it perfect. Neither the subsequent deliberate, and intelligent decision nor careful obedience to the law could alter the initial deliberate, intelligent decision. An evil spirit could not make a good decision after he became a sinner. The sinful spirit could not live forever because it could not make a good intelligent decision to correct the first one. If a sinner were to live forever he or she could not be saved.

Even the best performance and behavior in human terms would be a violation of the law. That is the reason that a Christian must deny self and accept the life of Jesus Christ. Such a Christian literally becomes a new creation in the spirit. Because he now has the new spirit, the spirit of Jesus Christ, he receives the Holy Spirit to reside with the new human spirit. Therefore, the newborn Christian has a sanctified body. He or she then becomes a yielded believer and a slave to the righteousness from God forever. The righteousness in Jesus Christ is irrevocable.

However, a yielded believer has not been freed from possibility of sinning against the Ten Commandments. The new spirit, a new person, resides and functions in the old body. Therefore, a yielded believer does not sin deliberately, and he does not continue in sin. However, a newborn believer will sin against the law because of the old body it has. The good news is, that God accepts the old body's inadequate responses when it is commanded by the new spirit and guided by the Holy Spirit. The newborn believer must always say and live daily by the motto, "Not I but Christ." By saying this, we die to ourselves each day, and Christ lives in us. Such a state becomes visible in the life of a yielded believer.

Because the first spirit that God gave to the humankind at creation sinned, it became subject to condemnation by the Law. However, the new spirit that we have through Jesus Christ is not subject to the law's condemnation. Because of the old body, a newborn or yielded believer will sin against the Ten Commandments, but not against grace—Jesus Christ. We must not sin against grace by not believing that God has destroyed our sin and our sinful life forever and that he has given us the righteous and eternal life of Jesus Christ.

God accomplished the re-creation of humankind by putting a new spirit in the existing human body. The new human spirit had to make a deliberate decision. Jesus made a correct decision in the desert; therefore, his body became sanctified. By conquering the temptation, the new life that God put in Jesus became perfect. The Holy Spirit resided in the mind of Jesus. The Holy Spirit and the perfect life of Jesus sanctified his body.

When we accept Christ as our Savior, we accept his life as ours; therefore, Jesus Christ lives in us through the Holy Spirit that the Father gave us. God gave us a new spirit in Jesus Christ (the order of spirit called Man), which was the same as given to the first man, Adam at creation. Therefore, the new spirit that God gave us must have the same body God made on the sixth day of creation. The Holy Spirit, whom God gives to yielded believers, translates the inadequate words and response to commands by the new spirit into what is acceptable to God who loves us.

God has fulfilled his promise to give a new spirit to humankind. He also promised to give a new heart to humanity and to enable them to obey him. God told the people that he would remove their heart of stone. The heart of stone in the Bible denotes a stubborn or unresponsive attitude. It symbolizes the sinful human nature bent on doing what is wrong. Therefore, God promised to remove both the bent to sin and the sinful spirit from humankind. He accomplished it by destroying humankind's sinful spirit and their natural inclination to sin forever. Therefore, the new humankind created in Jesus Christ has a new life, beginning, and history in Jesus Christ.

Jesus Christ, as the representative of new humankind, had to decide what new humankind will be. Adam, the first humankind's representative, had to decide what the first humankind would be. It has not been revealed to humankind whether other intelligence orders, which have a representative, might exist in a universe suitable for them. Angels are ministering spirits, and they do not procreate; therefore, each angel decides for itself only. We cannot conclusively state the reason that the first human being, Adam, had to decide for all humanity.

However, we must accept that Adam did decide for all humanity and that his decision became irreversible. Jesus decided for the new humanity and his decision became irreversible. The members of the old humanity inherited the decision of its representative, Adam. However, the members of new humanity do not inherit Jesus' decision, but we must accept it by trusting him. The new humankind will not procreate at the renewal of things, according to Jesus. Therefore, there will not be an inheritance of human nature for the new humankind. The new spirit (nature) is an eternal gift to us.

God proclaimed everything that he created good, including Adam and the woman. Adam's responsibility was to determine whether he and all of humankind would be perfect or sinners. The life (the spirit) that God put in Jesus at Incarnation, was good also. Jesus, by intelligent decision, was to decide whether the new spirit would be perfect or not. Jesus conquered temptation, and the new life of humankind became perfect. However, we do not inherit the perfect life. We receive it through the new birth—the birth by the Holy Spirit that God gave us.

Representatives of the first and the new humankind received life (the spirit) from God; therefore, both are the sons of God. In his book, Luke traces the genealogy of Jesus back to Adam, whom he identifies as a son of God."

> Now Jesus himself was about thirty year old when he began his ministry. He was the son, so it was thought, of Joseph, the son of Heli, …the son of Enosh, the son of Set, the son of Adam, the son of God." (Luke 3:23–38 NIV)

Jesus could not have taken the life (spirit) from Adam because Adam became a sinner. Jesus shared the body of Adam's descendants, but his spirit was a new human one, which God gave him. Therefore, we cannot say that he took on himself the sinful nature (the sinful human spirit). He had the body (the biological nature) that was subjected to the consequences of sin. The biological nature of humankind did not commit sin, in the Garden of Eden. The human spirit sinned and subjected the biological human nature to decay. Therefore, the biological nature did not have to die forever but be transformed.

The way concerning the birth of the Messiah, the world's Savior, has not been hidden. Long before the birth of Jesus Christ, God informed his people of the way he would bring the Savior into the world. Approximately seven centuries before the birth of Jesus, God announced through the prophet Isaiah.

> Therefore the Lord himself will give you sign: The virgin will conceive and give birth to a son, and will call him Immanuel. (Isaiah 7:14 NIV)

The New International Version's Bible translators relied on the Hebrew Masoretic Text which says that Mary named Jesus Immanuel. However, the Septuagint, (the Hebrew Scriptures' translation into the Greek language before the birth of Jesus) states, "And you shall call his name Immanuel." The Septuagint existed about eight hundred years before the Masoretic text did. Some of the Christian exegetes of the scriptures apply the "you" to Mary, the mother of Jesus. However, Isaiah wrote this message from God about seven centuries before Mary was born. He could not have addressed her then as "You." Isaiah did not know that the name of the Messiah's mother would be Mary. Immanuel means "God with us." God instructed the people of Israel to name Jesus the Immanuel.

God promised to redeem his creation and be with them forever. God is forever united with new humankind, in the body of Jesus Christ, the Immanuel. There is increasing acceptance that virgin refers to a young or unmarried woman. The Hebrew could be translated as a young woman. However, the message in the above verse may not be that a young woman would conceive. Whether virgin or not, any a female, who is in her childbearing age, could conceive by a foreplay without physical penetration. However, a virgin woman could not naturally give birth to a child and remain virgin.

The "young woman will conceive" could be translated "a virgin will be with child." The New American Standard Bible translates it this way. It means that a virgin will hold her child in her hands. An early Christian writing, which was not included into the new canon, states that a midwife examined Mary after she gave birth to Jesus to verify that she remained a virgin. We could credibly conclude that Mary remained a virgin after giving birth to Jesus.

The Messiah shares the body with humankind; however, his birth was not a common one. The son whom God promised to Abraham was not born in an ordinary way. Therefore, the Son of God who was promised to humankind was not born in an ordinary way. That a young female conceives without the male's involvement was not a common occurrence. However, Mary conceived without being with a male member of humanity.

The birth of Jesus did not happen in a common way. For example, Mary did not have birth pains when delivering the baby Jesus.

> Before she goes into labor, she gives birth; before the pains
> come upon her, she delivers a Son. (Isaiah 66:7)

Such a birth is a real miracle. A female giving birth to a child without experiencing birth pains is not a common occurrence.

A virgin conceiving is not a miracle in the same sense as giving birth to a child and remaining a virgin. The birth of the world's Savior is the most significant event that happened until the cross at Golgotha. We should not maintain that the birth of Jesus was the same as any other human being. God, the Creator, made new humanity in Jesus Christ. That could not be viewed as an ordinary or common accomplishment. The creation of new humankind was a task impossible and unimaginable for the fallen humanity to accomplish.

The prophet Isaiah spoke to the nation of Juda when he wrote Isaiah 7:14. He did not speak to a young or a virgin woman. The variants in translations create a tension that diverts the reader from the message to a person. God informed his people that he would bring the Savior into the world in the fullness of time. God specified that the Savior of the world would be born of a virgin and that the Savior would be called Immanuel. Instead of determining the precise grammatical form of the statement "You shall call him," we should concentrate on the message. The message is that we should not fear because God was bringing a Savior. A detailed assessment of the exact way the Savior came is not good news. The good news is that Jesus Christ takes away the sin of the world.

God told the nation of Juda and the world that the son born of a virgin would be the Immanuel (the Messiah). He informed the people that in the Immanuel, he would be with humankind forever. The Immanuel, Jesus Christ, is God's eternal dwelling among his people. Often Jesus Christ is presented as a first and last name. However, Jesus is our kinsman redeemer, whose human name is Jesus. The Christ denotes what Jesus is. He is the Christ, the Savior of the sinful and helpless humankind. God of Israel, whose glory resided in the tabernacle in Jerusalem, has come back in Jesus Christ's person to dwell with the re-created humankind forever.

Joseph adopted Jesus, so he is also known as the son of Joseph. Mary and Joseph did not name the Immanuel, Jesus. Angel instructed them to give him the name Jesus. The name Jesus indicated what he would do.

> "She will give birth to male son, and you are to give him the name Jesus, because he will save his people from their sins." (Mathew 1:21 NIV)

Jesus was born of Mary, a human being. He conquered the temptation in the desert. On the cross at Golgotha, Jesus was the Christ, the Savior of the world. Through Jesus Christ, God created new humanity and gave it the perfect and eternal life of Jesus Christ. This treatise will address the wonderful exchange later.

Humankind was in darkness because of sin in the Garden of Eden. They lost the true knowledge of God, the Creator. The Creator only had the power to say again, "Let there be light."

> In him was life, and that life was the light of all mankind. The light shines in the darkness, and the darkness has not overcome it. (John 1:4–5 NIV)

The light, the new life of humankind, come from God because he is the source of all light. Sinful humanity could not have done anything to disperse the darkness that sin brought. However, God had a plan for the way to disperse the darkness which covered humankind.

At just the right time, God sent an angel to Nazareth to inform a young virgin that she had been chosen to give human birth to the Savior of the world. The angel's announcement to Mary happened when John the Baptist's mother was in her sixth month of pregnancy.

> In the sixth month of Elizabeth's pregnancy, God sent the angel Gabriel to Nazareth, a town in Galilee, to a virgin pledged to be married to a man named Joseph, a descendant of David. The virgin's name was Mary. (Luke 1:26-27 NIV)

The angel Gabriel informed Mary that the son she would give birth to will be called Son of God. Mary did not understand how she could get pregnant without a man. The angel told her.

> The angel answered, "The Holy Spirit will come on you, and the power of the Most High will overshadow you. So the holy one to be born will be called Son of God." (Luke 1:35 NIV)

The names Son of man and the Son of God have caused much misunderstanding of the person who Jesus was. Why was he called the Christ? Jesus Christ was the Son of Man in his biological nature (the flesh). In his spiritual nature, his life was from God; therefore, he is the Son of God. Curiously, the angel told Mary that the child would be called Son of God. He did not say that the child to be born was the Son of God but that he would be called so. The angel spoke to Mary in the future tense and not in the present or past. Granted, the birth of Jesus was in the future, beginning from the time the angel spoke to Mary. However, Isaiah, who lived centuries before Mary, used the future tense also.

> For to us a child is born, to us a son is given, and the government will be on his shoulders. And he will be called Wonderful Counselor, Mighty God, Everlasting Father, Prince of Peace. (Isaiah 9:6 NIV)

However, God could not be born. He is the Creator of everything that exists. God has no beginning. He was neither born nor made. He *is*. Also, God was not nailed to the cross at Golgotha. The body of Jesus, the Son of Man, was nailed to the cross. His life was perfect, eternal, and in a sanctified body. Therefore, the perfect life of Jesus Christ could not be crucified. The sinful life of humankind was in the body of Jesus on the cross. He set aside his perfect and indestructible life so that the sinful human life could be in his body. To say that God died on the cross, as some do, is inappropriate.

Historically, most of the Christian students of the Scriptures and exegetes conclude that the names of Jesus apply to a preexistent deity in heaven. Biblical texts do not present a similar description of Jesus or conform clearly to traditional Christian thought. This treatise will address the nature of Jesus at Incarnation in more detail later.

The real nature of Jesus Christ presented various degrees of conflict throughout the history of Christianity. The diversity of opinion stems mostly from the misunderstanding of Jesus's nature. The words *nature of Jesus* are employed without a definition of what we mean when we say *divine nature*. What do we mean by *divine nature*? What is *human nature*? Human beings have a dual nature forever. Humans have a body and soul (biological nature and life (the spirit nature). At the renewal of everything, both natures will be perfect. In terms of physics, humans have a nature made of matter (body and soul) and nature that is not from matter (spirit). It is proper to understand that the new humankind's representative has dual nature also. The new human spirit is eternal; however, the restored body will be forever.

The duality of nature is a property of matter in our universe. Particles of the class called fermions, such as photons and electrons, have two natures concurrently. They are both particle and a wave until one of them is observed by intelligent being. When seen by an intelligent observer, the particle displays one nature—the nature that is chosen by an intelligent observer. However, an intelligent observer must decide in advance which nature of a particle he wants to study. Accordingly, we must be clear about which nature is being considered when discussing the nature of Jesus Christ.

This property of subatomic particles is analogous to human beings. Human beings have two unique but interdependent parts: the spirit, and the body. The third part of human beings is the product of spirit and body: the human soul. The human spirit (intelligence), which is not made of matter, employs the brain, which is of matter. The human intelligence (spirit) employs the brain to process information and command the body to execute its decisions. This interaction of spirit and body produces chemistry displayed in human feeling (soul). If the human spirit is perfect, its interaction with the human body is good. If the spirit is sinful, its interactions are sinful. The human body does not have the power to deny the spirit, whether the spirit is good or sinful.

It would be highly inappropriate to assign to God, the Creator, the attributes and the description of human nature. It would be especially misleading if we did not even know what we mean by nature. God is the Absolute Spirit; therefore, he is not dependent, and he does not possess the properties of matter. Created human beings were given a spirit, and they possess it. God, however, is Spirit. The created intelligence could not refer to God, the Absolute Spirit, as being at a specific location. God accepted the human definition that he is in heaven because that is the only way humans could understand.

> "God is spirit, and those who worship Him must worship in Spirit and truth." (John 4:24 NKJV)

God has never revealed to humankind that he has a human body. God made the human body from the dust that he created. Therefore, to say that God has the human body is not logical. Jesus Christ did not present God the Father as a physical being, but as the Absolute Spirit

Humankind by its spirit is created in God's image. The human spirit (intelligence) is from God. He gave it to us. God did not give humanity the human body because it did not exist before making it from dust. Therefore, the image of God when acting on the created body produces God-like results. At the resurrection of human beings, we will have the spirit that we received through Jesus Christ. The human body, at the resurrection, will be the body Jesus Christ has. While praying to Father, Jesus said, "I have revealed you to those whom you gave to me out of the world" (John 17:6 NIV). Jesus revealed to people a God who loved them. He did not reveal God's physical appearance. God is invisible to human beings.

On the earth, he referred to himself as "I am," a name the old covenant scriptures attribute to God the Father.

"Very truly I tell you, Jesus answered, before Abraham was born, I am!" (John 8:58 NIV)

Additionally, Jesus claimed that he and the Father were the same.

"I and the Father are one." (John 10:30)

The Greek word translated *one* also means *one and the same*. Traditionally, Christians maintained that Jesus was fully God and fully man on the earth. However, being one does not mean the union of two unique beings. The Greek word means one in a literal sense.

The coming of the Messiah (Christ) in the human body has not been adequately understood within Christianity. The Incarnation refers to spirit (intelligence) taking on the human body. The human spirit is the identity of humankind. The representative of the new humankind had to have the human body. The exegetes of the scriptures do not present a coherent meaning of the Incarnation. Opinions vary, and debates are endless. Accordingly, Christianity does not have an unambiguous definition of the Incarnation and the nature of Jesus Christ. The various conclusions generate more questions than answers.

Jesus and the Father being one is not the same as one humankind. They are one and the same. One humankind refers to many human beings having the same language and the way of thinking. Our current knowledge about the universe implies that there could be only one Absolute Intelligence (Spirit). God is the Absolute Spirit. Therefore, there is only one God.

The new humankind will be one. Jesus prayed to the Father that those who followed him would be one, as he and the Father are. The new humankind will be one or of one mind. However, members of the new humankind are not one and the same but one in the thought process. The one humankind will be able to make a single intelligent decision even though many minds are involved. While there are many minds, the spirit (intelligence) is the same. New humankind will not be a union of diverse parts. Diversity or individuality rises from the same spirit expressing itself through many physical minds. A degree of diversity is necessary for humanity. The ability to make a single intelligent decision in such diversity is necessary for our universe's proper administration.

Advanced studies concerning anthropic cosmological principles imply that a single intelligent decision by many parts is essential for human activity in our universe. A union, in classical nature, could not accomplish anything concerning our universe. However, we could not apply the nature of new humankind to the Absolute Intelligence, God. There is only one Absolute Spirit, God. For fallen and redeemed humanity, he is God the Father (our Creator), God the Son (our Savior), and the God the Spirit (our Comforter and guide) However, he is the one and the same God always.

The difficulty that is relative to the Incarnation and the Absolute Spirit, may stem from applying a modern-time's worldview to the ancient worldview. The readers of the scriptures should be aware of the circumstance that is relative to biblical authors. They lived and functioned in a time of limited worldview. They had to present the message in a way that the people they lived among could understand. The biblical authors could not have anticipated the concerns that the modern-day readers would have. however, we should not view the methods and styles employed by the biblical authors in a negative way. They did the only way they could, considering the time that they lived in and the knowledge that was available to them.

A supportable and more logical worldview can assist in understanding their writing style. The biblical authors, to their credit, have preserved the knowledge of one true God. Their knowledge of God was not perfect. They display similarities with the surrounding nations; nevertheless, they kept the knowledge of one God distinct. They conveyed the message concerning God's plans for humankind in a way that the people could understand. The biblical authors did so because the Holy Spirit guided them. The better way and a full message had to wait until the time when God would speak through his Son. God, the Creator, revealed himself fully through Jesus Christ at just the right time.

Readers of the old covenant scriptures should be aware that biblical authors wrote the message in human words. They employed words common in their time and words that their contemporaries could understand. Biblical authors could not envision that in millennia after them, a different brand of people would be reading it. They could not envision and possibly did not expect the critical analyses of their writings that were employed in modern times. Biblical authors did not possess knowledge of literary rules and analytical tools, which modern readers depend on. They could not have been aware of and familiar with the modern-day rules and practices concerning critical analyses. The Bible students should not apply the modern-time literary rules and analytical tools to the biblical-time writings. Modern-day analytical tools will create more tensions than explanations. The readers of the scriptures should visualize themselves in the shoes of the biblical authors.

Biblical authors had to employ their everyday experiences and knowledge when presenting God to the people. They employed things that ordinary people were familiar with so that they could understand the message from God correctly. Had the authors done it the way that we want them to, the people in their time would not have accepted the message. Readers in ancient times did not require that the messages be written in a particular way. Literary skill as we understand it did not exist in ancient time. Biblical and ancient-time authors had to employ illustrations and comparisons with which people were familiar.

Biblical authors did not possess the global worldview available today. Had they known the global worldview and employed it, no one would have understood the message. The universe we observe did not exist for those people and biblical authors. The earth was flat and the only inhabited place outside heaven. A vast spherical universe full of spherical bodies, the earth included, is a modern-day discovery. The ancient and biblical time, people could not observe the universe that we see. Had any author in ancient times written about it, no one would have believed it.

Historically, people viewed everything above the earth as the heavens. Heaven was a place where God and other heavenly beings lived. Their concept concerning God and heavenly beings conformed to their limited worldview. For people in ancient time and biblical authors, God and heavenly beings had physical form like humans. Heavenly activities and arrangements were like human practices on the earth. For ancient-time people God was like an earthly king, although more powerful. For the ancient understanding, God had to employ servants, advisors, and the executors of his plans for humankind on Earth. The earth and its inhabitants were the only objects of God's attention. There was no one else outside heaven.

God through his messengers the prophets, gave the people a description of himself in a form that they could understand. Nevertheless, people persisted in their human-centered concept of God and heavenly beings.

"With whom will you compare me or count me equal?
To whom will you liken me that we may be compared?"
(Isaiah 46:5 NIV)

Ancient-time people could not visualize anything greater than their surroundings and practice.

Modern-day readers of the scriptures do not have an excuse for presenting God in an anthropomorphic way. God is far more than we could ever conceive.

"As the heavens are higher than the earth, so are my ways higher than your ways and my thoughts than your thoughts." (Isaiah 55:9 NIV)

However, people in ancient time could not understand God in a nonhuman way. Ancient people believed that their gods must reside in their temples and sitting on their thrones. Biblical authors did the same thing. This concept of God persists in modern time. However, human beings should not present God in a physical form, sitting on a physical throne made of matter in a physical heaven. We do not know, and we could not know if God resides in a temple made of some form of matter. God is the Absolute Spirit. As such, he could be anywhere and nowhere in a created dominion at the same time. This possibility means that we cannot specify God's location.

Biblical authors presented God sitting on a throne in a temple. They had to present it all in a way that was familiar to them and the people. God himself spoke to the people in a way that they could understand. However, God's condescension to the human level should not be maintained as God's absolute nature. The created being cannot understand the true nature of the absolute. Such practices were considered correct in ancient time because there were no other ways to present God to people who were living with a limited worldview. Modern-day readers of the scriptures should not consider such practices as incorrect. However, for us today, there is no excuse for insisting on a limited view of the Absolute Spirit, God. God has in the past, and he may today, present himself at a level that humans can understand. However, we should never maintain that it is so in the Absolute.

God lowers himself to our level because he loves and wants us to be comfortable in his presence. We should not abuse such a privilege. God is much more than we could comprehend. God is not limited in any sense, and he could not be localized to a physical structure and place. God told us this through the prophet Isaiah.

> This is what the LORD says: "Heaven is my throne, and the earth is my footstool. Where is the house you will build for me? Where will my resting place be? Has not my hand made all these things, and so they came into being? Declares the Lord..." (Isaiah 66:1–2 NIV)

God, the Creator, made everything that does and could exist. There is not a physical place or location that we could describe as God's residence. He is with us through Jesus Christ, and he resides in our hearts. Yielded believers should venture this far when describing God, the Creator. We do not know where the perceived heaven is. Yet we say God is in heaven because that is how we understand it. God understands our limits. Some believe that God has localized himself somewhere in our universe. However, God's dominion is infinitely greater than our universe. It is highly inappropriate to localize the Absolute Spirit within the universe that he created.

Modern-day humans are limited in what they can know, even though we live in an advanced time. Unfortunately, some do not recognize the limits to our knowledge and understanding. Accordingly, they insist on presenting the unreachable in unacceptable ways. They present God, the Creator and the Savior, in human terms including with human limits. Accordingly, they present God and the Savior's nature in limited human terms and insist it is so. However, students, teachers, and the exegetes should avoid the temptation of thinking they have true knowledge and interpretation.

Modern-Day Misconceptions Concerning God?

Often, the readers of the scriptures are not aware of limitations concerning human knowledge. Therefore, the creation, the Incarnation, and the re-creation of humankind are misrepresented. An example of misconceptions is human knowledge and conclusions concerning our universe. Through advanced modern-day study and observation, we have gained more knowledge about our universe than humankind had in its history. We became aware of space and time.

Humans talk about space and time as if they know exactly what they are. However, our everyday experience of space and time is not an indication of real knowledge about them. Our everyday experience of spacetime is not an indication of the nature of space and time. Humankind is clueless concerning the nature of space and time. There is no known particle of matter that mediates or transmits space and time. We accept that they exist and they are real to us, despite the absence of physical evidence. The only evidence is our experience.

We do not know how space and time enable the transmission of various forms of information,. We simply accept it as real. Advanced studies show that space and time are the underlying structures of our universe. Matter is being created from the expansion of space in time continuously. Advanced study in the field of quantum cosmology indicates that space and time are inseparable. Together, they form the *fabric* of our universe. Quantum cosmology implies that the creation of our universe is the creation of time. An increasing practice by modern scientists is to present space and time as a single entity—spacetime. People generally assume that they know what space and time are. They accept that they experience the true nature of space and time every day. Nevertheless, humans do not have a clue concerning the nature of what they experience.

Are space and time what we perceive and observe? No one could with reliable confidence define the foundation of our universe. People study and discuss space without a definition of what it is. We accept and perceive space as a distance that we measure in various ways. However, space is not just the distance. It is what our universe is. Matter deforms the space, and space tells matter how to move. We observe and study the objects made of matter without being concerned about the regions of the absent visible matter. Traditionally, humans accept the notion that time flows. It passes from the past to the present to the future. However, humans do not have a clue what time is. Human history and experience are distinguished by the past, present, and future. However, this distinction may not apply to time. The humans perceive to travel through time without knowing if it is so.

If our location in space does not change, did time flow? We cannot know. We accept in our mind that future time exists in the absence of motion. Humans accept their local experiences as sufficient indications of what space and time are. We accept our local experiences of space and time as the universal fact and without confirmation that it is so. The events outside a local region are accepted as real, even though we did not observe them. The readers and listeners of a definition of space and time are certain that it is real. Yet no one could prove that a is as described.

A similar misconception of what is real exists when we read the scriptures. We read the scriptures, which were written in ancient time, as if they were written in modern time. However, readers and exegetes of the scriptures must be aware of time, circumstance, and the readers to whom the scriptures were given. Concepts and concerns that existed at the time of its writing were considerably different from the things that modern-day readers are conscious of or experience. The concept of God, the Creator, was quite different in ancient time. Human limitations were quite different in ancient time also. Their experiences were limited and different from modern-day humans. However, modern-day readers, students, and exegetes of the scriptures accept the ancient time's concept of God as the correct definition of the Absolute. Nevertheless, human limitations and misunderstandings have not altered the nature of the message.

The modern-day definition of God's nature is as if it exists in the same space and time as the one that we perceive. However, God created space and time. Therefore, we must present God apart from created things. God is Absolute Spirit, and he is with us always. However, God's presence with us does not justify our concept of him as existing in space and time. It would be inappropriate to describe the Creator in material form and assume that he limited in ways like humans are. God, the Creator, created the universe for us (the carbon-based intelligent life). God did not create our universe as his residence, but ours. The Creator (the Absolute Spirit) is separate from all he created. God sees all his creation at all times without being physically present in it. God is Absolute Spirit. Therefore, he can be present everywhere and nowhere physically at the same time. However, it is not ours to say so.

People in ancient times and biblical authors did not know the nature of our universe. They did not know that the universe that we observe existed. The biblical authors did not know that protons, neutrons, and electrons existed as particles of matter. Their bodies, like ours, are made of these particles of matter. However, humans do not think of the body in terms of particles of matter.

Because humans are made of matter, which is still subject to sin's consequences, we cannot understand the Absolute Spirit's true nature. We cannot be certain that the Absolute Spirit has nature as humans understand it. We do not understand our nature; therefore, we cannot say that we understand the Absolute Spirit. We must always realize that our lack of understanding is because of our condition, which results from our choice, not because of God's design.

The probability exists that humankind in its present state cannot correctly understand the events before human history began. Likewise, we cannot fully understand what God has accomplished on our behalf at the supreme level. God's coming down to the human level to save it contains information well beyond humankind's capability to understand. What God accomplished on the cross in the body of Jesus Christ and on our behalf is apart from all laws that are known to humankind.

Our salvation was accomplished in conformity to a law that we cannot understand. In our present state, the human mind could not process information that is related to events that are governed by laws that are above our universe. Therefore, it would be inappropriate to either maintain or imply that the Incarnation impacted God's absolute nature. God is the Absolute Spirit, and he cannot be impacted by his actions on behalf of his Creation.

Any ideas and concepts that God has been impacted in some way by what he has accomplished on behalf of sinful humanity should be removed from the theological vocabulary. God, the Creator, can assume the form of all created intelligence at the same time without experiencing any impact on his absolute nature. Anthropic cosmology implies that God can take on him the form of all created intelligence at the same time and yet not be anyone of them. This probability implies that it is extremely inappropriate for human beings to attribute human characteristics to God.

God's is able to be God in heaven and a man on the earth at the same time without being limited. God did not need another being to go in his place and assume a human form to save humanity. God is all-knowing and all-powerful; therefore, he is beyond our understanding. By trusting him, we accept that what he has accomplished on our behalf while being in human body here on earth is all we need for eternity with him. We should present and discuss the Incarnation while considering human needs for such an act and maintaining that God's Absolute Nature is always off-limits for human discussion.

Created intelligent beings in the universe of spacetime should not discuss and present God in terms of *was* and *will be*. God, our Father, the Almighty Creator, always *is*, with no exceptions. He does not ever change in any conceivable way. For God, the Creator, there is neither past nor future, but only the eternal present, as it concerns the universe of spacetime. God should always be now for the fallen and redeemed human beings. Human beings, especially Christians, should never present the Absolute God in space and time because he created all. God is above everything he has created.

God, our Father, will interact with and on behalf of humankind in many ways and circumstances. He acts on behalf of humanity according to its needs always. God does not act on our behalf in various ways because he is somehow limited, and therefore, he is searching for what is best. God, the Creator, is not subject to human limitations. Fallen humankind, by its decisions, always progresses toward self-destruction. Therefore, God acts appropriately for the situation because he loves humanity and wants to preserve it. (All of the above is in human terms because what God has done on our behalf is beyond understanding). God loves humankind; therefore, he is patiently acting on its behalf at its level.

Sometimes, it may be something that we do not expect or ask for; however, God acts in ways that are always best for us. We must understand and believe that God is always intimately involved on our behalf. Without His constant care for humanity, we would not exist. Our union with God, the Father, in the body of Jesus Christ, contains truths infinitely greater than what the sin-impacted humanity can understand. Our heavenly

Father urges us to believe and trust him. At just the right time, he will restore all the privileges he bestows on his children to us. Yielded believers must join the apostle Paul in saying:

> And we know that in all things God works for the good
> of those who love him, who have been called according to
> his purpose. (Romans 8:28, NIV)

How Should We Understand the Incarnation?

Traditionally, discussions and debates concerning the Incarnation have centered on the nature of Jesus Christ. The absence of a definition of what we mean by *nature* has led to conflicting conclusions. The Christian exegetes have merged the divine nature with the sinful human nature in one body: Jesus Christ's body. They do not realize that the perfect and holy nature of Jesus on the earth is new humankind's spirit. The nature of the new humanity is the same order of spirit as the human spirit that God put in Adam at creation. However, the human spirit God put in Jesus at Incarnation did not sin. It only resides in the body that was subjected to the consequences of sin. The sinful human spirit (life) and the perfect spirit of Jesus Christ could not have been in the sanctified body of Jesus simultaneously. The sinful spirit could not function in the sanctified body. The body of Jesus Christ was sanctified by the Holy Spirit who resided in his mind together with the perfect spirit of new humankind.

The biological nature of humankind did not sin in the Garden of Eden. The human spirit sinned. The spirit, as stated earlier, is the identity and life of humankind. The human life (spirit) that God put in Adam sinned in the human biological nature. The human body and soul (the biological nature) were not condemned for the sin. Therefore, only the spirit that sinned had to die forever as wages for sin.

The assertion that God united a divine nature with a human fallen nature (fallen spirit) creates confusion concerning which nature died on the cross. Accordingly, some Christians believe that the divine nature died as wages for sin on humankind's behalf. However, the divine Spirit (nature) was eternal and it could not die.

Also, the moral law does not accept the substitution, as presented earlier in this treatise. Had the perfect human spirit of Jesus Christ died on the cross, humankind would not exist today. The spirit which sinned could not be made righteous. Such an option did not exist. A sinner is always a sinner, regardless of the quality of his behavior. The only hope for humanity has always been that God replaces its sinful spirit with a righteous one. That is what God accomplished for humankind in the body of Jesus Christ on the cross at Golgotha.

Understanding the exchange of spirit in the body of Jesus Christ on the cross is essential to our understanding of what God accomplished on our behalf. We must understand and accept that when we sinned in the Garden of Eden, we had to die the second death, and there was no way out. However, God, who loved us, determined that he would replace our sinful spirit (life) with the righteous human spirit of his Son. He accomplished it in the sanctified body of Jesus Christ because the human spirit, whether good or evil, could function only in the body that God made on the sixth day of creation and no other. To say that the righteous nature or the righteous spirit of Jesus Christ died on the cross in our stead would indicate that God died for humanity on the cross. Some Christians insist that God died for us on the cross at Golgotha. Such a conclusion presents a logical contradiction.

A more detailed description of the great exchange on the cross will be presented later in this treatise.

The assertion that Jesus Christ came with two natures united in one body is a dangerous one. The law of intelligence and the quantum law do not allow two opposites to reside in the same place in our universe. Matter in our universe consists of both matter and antimatter. The two forms of matter cannot remain in the same place without consequences. The same applies to the order of spirit called human. Based on our universe's laws, we can conclude that an evil spirit and a righteous spirit cannot coexist in the one human mind. By definition, they must have different minds and bodies. Also, the two opposite spirits cannot coexist in our universe forever.

However, there could be only one Jesus Christ; therefore, there was one spirit in his body, not two. Jesus had a sanctified body. His body was as good as God declared at the creation. The righteous spirit and the evil spirit cannot reside together in a good house. Quantum cosmology implies that good and evil cannot coexist forever. Whatever men conclude concerning the Incarnation, they should refrain from placing the holy nature of Jesus Christ with the sinful human nature in one body.

Therefore, this treatise presents a view that avoids the contradictions concerning the true nature of the Incarnation. This author finds it logical and helpful to present the Incarnation as the re-creation of humankind. The Incarnation is, in fact, the creation of new humanity. The unalterable and undeniable biblical fact is that humankind sinned in Adam in the Garden of Eden. Therefore, all of humanity became utterly helpless concerning its status. It sinned; therefore, it must die eternally. Humankind had to die the eternal death or the second death, with no way out. However, because he loves humankind, God was determined to create the new humankind in Jesus Christ at just the right time.

Please note that the moral law mentioned above does not refer to the Ten Commandments. They are a practical presentation of what the moral law requires. Advanced study concerning anthropic cosmological principles implies that the moral code (law) is required when intelligent processing of information arises in a universe of spacetime and matter. Such a moral code could be summarized in one sentence: You are free to do as you please but not at someone else's expense. The moral law applies to all of God's dominion. It is the universal principle of selfless love. It exists because God is the Selfless Love (Agape) in the Bible.

In its representative Adam, humankind became a sinner by a deliberate, intelligent decision in Eden's garden. The spirit that God put in Adam made a deliberate decision for all humankind. By an irrevocable decision, the human spirit (life) subjected the human body and all nature to the consequences of sin. The replacement of the sinful human life with a perfect life needed a sanctified body. Jesus conquered the temptation, and his life (spirit of new humankind) became perfect. The Holy Spirit resided with the perfect new human life in the mind of Jesus. Therefore, Jesus's body was sanctified by the Holy Spirit inside him. If he had had a sinful and perfect human nature, he could not have had a sanctified body. Because Jesus's human spirit at the Incarnation was good, the Holy Spirit resided in his mind. The sinful human spirit (nature) could not reside with the Holy Spirit in the same body.

Only God, the Creator, could replace the sinful spirit with a righteous one. God accomplished it in the body of Jesus Christ on the cross at Golgotha. He accomplished it at just the right time for helpless humanity.

> But when the set time had fully come, God sent his Son, born of a woman, born under the law, to redeem those under the law, that we might receive adoption to sonship. (Galatians 4:4–5 NIV)

Members of the first or old humankind are biological descendants of their representative, Adam. Therefore, they inherit their sinful nature from him. Accordingly, a member of the first humankind remains a sinner even though he or she obeys the law. However, members of new humankind, who are created in Jesus Christ, do not inherit their righteousness. Members of the new humankind are not the biological descendants of Jesus Christ. They are his brothers and sisters. The righteousness of the new humankind is a gift from God, the Father. God removed the sin of the whole world through Jesus Christ.

> Both the one who makes people holy and those who are made holy are of the same family. So Jesus is not ashamed to call them brothers and sisters. He says, I will declare your name to my brothers and sisters; in the assembly I will sing your praise. (Hebrews 2:11–12 NIV)

The Last Adam, Jesus Christ, did not have a helper for biological procreation. Biological procreation was the option that the first humankind selected in Adam. Because the first humankind became a sinner by nature, it and everything associated with it had to die an eternal death. The old (first) humankind and all its choices died the second death in the body of Jesus Christ on the cross at Golgotha.

Therefore, no one is guilty of sin anymore, if they trust God and Jesus Christ that it has been accomplished as promised. If he does not trust or believe in God and Jesus Christ, he remains condemned because he refuses the gift. His guilt is because of his unbelief and not because of a violation of the law. Deliberate sin is irrevocable. In like manner, the gift from God is irrevocable. God removed the irrevocable sin from us because only he has the power to do so. The gift of righteousness is irrevocable because only God has the power to give it. He gave it to us, and he does not change his mind. The new humankind's members must walk the Via Dolorosa of self-denial to Golgotha and be crucified so that Christ could live in them. Members of the first humankind are the children of Adam, who made them sinners by nature. However, the new humankind's members are children of God, who made them righteous in Jesus Christ.

13

Jesus at Incarnation

WE CONCLUDED THAT the only option concerning humankind's continuing existence was to replace its sinful life (spirit). A human being could not have accomplished such a task. Only God had the power to destroy the evil spirit and replace it with the righteous one. The human spirit comes from God. There is no other source. Looking at Illustration 6, we see that God accomplished it by preserving the human body through a female part of humanity. However, the spirit, (human intelligence) came from God, not from humankind's male role.

How did God accomplish the creation of new humankind? The following Illustration 6 may help us understand this incredible act by God, who loves us.

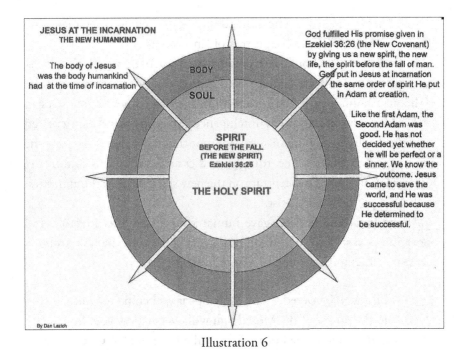

Illustration 6

The circles above are for illustration only. There is no other purpose.

At his birth, Jesus shared the body that humankind had at the time of Incarnation. He shared the body that God had made on the sixth day of creation week with humankind. Therefore, he is the Son of Man. The body Jesus shared with humanity had been subject to sin's consequences for thousands of years before the Incarnation. How much has the human body suffered? We do not know. However, Jesus did not inherit the life of Adam. He had a life of new humankind that came from God and not from man. Therefore, Jesus is also the Son of God, as the representative of a new humanity. Even Adam, at the resurrection, will receive the life of Jesus Christ. Adam's life, he received from God, died forever in the body of Jesus on the cross because it became irrevocably sinful.

The spirit of Adam, who was the representative of the first humankind, was good before he made a deliberate decision to disobey God. His body was also good. The body of the Second Adam, the new humankind, came through Mary, who was a sinner by nature. She inherited the sinful spirit from the first man Adam. Therefore, despite strict religious regimens, her body was subject to the consequences of sin.

Accordingly, we should not present the Incarnation of Jesus Christ from a physical perspective. God, the Creator, did not make a new body for the new humanity at the Incarnation. He gave a new human spirit, which was a new life and new intelligence for humankind. Sin entered the world through the human spirit and not the body; therefore, only the spirit had to be replaced. Accordingly, studies and discussions concerning the Incarnation should concentrate on the new spirit or life of humankind, which God put in Jesus Christ.

At the Incarnation, God gave humankind a new life, identity, and history in his vast dominion. God put a new spirit into the human body that was formed in the womb of a human being (Mary).

> The angel answered, "The Holy Spirit will come on you, and the power of the Most High will overshadow you. So the holy one to be born will be called the Son of God." (Luke 1:35 NIV)

By putting a new spirit in the body of Jesus at the Incarnation, God made the new humankind the same way that he made the old one in Adam. God made the human body at creation and gave it a new spirit at the Incarnation. However, at the Incarnation, the human body was not a new one. Therefore, Jesus is the Son of God in the same way that Adam was the son of God.

> In the same way, Christ also did not take upon himself the glory of becoming a high priest. But God said to him, You are my Son; today I have become your Father. (Hebrews 5:5 NIV)

The human spirit that God put in Jesus at the Incarnation is the same order as the spirit he put in Adam at creation. Both spirits are in the order that is called mankind. The order of spirit called man applies to all humankind, male and female. However, the new human spirit was not under condemnation by the law. The spirit God put in Adam sinned, and was condemned by the law to eternal death. The spirit that God put in the body that he made at creation did not have any deficiency. Likewise, the human spirit in the body of the Second Adam, Jesus, did not have any deficiency. Both spirits were good before they made an intelligent decision.

The humankind that God created in the first Adam was declared good. Likewise, the new humankind that God created in Jesus Christ was good also. However, in human terms, we could say that the body of Jesus had some disadvantages because it came through a fallen human being. The representative of the first humankind had everything that was good in the Garden of Eden, including the body. Jesus, however, was born and lived in a world that had been subjected to corruption. In the garden of Gethsemane, Jesus indicated that his body was not as strong as it had been in the Garden of Eden.

> Then he returned to his disciples and found them sleeping. "Couldn't you men keep watch with me for one hour? He asked Peter. Watch and pray so that you will not fall into temptation. The spirit is willing, but the flesh is weak." (Matthew 26: 40–41 NIV)

Jesus's new human spirit was willing. The spirit in the apostles could not be willing because they became sinners in Adam and lost the ability to be willing. Jesus asked the apostles to watch and pray; however, they slept. This shows that their spirit was not willing. Jesus's willing spirit kept his body from falling asleep.

Christians have debated the nature of Jesus at Incarnation throughout the history of Christianity. However, the confusion persists because they lack a definition of which nature is being discussed. Human beings have three components, as stated earlier in this treatise. They are the body, the spirit, and the soul. God made the human body. He gave it the spirit, and the body became the living soul. When the spirit (intelligence) acts on the body, it produces the chemistry (feelings that we know as the soul).

Therefore, the spirit and the body are the two natures of human beings. However, the new spirit is Jesus's nature, which we should study and discuss, not the body. We should view the human spirit or intelligence as spiritual or intelligent human nature. The human body is the biological human nature. The human spirit, given at creation, sinned and subjected the human body (the biological nature) to corruption. Therefore, the human body did not sin in the Garden of Eden. The human body had to execute the commands of the sinful spirit. Command by sinful spirit results in a sinful response. The spirit could not alter its state; therefore, its decisions were not good. The sinful human spirit only does evil. The perfect spirit of the new humankind only does the righteous deeds and thinks righteous thoughts. Neither one can change its nature or the things that is accustomed to doing.

The spirit of the first man, Adam, was from God. Therefore on the earth, he was 100 percent man (the son of God). Likewise, the spirit of the second Man, Jesus, was from God. Therefore on the earth, he was 100 percent man (the Son of God). Being from God, however, does not imply being God. Jesus, as the representative of new humankind, was fully man. However, in the Absolute at the same time, he was the Almighty.

God does not have a physical form. God is Spirit. He created everything that exists; therefore, he could not be made of created matter. He existed as God Almighty before the creation of matter. Jesus told us that God is Spirit.

> "God is spirit, and those who worship Him must worship in Spirit and truth." (John 4:24 NKJV)

Jesus was the firstborn member of a new humankind. Adam was the firstborn member of the old or first humankind. The first man, Adam, lost his firstborn standing because he sinned. Adam had to surrender his standing as a firstborn to Jesus Christ. He did so for a piece of forbidden fruit, even though he was not hungry.

Some Christians support the conclusion that Jesus was fully God and fully man at the Incarnation. However, the *God with us* does not mean that God was born of Mary. God could not be born, and he does not have a beginning. Concerning such statements, it would help if we could differentiate between what is in the absolute (heaven) and what is on the earth. Immanuel presents the message that God sent the Savior of the world in Jesus at the Incarnation. He gave new life to helpless humanity in Jesus Christ at the Incarnation. All this is from God; however, it became reality in the physical sense here on the earth. Mary was a sinful human being, even though she grew up under careful control, and she had not physically violated the Ten Commandments. However, growing up under strict control could not remove the sinful nature from her. All descendants of Adam are born with sinful nature (the sinful Spirit).

God did not put the divine nature (the spirit) in Jesus at the Incarnation. Jesus shared the human body through Mary. However, the human body had been subject to the consequences of sin. Living in strict compliance with the law could not make a sinner good. The body of Mary was subject to the consequences of sin that Adam committed in the Garden of Eden. Mary inherited the spirit of Adam, which sinned. So Jesus was also the Savior of Mary, his earthly mother.

Therefore, we cannot say that the divine nature entered the body that was subjected to consequences of sin. God put the order of spirit called man, who is not divine, in Jesus,. The orders of spirit that come from the Absolute Spirit are not divine spirits. They are spirits of the created beings. If the given spirits do not sin they become perfect and eternal. However, they are not absolute. The Absolute Spirit (Nature) is not an order of spirit. He is the source of all spirit orders. Jesus's body became sanctified when he conquered the temptation, and his new human spirit was made perfect. This treatise will explore this fact later.

Additionally, the holy divine nature (Spirit) and the sinful human nature (spirit) could not reside together in the human body, whether sanctified or not. They could not reside together because the sinful spirit could not reside in the sanctified body. The sinful spirit would die instantly in the presence of the divine Spirit in the same body. The Bible does not tell us that there is a divine body. God is the Absolute Spirit, and his angels are ministering orders of spirit.

> Are not all angels ministering spirits sent to serve those
> who will inherit salvation? (Hebrews 1:14 NIV)

The apostle Paul stated that the angels are spirits, in the plural. It implies that each angel is a unique order of spirit. Jesus was born with a new human spirit, who has not made a deliberate, intelligent decision.

Therefore, Jesus, the representative of new humankind, had the same spirit that Adam had at creation.

Jesus did not come to serve as a substitute for sinners. He came to bring new, perfect, and eternal life for the new humanity. The sinful humankind had to die eternal death for its sin. No one could have died in its place. The sinful human spirit has died the second eternal death in Jesus Christ on the cross. Jesus' perfect spirit reentered his body at his resurrection, confirming that the new humanity would live forever free from sin and condemnation. Therefore, Jesus Christ is the Savior of the world. He is not the Savior as a substitute and an example. He is the Savior of the world because he is the new and perfect life for new humankind. God announced it through the prophet Jeremiah.

> "The days are coming," declares the LORD, "when I will raise up for David a righteous Branch, a King who will reign wisely and do what is just and right in the land. In his days Judah will be saved And Israel will live in safety. This is the name by which he will be called: The LORD Our Righteous Savior." (Jeremiah 23:5–6 NIV)

If Jesus had come into the world with a sinful spirit (a sinful human nature), as some think, he would need a Savior himself. Jesus could not have saved himself and the world. If he had a sinful human nature that had to die forever, there would be no resurrection and no humankind. It helps to repeat what was stated earlier in this treatise. The sinful human nature (spirit) could not be made good again. It had to die the eternal death. There was no way out. Humankind lost both the desire and the ability to do good when it sinned in the Garden of Eden.

The human spirit God put in the first man, Adam, made a deliberate decision to disobey. Therefore, he and all humankind that was created in him lost the possibility of returning to its original state forever. Once a sinner, always a sinner. Likewise, once righteous in Jesus Christ, always righteous in him alone. Consequently, the sinful humankind could obey the letter of the law but not the spirit of it.

However, the Law demands perfect obedience, including the letter and the spirit of the law. The imperfect humanity could not render perfect obedience, even with the best of intentions and effort. Therefore, if Jesus had come with a sinful human nature, he would have been of no use for the fallen humanity. The fallen human spirit (nature) could not resist temptation ever. It had to be replaced with a perfect spirit, which was the nature God gave us in Jesus Christ.

The sinful human spirit could not do good even had it received a new body at the Incarnation. Jesus Christ received the same body that humans had at the time of his conception. He did not possess an extraordinary advantage over humankind. Jesus shared a body that has been subject to the consequences of sin for millennia with humanity. However, the new human spirit of the same order that God put in Adam commanded the body of Jesus. The new human spirit God gave us in Jesus could make only good demands from the human body, which Jesus shares with us.

Since the new human spirit that God put in Jesus at conception was good, the Holy Spirit resided in Jesus's mind. The Holy Spirit educated and guided young Jesus to prepare for a deliberate decision that was essential for humankind. God educated first man, Adam, concerning the enemy and Adam's duty to make a deliberate, intelligent decision on humankind's behalf. Therefore, God educated the new humanity's representative to give him all the knowledge that he needed for a deliberate, intelligent decision on behalf of the new humanity. God announces it through his prophet.

> He will be eating curds and honey when he knows enough
> to reject the wrong and choose the right, for before the boy
> knows enough to reject the wrong and choose the right the
> land of the two kings you dread will be laid waste. (Isaiah
> 7:15–16 NKJV)

God selflessly loved the humankind that he created in Adam. Therefore, he educated the first human pair concerning the enemy, who had gone out of heaven bent on conquering. God did not leave Adam in the darkness to face this unknown enemy. Likewise, God loves the new humankind he created in Jesus Christ. Therefore, he gave Jesus all the knowledge that he needed to make a good decision. God prepared Jesus to conquer the temptation, defeat the enemy, and secure a perfect life for the new humankind.

Sinful human beings on the earth could not educate Jesus, the Savior of fallen humanity. Utterly helpless sinners could not educate their Savior. Humankind failed in Eden's garden; therefore, it could not have sufficient knowledge to resist temptation. Jesus knew more than all human beings put together, including Solomon. He was the most knowledgeable person on the earth because God gave him everything that he needed to say and how to say it. Some Christians maintain that Marry educated Jesus. However, the Bible does not tell us that Mary knew how to read the scriptures. Jews did not train female children in the same manner as male children.

> "For I have not spoken on My own authority; but the Father who sent Me gave Me a command what I should say and what I should speak. And I know that His command is everlasting life. Therefore, whatever I speak, just as the Father has told Me, so I speak." (John 12:49–50 NKJV)

Jesus Christ gave the apostles all that they needed to know to continue his mission on the earth. Under the Holy Spirit's guidance, the apostles passed on to us everything that we need to know concerning our salvation. Our mission here on the earth is to be good lampstands from which the Light of the world can shine. Jesus Christ revealed to us all that we need to know about God, the Father. No new knowledge needs to be added to what Jesus has revealed by his words and deeds. No human being, however devout a Christian he might be, could add knowledge and instructions concerning our salvation and witness.

We disobeyed God in the Garden of Eden, in the first man Adam. Therefore, we lost the image of God that we had at creation. Our sin of disobedience separated us from the Creator, who is our only source of life. We did not die in the Garden of Eden, as the law required. We did not die because God, the Father, loved us and he was determined to save us. Accordingly, God the Father, came to the earth in human form (Jesus Christ). The Incarnation gave a new life (spirit) to the helpless humanity.

The new humankind obeyed God in its representative, Jesus Christ. Therefore, God restored his image in humanity through the body of Jesus Christ. The Incarnation began the restoration of humankind to God as his children, with full inheritance in his dominion. Unfortunately, not all people want to accept God as their Father. The Incarnation began the re-creation of humankind in Christ Jesus. God, the Creator, gave us the ability to grow in the knowledge of him and the things that he has accomplished on our behalf. Therefore, our life of witness should demonstrate that God re-created us and has restored his image in us.

14

The Re-Created Humankind Is Tested

BEFORE JESUS BEGAN his mission on the earth, God sent a messenger to inform the people that the re-creation of humankind is at hand. At just the right time, God sent his messenger to tell the people that the Messiah, the kingdom of God, has arrived.

> A voice of one calling: "In the wilderness prepare the way for the LORD; make straight in the desert a highway for our God." (Isaiah 40:3 NIV)

However, neither John nor the people knew who he was. John the Baptist called on people to repent and be baptized because the kingdom of God has arrived. There is no more waiting. John the Baptist announced that the promised Messiah was among the people.

> In those days John the Baptist came, preaching in the wilderness of Judah and saying, "Repent, for the kingdom of heaven has come near." (Mathew 3:1–2 NIV)

John the Baptist stated, "The kingdom of heaven has come." On another occasion, he would refer to a person who was not yet recognized.

What is the kingdom of heaven?

> Once, on being asked by the Pharisees when the kingdom of God would come, Jesus replied. "The coming of the kingdom of God is not something that can be observed, nor will the people say, 'Here it is,' or 'There it is,' because the kingdom of God is in your midst." Luke 17:20, NIV.

Jesus referred to himself as the kingdom of God. In Jesus Christ, all people belong to God because he has rescued them from slavery in the enemy's kingdom. When John the Baptist said, the kingdom of God has come near; John referred to a person. He was not referring to a geographic region or a royal dominion. Therefore, the question should be who is the kingdom of God, and not what it is.

People go to a geographic region or a country. The geographic region does not come to the people. Therefore, the kingdom of God referred to Jesus Christ, who is God with us. God came to his enemies and made them his friends. He gave them the eternal life of Jesus Christ. God came to his enemies because his enemies could not come to him. Their sin separated them from God. Jesus Christ is the Savior of the world. He is the Lamb of God.

> The next day John was there again with two of his disciples. When he saw Jesus passing by, he said, "Look, the Lamb of God." (John 3:35– 6)

Jesus is also the first among many who would accept him and join the kingdom of God. Jesus came to conquer death and secure eternal life for all who denied themselves and trusted Jesus Christ.

The kingdom of God became a reality in Jesus Christ. We do not know how long John has preached in the wilderness of Judah. We do not know how many years God has been preparing Jesus to face the enemy of God. How long did it take until Jesus knew enough to refuse evil and choose good? We do not know. We only know that John the Baptist was six months older than Jesus was. John asserted that he did not know Jesus before he baptized him. The mother of John and Mary, the mother of

Jesus, were cousins. However, John and Jesus never met, even though their mothers were related. John's parents lived in the countryside of Judea, which was mostly a wilderness.

> And the child grew and became strong in spirit; and he
> lived in the wilderness until he appeared publicly to Israel.
> (Luke 1:80 NIV)

We can be certain that God acted at just the right time on behalf of rebellious humankind. Accordingly, when Jesus was ready for an essential decision and choice, he went to be baptized by John the Baptist.

The baptism of Jesus is not a baptism of repentance. Jesus has not sinned. The enemy of God had not confronted him before his baptism. John the Baptist hesitated to baptize Jesus; however, Jesus said that John should baptize him to fulfill all righteousness. Therefore, all who accept Jesus Christ must fulfill all righteousness. They must trust God, the Father, that in Jesus Christ, they are irrevocably the children of God. They must be baptized in the same way that Jesus was. In such a way, they testify that they no longer live, but that Christ lives in them. They must join the apostle Paul in asserting,

> For through the law, I died to the law so that I might live
> for God. I have been crucified with Christ and I no longer
> live, but Christ lives in me. The life I now live in the body,
> I live by faith in the Son of God, who loved me and gave
> himself for me. (Galatians 2:19–20 NIV)

A committed adherence to the universal principle of selfless love remains forever a single requirement for enjoyment of eternity with God for new humanity in Jesus Christ. Jesus went from Galilee to the place where John the Baptist was baptizing in the river of Jordan so that he could be baptized. Jesus did so to show that he has come as the second Adam, the representative of a new humankind. Baptism was Jesus's first act in his ministry that would lead to the re-creation of humankind.

> Then Jesus came from Galilee to the Jordan to be baptized
> by John. But John tried to deter him, saying, "I need to

be baptized by you, and you came to me?" Jesus replied, "Let it be so now; it is proper for us to do this to fulfill all righteousness." Then John consented. (Mathew 3:13-15 NIV)

The baptism was the beginning of John's introduction of Jesus to the people. John did not meet Jesus before his baptism. Because Jesus was unknown to him, John could not have affirmed that Jesus was the one before he baptized him. The Jewish leaders asked John if he were the one to come? John, however, assured them that he was not the Messiah. John told them that the Messiah was coming after him. When questioned, John assured the Jewish leaders that the Messiah was among them, but they do not recognize him. However, God gave the sign to John so he could recognize the Messiah. God had fulfilled his promise to John.

As soon as Jesus was baptized, he went up out of the water. At that moment heaven was opened, and he saw the Spirit of God descending like a dove and alighting on him. And a voice from heaven said, "This is my Son, whom I love; with him I am well pleased." Mathew 3:16–17 NIV)

Other people were present as Jesus was baptized by John the Baptist. However, only John saw the Spirit descending on Jesus in the form of a dove. The next day after the baptism, Jesus passed by, and John the Baptist saw him. Then John told the people that Jesus was the man he has been announcing.

The next day John saw Jesus coming toward him and said, "Look, the Lamb of God, who takes away the sin of the world!" (John 1:29 NIV)

John the Baptist confirmed that that he had not known who the Messiah was. But God gave him the sign by which he could identify the Messiah. The following day, John saw Jesus again, and he assured his disciples that Jesus was the one whom he had come to introduce to the world.

"And I myself did not know him, but the one who sent me to baptize with water told me, 'The man on whom you see the Spirit come down and remain is the one who will baptize with the Holy Spirit.' I have seen and I testify that this is God's Chosen One." (John 1:33–34 NIV)

John saw Jesus one more time and testified that he was the One. He may have continued his mission of baptism of repentance while Jesus was in the wilderness being tempted. Perhaps soon after that, John the Baptist was arrested and put in prison. We do not know how long he was in prison before his execution. After John the Baptist was put in prison, Jesus returned to Galilee to begin his mission.

The representative of the new humankind had to decide if the new human spirit would be perfect. Illustration 7 depicts the nature of the new life (new spirit) of humankind.

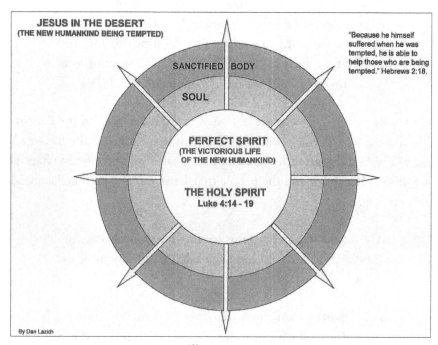

Illustration 7

As the representative of new humankind, Jesus Christ had to make a deliberate, intelligent, or spirit decision. He had to face the enemy, conquer the temptation, and secure a perfect and eternal life for the new humanity.

> Jesus, full of the Holy Spirit, left the Jordan and was led by the Spirit into the wilderness, where for forty days he was tempted by the devil. He ate nothing during those days, and at the end of them he was hungry. (Luke 4:1–2 NIV)

The devil, Satan, exploited the fact that Jesus got hungry. He attempted to entice Jesus to show more concern about his condition than for humankind's life. However, Jesus loved both the old and the new humankind. Accordingly, he resisted the devil and gained the victory for the new humanity. By resisting the devil's enticement, Jesus demonstrated his selfless love for humankind that he came to save.

The devil attempted to entice Jesus to turn his attention and love to himself and satisfy the needs of his body. The devil may have suggested that he first take care of his own needs. He could not help others if he was suffering.

There was nothing in the wilderness that was suitable for food. The only recourse for Jesus would have been to use his own divine origin to his advantage. However, Jesus came to be the Savior of the world and not to ensure his own comfort. Because Jesus loved humankind more than himself, he resisted the devil's suggestions.

> The tempter came to him and said, "If you are the Son of God, tell these stones to become bread." Jesus answered, "It is written: 'Man shall not live on bread alone, but on every word that comes from the mouth of God.'" (Mathew 4:3–4 NIV)

The three categories of sin that are described in 1 John 2:16 are the father of all sins. The first human pair was tested in these three categories of sin in the Garden of Eden. Therefore, the second Adam, Jesus Christ, had to be tempted in these three categories of sin. These are the categories.

> For everything in the world—the lust of the flesh, the
> lust of the eyes, and the pride of life—comes not from the
> father but from the world. (1 John 2:16 NIV)

The first temptation of Jesus concerned the lust of the flesh. This category of sin leads to determination. I must take care of number one before helping others. However, Jesus came to save the helpless humanity and not to take care of himself.

Satan knew that Jesus was the Son of God. However, he said that *if* Jesus was the Son of God. Perhaps Satan tried to put doubt in the mind of Jesus. Satan implied that the Son of God does not get hungry. Perhaps the devil attempted to entice Jesus in a conversation like he had done with Eve in the garden. He may have hoped Jesus would try to correct him by saying, "I am the Son of God, not if." However, Jesus understood a subtle difference in Satan's words. Therefore, Jesus quoted the scriptures instead of correcting the devil's statement. Jesus did not need to explain to Satan who he was on the earth.

Satan employed the same categories of sin in his temptation of Jesus that he employed in Eden's garden. He successfully tempted the first human pair. Therefore, he hoped to succeed with the new humankind's representative. The first category Satan employed was the lust of the flesh. Satan said to Jesus, "You are hungry; the Sons of God do not get hungry. Therefore, if you are one of them, make bread of these stones." To the Woman in Eden's garden, Satan showed that the forbidden fruit was good for her body. In the case of the woman in Eden, the lust of the flesh temptation was successful. However, Jesus resisted the devil, even if it meant he would remain hungry. Jesus had the need of the helpless humanity in his mind, not his temporary needs. The lust of the flesh is still a powerful category of sin that traps many.

Satan lost the first round of temptation. Because Jesus quoted the scriptures in the first round, Satan wanted to show Jesus that he too knew the scriptures. Therefore, he quoted scripture in his second temptation of Jesus.

> Then the devil took him to the holy city and had him
> stand on the highest point of the Temple. "If you are the

Son of God," he said, "Throw yourself down. For it is written: He will command angels concerning you, and they will lift you up in their hands, so that you will not strike your foot against a stone." Jesus answered him, "It is also written: Do not put the Lord your God to the test.'" (Mathew 4:5–7 NIV)

Satan quoted the scriptures to remind Jesus that his Father always keeps his promise. However, Satan's chief goal was to elevate doubt in the mind of Jesus. Perhaps he tried to tell Jesus that it was his chance to test the loyalty of those who should protect him. He insinuated that Jesus wanted people to accept him as the Son of God. This would be his chance to demonstrate it. However, Jesus did not seek and value what was good for his body and his life. Jesus came to be the Savior of the world and not to entertain it.

The woman in the Garden of Eden saw that the forbidden fruit was good for gaining knowledge, so she ate it. She already had the necessary knowledge about evil; however, she also wanted to know evil. To know evil is to experience it. Therefore, the woman wanted to experience evil in her body. However, her experience of evil has not increased her knowledge, but it gave her more trouble.

The woman offered the forbidden fruit to her husband. Adam knew what the woman had done. However, he made a deliberate, intelligent decision to eat the forbidden fruit. By his decision, Adam made all humankind a sinner by nature.

Satan lost the second round of temptation to Jesus. Quoting the scriptures did not help him. Therefore, he proceeded to employ the third category of sin, the lust of eyes.

Again the devil took him to a very high mountain and showed him all the kingdoms of the world and their splendor. "All this I will give you," he said, "if you will bow down and worship me." Jesus said to him, "Away from me, Satan! For it is written: Worship the Lord your God, and serve him only." (Mathew 4:8–10 NIV)

Satan reminded Jesus that he had come to redeem the earth from the kingdom of sin and darkness. Accordingly, he suggested that Jesus did not have to suffer the cross to achieve his goal. All he needed to do was worship Satan. Satan here displayed his *pride of life*. He wanted the Son of God to worship him, which could have made Satan equal to God. Satan attempted to entice Jesus to choose an easier way to gain earth. He said that if Jesus bowed and worship him just one time, he would give it to him.

However, Jesus came to overthrow the prince of this world (Satan) and remove the sin of the world's inhabitants. Jesus remained faithful to his mission so that by his faithfulness, he might justify humankind. Jesus conquered the third category of sin (the lust of eyes). He rescued the earth and its people for God. The woman in the Garden of Eden saw that the forbidden fruit was pleasing to the eyes, so she ate it and therefore, became a sinner.

Jesus conquered three categories of temptation. The representative of the first humankind failed, but Jesus, the representative of the new humanity, succeeded. By his victory, Jesus secured a perfect life for the new humankind that God created in him.

The life God put in the first man, Adam, was good until his deliberate decision to disobey. The new life (new spirit) that God put in Jesus at conception was good. By conquering temptation, Jesus irrevocably made new human life perfect and eternal,. Therefore, Jesus Christ is the source of salvation for all who die to self so that Christ can live in them.

> Son though he was, he learned obedience from what he suffered and, once made perfect, he became the source of eternal salvation for all who obey him and was designated by God to be the high priest in the order of Melchizedek. (Hebrews 5:8–10 NIV)

What suffering made Jesus' life perfect?

> Because he himself suffered when he was tempted, he is able to help those who are being tempted. Hebrews 2:18 NIV)

Jesus suffered the temptation, and he conquered it, which made the new life of humankind perfect. By trusting Jesus, we receive his perfect life. We could never make our life perfect by careful and sustained obedience. Because we have become sinners by nature, we lost the ability to obey the spirit of the law. Our effort to obey the letter of the law only reveals more of our sinfulness. God destroyed our sinful spirit (our sinful life) so that he could give us the perfect life of Jesus Christ. Jesus' victory in the wilderness is our victory when we trust him and have faith in him.

By his deliberate, intelligent decision, Adam (the first man) estranged us from God and made us his enemies. By his obedience and sacrifice, the Second Man, Jesus Christ, restored us to God as his children with the right of inheritance. We are the newborns (born of Spirit) children of God. We are not his foster children. We have all this because God gave humankind a Second Adam, who brought new life to humanity.

There are two Adams, two deliberate decisions, and two eternal consequences. By his deliberate decision, the first Adam made humankind a sinner by nature and condemned to eternal death irrevocably. By his deliberate decision in the wilderness, the Second Adam made the new humankind perfect in the eyes of God and gave it eternal life irrevocably. By the act of his selfless love, God made us righteous in Jesus Christ irrevocably.

Jesus went to the wilderness in the human body that he received through Mary at conception. However, he received good spirit (good intelligence) from God. His new spirit was good because it came from God, which was the same as the first Adam's spirit at creation. Jesus did not need to make a deliberate decision until he knew enough to do so. The Holy Spirit resided in and guided Jesus before he was ready for a deliberate decision. Jesus went into the wilderness full of the Holy Spirit. However, in the wilderness, he faced the enemy on his own. On behalf of the new humankind in him, his decision in the wilderness had to be on his initiative.

In the wilderness, Jesus remained resolutely faithful and committed to his mission as the Savior of the world. Therefore, he emerged from the wilderness, a victorious representative of the re-created humankind. Because Jesus's spirit (life) was made perfect through suffering temptation, the Holy Spirit entered him and remained with him forever. By trusting

Jesus, the yielded believers have the promised Holy Spirit in them forever. Not only has the life (spirit of Jesus Christ) become perfect through his victory, but it also became indestructible.

> And what we have said is even more clear if another priest like Melchizedek appears, one who has become a priest not on basis of a regulation as to his ancestry but on the basis of the power of an indestructible life. (Hebrews 7:15–16 NIV)

The life of the representative of new humankind is indestructible because God granted him such a life.

> For as the Father has life in himself, so he granted the Son also to have life in himself. (John 5:26 NIV)

Therefore, Jesus's human body became sanctified and ready for the wonderful exchange on the cross. The re-created humankind received in Jesus Christ much more than had been lost in the Garden of Eden. Those who surrender themselves and accept Jesus Christ have an indestructible life, here and now. After the temptation, Jesus preached the good news of the kingdom for three and a half years. On numerous occasions, He demonstrated that he was the Son whom God had promised to send.

15

Jesus Christ, the New High Priest

WHEN JESUS FINISHED his mission of preaching the good news of the kingdom, he went to Jerusalem. The time has come for him to suffer the cross of Christ. Time has come for the old, sinful humankind to die the eternal death so that the new humanity could have eternal life in Jesus Christ.

The new humankind, with a new spirit, lives in a temporary body. When Jesus Christ returns to take his bride to his Father's house, we will receive the glorified body of Jesus Christ.

> And just as we have born the image of the earthly man, so shall we bear the image of the heavenly man. (1 Corinthians 15:49 NIV)

The *cross of Christ* refers to what he suffered while nailed to the cross at Golgotha. Separation from the Father was the *cross of Christ*.

The most significant day ever was on Friday that was almost two thousand years ago. The event that transpired on the cross at Golgotha cannot be explained by any law known to humankind. What God did on our behalf, through the body of Jesus Christ, conforms to a low that is not in our universe. God acted on behalf of sinful humanity at a level inconceivable for earthly beings. Our God, the Father, himself came down to Golgotha to restore to him the rebellious humankind as his children. Only God, the Creator, could destroy humanity's sinful spirit and replace it with a perfect spirit that he put in Jesus Christ at conception. The old is gone; the new has begun.

> Therefore, if anyone is in Christ, the new creation has come: The old has gone, the new is here! All this is from God, who reconciled us to himself through Christ and gave us the ministry of reconciliation: that God was reconciling the world to himself in Christ, not counting people's sins against them. And has committed to us the message of reconciliation. (2 Corinthians 5:17– 9 NIV)

On that day, God destroyed the sinful spirit (life) and the sinful history of humankind forever. He replaced them with a new and perfect life and the holy history of Jesus Christ.

After his temptation, for three and a half years, Jesus lived a perfect life in his sanctified body. On several occasions, Satan tried to distract Jesus from his mission. However, Jesus recognized the evil attempts by the enemy. He resisted the devil and remained faithful to his mission as the Savior of the world. Jesus successfully secured a perfect life for the new humankind that God created in him. The sinful life (sinful spirit) that humankind inherited from the first man, Adam, had to die an eternal death. However, God had determined to preserve the humankind that he loved; therefore, he gave humanity a new and eternal life in Jesus Christ. We shall show that humankind's sinful life has died forever, in the body of Jesus Christ on the cross.

The great exchange of life (spirit) and making all of humanity his children is God's mystery that he announced through his servants, the prophets.

> "But in the days when the seventh angel is about to sound his trumpet, the mystery of God will be accomplished, just as he announced to his servants the prophets." (Revelation 10:7 NIV)

Throughout the history of Christianity, the mystery of God has been misunderstood. Misunderstanding of the mystery of God led to the misunderstanding of the cross of Christ. Soon after the apostles had died, or been martyred, the knowledge of the cross of Christ began to fade. Therefore, much of the central message in God's mystery was overtaken by various human interpretations. What is the message that is central to the mystery of God?

> The seventh angel sounded his trumpet, and there were loud voices in heaven, which said: "The kingdom of the world has become the kingdom of our Lord and his Messiah, and he will reign for ever and ever." (Revelation 11:15 NIV)

The mystery that the seventh angel announced is that the Messiah is victorious. He has defeated the enemy of God and has restored the principality of Satan to God the Creator. Lucifer gained this world as his principality by a deceptive method. However, hi is not its prince anymore. Now Jesus rules as the King of kings and Lord of lords.

> "Very truly I tell you Pharisees, anyone who does not enter the sheep pen by the gate, but climbs in by some other way, is a thief and a robber. The one who enters by the gate is the shepherd of the sheep." (John 10:1–2 NIV)

Therefore, what Lucifer did in the garden of Eden is robbery. He dishonestly entered this world. Jesus Christ came to restore the stolen property to its rightful owner. God announced it through his servant long before the birth of the Messiah.

> Those who hate me without reason outnumber the hairs of my head; many are my enemies without cause, those who seek to destroy me. I am forced to restore what I did not steal. (Psalm 69:4 NIV)

Not only did the representative of the re-created humankind restore the stolen property, but he also banished the thief forever. God announced it in advance, through his servant, the prophet.

> He asked me, "What do you see?" I answered, I see a flying scroll, twenty cubits long and ten cubits wide. And he said to me, "This is the curse that is going out over the whole land; for according to what it says on one side, every thief will be banished, and according to what it says on the other, everyone who swears falsely will be banished?" (Zechariah 5:2–3 NIV)

Jesus accomplished all the above while he was in the human body on the earth. He conquered the temptation from the thief and has banished him from the sheep pen. Satan is no longer the prince of this world. Jesus assured his disciples that he would do it.

> "Now is the time for judgment on this world; now the prince of this world will be driven out. And I, when I am lifted up from the earth, will draw all people to myself." (John 12:31–32 NIV)

The victorious Jesus Christ is our true gate to the Father. The true gate to heaven is forever open for all. The thief does not have the authority to come to the sheep pen anymore.

> "I am the gate; whoever enters through me will be saved. They will come and go out and find pasture. (John 10:9 NIV)

Not only has Jesus banish the thief (Satan) but he also saved humankind from guilt and eternal punishment for sin. He accomplished it in his body while he was nailed to the cross at Golgotha. How did God accomplish his mystery in the body of Jesus Christ on the cross? Historically, this selfless act of God has been misunderstood within Christianity.

The Cross of Christ Is Misunderstood

Historically, Christians have debated and discussed the nature and significance of the cross of Christ endlessly. Opinions are as diverse as the Christian landscape is. The wonderful exchange on the cross at Golgotha is very simple, yet it has confounded the minds of readers and students of the scriptures. Understanding the simple yet profoundly pivotal truth to the re-creation of humankind has eluded many sincere minds. The profoundly complex nature of the cross of Christ is not complicated. When we say, "The cross of Christ," we speak of what he suffered while nailed to the cross at Golgotha. What took place on the cross at Golgotha is the most crucial event in human history.

What then is the obstacle to understanding the cross of Christ? Concentration on the soul as the human identity is a leading obstacle to a fuller understanding of Christ's cross. The order of spirit called mankind is the life of human beings. Jesus told us that spirit gives life. Our spirit is our intelligence. Because it is not from matter, the spirit (intelligence) is fixed. It neither varies nor changes. Human knowledge increases; however, knowledge is not human intelligence. Human intelligence generates human knowledge. Therefore, the spirit that God put in the first man, Adam, is the human identity. The human spirit commands the body, and thus, it produces chemistry that displays the uniqueness of personal identity. The identity of the old (first) humankind is the spirit that was given by the Creator at creation. The identity of the new humanity is its spirit that God put into Jesus Christ at the Incarnation.

The spirit that resides in the human brain generates thoughts, choices, and decisions through the brain's statistical process. Decisions made by the human spirit (the intelligence) are irrevocable. When a deliberate, intelligent decision, is made, all other options cease to exist. The intelligent decision cannot be revoked or destroyed. The irrevocable nature of intelligent decisions makes human beings powerless to avoid and change the consequences. Decisions based on feelings (or soul) are unreliable and are subject to change and elimination. Decisions based on feelings are often amended, modified or replaced by other decisions. Therefore, decisions based on the human soul are unreliable. Intelligent decisions, whether made for sin or righteousness, are equally irrevocable.

Therefore, the study and contemplation of the creation and the re-creation of humankind should always be based on the spirit, not the soul.

The second obstacle to a fruitful understanding of the cross of Christ results from the concentration of the earthly Temple and its priesthood. With its priesthood and the annual *day of atonement* ritual, the earthly Temple was only a shadow pointing to reality. The reality is in Jesus Christ, who superseded the shadow. Often the students and the exegetes of the scriptures portray Jesus Christ and his mission, as a High Priest, in light of Aron's order of the priesthood. However, the law, the stipulations, and practices, that were followed by Aaron's priesthood do not apply to Jesus Christ. While both Aaron and Jesus are presented as high priests, they differ fundamentally. Aaron's priesthood was temporary. Jesus' priesthood is permanent. Aaron had successors. Jesus does not have a successor.

The high priest's critical function in the earthly temple system has been to represent the people before God. To symbolically make the people acceptable to God, Aaron's order high priests had to repeat the atonement ritual annually. However, in Jesus Christ, who is the permanent High Priest, the people belong to God forever. People are free to approach God, in prayer, without an intercessor. The earthly Temple's system needed the high priests because sinful human beings could not live in God's presence. Accordingly, God established a shadow priesthood to serve as a constant reminder that he will establish a permanent connection between himself and humankind at just the right time. In Jesus Christ, God is with his people permanently. Aaron's order of the high priests could not serve as a permanent connection to God because they were sinners themselves. They first had to offer a sacrifice for their sins and then for the people's sins. Aaron's order of high priests served temporarily. Death prevented them from serving indefinitely.

> Every high priest is selected from among the people and is appointed to represent the people in matter related to God, to offer gifts and sacrifices for sins. He is able to deal gently with those who are ignorant and are going astray, since he himself is subject to weakness. This is why he has to offer sacrifices for his own sins, as well as for the sins of the people. (Hebrews 5:1–3 NIV)

However, Jesus Christ, our permanent High Priest, did not have to offer a sacrifice for himself. He conquered temptation and obtained a perfect life eternally. Jesus Christ is a permanent High Priest because he lives forever.

> Unlike the other high priests, he does not need to offer
> sacrifices day after day, first for his own sins, and then for
> the sins of the people. He sacrificed for their sins once for
> all when he offered himself. (Hebrews 7:27 NIV)

All Levitical priests were sinful human beings who were appointed to sacred duties in the Temple. They were subject to death in the same way as other humans. They were a sinner by nature and condemned to eternal death. They were not exempt from the consequences of sin. They inherited their priestly function. Therefore, their priesthood had to be temporary. However, Jesus Christ did not inherit the designation of High Priest. God appointed him to be a permanent High priest. God has restored sinful humankind to himself as his children. The cross of Christ connected the re-created humankind with God forever, in Jesus Christ. Unfortunately, many do not accept God as their Father. Therefore, they reject Jesus Christ and the eternal life in him.

> Now there have been many of those priests, since death
> prevented them from continuing in office; but because
> Jesus lives forever, he has a permanent priesthood.
> Hebrews (7:23–24 NIV)

The old-covenant priesthood's laws, precepts, and regulations do not apply to the High Priest in Melchizedek's order—Jesus Christ. Therefore, it is not proper to depict Jesus Christ as the high priest in Aaron's order. Aaron's order of high priests could not officiate in their bodies because they were sinners by nature. Therefore, they had to perform their duties in a physical structure designated for sacred service.

The old covenant priesthood could not remove sins from the people. They only symbolically portrayed that the punishment for sin was held in abeyance until the Messiah would come. Aaron's order of high priests could not save anyone. They served as a shadow that pointed to the reality—Jesus Christ. To remove the sin from humankind, God appointed a better high priesthood, a High Priest in the order of Melchizedek, Jesus Christ. As a High Priest, Jesus officiated in his body, not in a physical structure, Temple. His body is the Temple God built, not men.

The old-covenant priesthood could not give the people a new and perfect life. The sinful high priest did not have a perfect life, even though he conformed to the laws and regulations.

> If perfection could have been attained through the Levitical priesthood – and indeed the law given to the people established that priesthood – why was there still need for another priest to come, one in the order of Melchizedek, not in the order of Aaron? For when the priesthood is changed, the law must be changed also. (Hebrews 7:11–12 NIV)

Aaron's order of priests had to offer sacrifices in conformity to the old-covenant law. The old covenant was an agreement between the people and God. The people were participants in the old covenant. The people proposed an agreement (a contract) with God. They told Moses to tell God that they would obey whatever he asks of them through Moses. They were afraid to have their God talk to them directly. The people were sincere in what they had offered. God accepted it with a caveat. Accordingly, God gave Moses the words that he was to speak to the people.

> So Moses went back and summoned the elders of the people and set before them all the words the LORD had commanded him to speak. The people all responded together. We will do everything the LORD has said. So Moses brought their answer back to the Lord. (Exodus 19:7–8 NIV)

However, the agreement that people made with God did not hold. They did the things that they inherited from the first man, Adam. They broke the covenant.

As at Adam, they have broken the covenant; they were
unfaithful to me there. (Hosea 6:7 NIV)

The people's unfaithfulness made the old covenant useless. The sinful
spirit (nature) could not obey God, no matter how hard it tried. The law
given for the old covenant could not change the sinful nature of the people.
The law given to Arron's priesthood could not help people obey the words
of God.

The former regulation is set aside because it was weak and
useless (for the law made nothing perfect, and a better
hope is introduced, by which we draw near to God.
(Hebrews 7:18–19 NIV)

Why did the old covenant system become useless? Was there anything
wrong with what God gave to the people?

For if there had been nothing wrong with that first
covenant, no place would have been sought for another.
But God found fault with the people and said: The days
are coming, declares the Lord, when I will make a new
covenant with the people of Israel and with the people of
Judah. (Hebrews 8:7–8 NIV)

There has been nothing wrong with what God required from the
people. God knew before he accepted the agreement that people would not
remain faithful to the covenant. He gave them the Ten Commandments
to show them that they (the sinful people) could not obey. The problem
always lay with people. The people were sinners by nature, therefore,
utterly helpless. All humankind was so helpless that it could not recognize
that it could not obey, no matter how hard it tried. The law requires
perfect obedience, which the sinful humankind could not render under
any circumstance. Even the people's best efforts were not sufficient. There
was no possibility of making humankind better under the old covenant
law. The re-creation of humankind was the only answer.

The re-creation of humankind required a radical change in the way
that the people related to God. The old Temple, with its priesthood, had

to be replaced with the better one. A better priesthood required a new covenant and the new law.

> By calling this covenant new, he has made the first one obsolete; and what is obsolete and outdated will soon disappear. (Hebrews 8:13 NIV)

Therefore, the new High Priest had to officiate in a new and better way. The new High Priest is the mediator of the new covenant. The new eternal High Priest is always a mediator of a new covenant because it is forever. The new covenant was established by unilateral act by God, the Father. It was not an agreement but the last will. Humankind was neither a party to nor a participant in it. Humankind is the beneficiary under the new covenant. The new covenant is a will left by someone who is soon to die. Jesus came to do the will of the Father. He remained faithful to what he willed. By his faithfulness, we stand justified from everything that we could not have done ourselves.

> Therefore, when Christ came into the world, he said: "Sacrifices and offering you did not desire, but a body you prepared for me; with burnt offerings and sin offerings you were not pleased. Then I said, here I am—it is written about me in the scroll—I have come to do your will, my God." (Hebrews 10:5–7 NIV)

Certainly, the old covenant priesthood with its law and sacrifices was only a temporary shadow. The reality is the new and better priesthood, in Melchizedek's order. The sun of our righteousness from God has risen to a noon-high position and dispelled the shadow. The High Priest of the new (the re-created) humankind said that he came to do the will of God. What is the will of God the Father?

> "For my Father's will is that everyone who looks to the Son and believes in him shall have eternal life, and I will raise them up at the last day." John 6:40 NIV)

We may not know all there is to know about our new High Priest. We may not understand everything about him. However, we must look to the Son and believe him. It is like the thief on the cross who did not know the good man who was nailed to the cross next to him. He only knew that the one nailed to the cross next to him was a good man who was crucified for something he had not done. So, he looked up to the good man and placed his trust in him. The good man, Jesus Christ, assured the thief that he would be with him in paradise. When Jesus returns, the first thing the thief will hear is the voice of the good man calling him to paradise.

Old covenant high priests could not do the will of God. They offered many sacrifices for sin; however, they could not secure eternal life for the fallen humanity. Only the High Priest of the new covenant could make eternal life a present reality for the yielded believers. The new High Priest is so superior to the old covenant system that he only had to offer one sacrifice for all time. He does not have to repeat it again and again. Nothing could be added to what God accomplished on behalf of the re-created humankind through the body of Jesus Christ. The will of the Father has been accomplished, and it is forever and irrevocable.

> And by that will, we have been made holy through the sacrifice of the body of Jesus Christ once for all. (Hebrews 10:10 NIV)

What the High Priest of the new covenant has accomplished on our behalf could not be compared in any way to what the high priests of the first covenant did. Therefore, maintaining that the new High Priest's ministry is the renewed first-covenant system is a disservice to the world's Savior. It is a disgrace to the cross of Christ.

16

Golgotha

THE ANNUAL ATONEMENT ritual performed by Aaron's priesthood had two parts. The first part was the sacrifice for the people's sins. By sprinkling the blood of the sacrifice for sins onto the most holy place, the high priest symbolically transferred the people's sins to the mercy seat. The second part removed the sins from the mercy seat to the wilderness via a scapegoat. The removal of the people's sins to a remote place, assured the people that their sins could not come back and count against them again. The removal of sins from the mercy seat also cleansed the Sanctuary.

The annual ritual in the earthly Temple was the shadow that pointed to the cross of Christ. It also reminded the people that God will remove the sin from humankind forever, at just the right time. God removed the sin of humankind through a better sacrifice and High Priest. God has accomplished it through the body of Jesus Christ at just the right time. Daily and on special occasions, sacrifices were a form of worship. They were not a shadow of the cross of Christ.

The law (the Ten Commandments) that God gave to the old covenant system served as a reminder that sinful human beings were helpless. Their effort to obey, however sincere, could not remove from them the stigma of sin. The requirements embedded in the Ten Commandments were to make people realize that they need a Savior. Their sincere efforts to obey were powerless to take care of their sins. Even the best efforts possible with utmost sincerity could not make the people righteous. Despite all the sacrifices and rituals, the people were still sinners by nature. The removal of the people's sins had to await a better priesthood, with a permanent High Priest. Only the High Priest who had a perfect life (spirit) could forever remove the people's sins. How did the new High Priest remove sins from the people? The illustration 8 may help visualize what transpired on the cross at Golgotha.

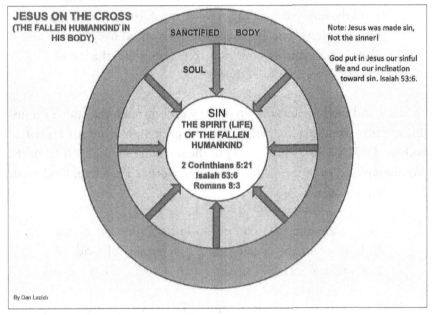

Illustration 8

Jesus is the representative of the new humankind. The first man Adam made the first humankind a sinner by nature. The Second Man, Jesus, made the new humankind righteous by nature in him. The re-creation of humankind was the only way possible for restoring humanity to God. Jesus, the Second Adam, lived a perfect life for three and a half years. Because his life had been made perfect, his body was sanctified and he could not undergo decay. Jesus's body did not have life in it from Friday afternoon until Sunday morning, and yet, it did not begin to decay. Therefore, in the sanctified body of Jesus Christ, the sinful humankind died the second death. Now the new humankind lives forever.

Justification or removing humankind's sin could be accomplished only through the new- humankind High Priest's body. The removal of sins forever could be accomplished through a High Priest who officiated in his body and not in a physical structure. The whole of humankind sinned in one man, Adam. Only one man, Jesus Christ, could remove the sin of humankind. Both the first and the Second Adam are representatives of their respective humankind.

> Therefore, my friends, I want you to know that through Jesus the forgiveness of sins is proclaimed to you. Through him everyone who believes is set free from every sin, a justification you were not able to obtain under the law of Moses. (Acts 13:38–39, NIV)

How did God remove the sin of the world through the body of Jesus? Jesus Christ separated his perfect human spirit (life) from his sanctified body and laid it aside. Then, God put the sinful human spirit (life) of the old humankind in Jesus on the cross at Golgotha. Therefore, God made Jesus what he was not.

> God made him who had no sin to be sin for us, so that in him we might become the righteousness of God. (2 Corinthians 5:21 NIV)

God made Jesus sin, not a sinner. The representative of the new humankind became Christ, the Savior of sinful humanity. The High Priest of the new humankind suffered the cross of Christ on the cross at Golgotha. The cross of Christ is the separation from the Father because of the sin of the world being on Jesus.

The old-covenant shadow depicted the placement of sin on Jesus Christ while he was on the cross at Golgotha. The annual earthly temple ritual deployed two goats for the removal of sins of the people. One goat was chosen to be a sacrifice for the sins of the people. The other goat became a scapegoat, which removed the people's sins from them into the wilderness, which was a place of no return. The scapegoat symbolically ensured the people that their sins would not come back and count against them.

"Aaron shall bring the goat whose lot falls to the LORD and sacrifice it for sin offering. But the goat chosen by lot as the scapegoat shall be presented alive before the LORD to be used for making atonement by sending it into the wilderness as a scapegoat." (Leviticus 16:9–10 NIV)

Both goats employed in the shadow's Day of Atonement represented, symbolically, Jesus Christ on the cross at Golgotha. The concept of Jesus being both a sacrifice for sin and the scapegoat presented a problem among Christians. Some could not visualize how Jesus could accomplish both functions at the same time on the cross.

Such difficulty persists today. Accordingly, some conclude that Jesus only offered a sacrifice on the cross at Golgotha. Therefore, this sacrifice was for past sins only. Present and future sins remained unforgiven. If this is true, then Jesus did not save anyone on the cross at Golgotha. Sinners would still have sinful life in them. They would be condemned to eternal death.

An unforgiven sinner could not have the perfect spirit of Jesus Christ in him. Therefore, there would be no newborn believers. Those who adhere to the concept that on the cross at Golgotha God forgave only the past sins imply that Jesus Christ died for nothing.

According to the conclusion that God forgave only the past sins, sinners must repent, obey the Ten Commandments, and ask God to forgive their present sins. No one could confess the sins he or she did not yet commit. Therefore, sinners could not repent for future sins, and yet, they are guilty of their future sins. If our confession of present sins and our repentance could bring forgiveness, then Jesus Christ died for nothing. If a sinner by nature were to be justified and be free to approach Holy God in prayer, all sins—past, present, and future—must be forgiven.

The concept that God forgave only the past sins implies that he forgave only the sins committed before Jesus died on the cross. No sins committed after the cross at Golgotha were forgiven. Therefore, by such a conclusion, they imply that humankind, after the cross at Golgotha, does not have a Savior because it committed the rest of its sins after Jesus Christ died on the cross. Those who adhere to such teaching do not realize that a sinner could not even recognize he is a sinner. If sinners cannot recognize they are sinners by nature, how can they ask God for forgiveness? In their mind, they have not committed an offense that requires repentance. Also, if we could repent and obtain forgiveness, why do we need Jesus? Why then did Jesus had to die?

The only solution to this dilemma is accepting Jesus's death, resurrection, and life as ours, here and now. We must always be sinners who are saved by Grace. Yielded believers in Jesus Christ repent because their sins have been forgiven through the body of Jesus on the cross at Golgotha. Yielded believers do not get forgiveness when they ask for it. Because he loves us, God has forgiven us all sins against the law. By forgiving our sins, God enabled us to recognize that we are sinners by nature. Now the law cannot condemn us for breaking a command because it has no authority over yielded believers. Yielded believers do not violate the laws that God has established because they love God and human beings selflessly. We love God because he has given us a perfect and eternal life in Jesus Christ.

> When you were dead in your sins and in uncircumcision
> of your flesh, God made you alive with Christ. He forgave
> us all our sins, having canceled the charge of our legal
> indebtedness, which stood against us and condemned us;
> he has taken it away, nailing it to the cross. (Colossians
> 2:13–14 NIV)

Paul states that God forgave us all our sins. All sins against the law—past, present, and future—were removed from us through the body of Jesus Christ, on the cross at Golgotha. Therefore, the re-created humankind remains justified forever. Unfortunately, all do not believe that God has accomplished it for us through the body of Jesus Christ on the cross. Because of their unbelief they remain condemned to eternal death.

However, God promised it to us long before the birth of Jesus Christ.

> "I, even I, am he who blots out your transgressions, for
> my own sake, and remembers your sins no more." (Isaiah
> 43:25 NIV)

The good news for the sinners is, not only has God remove their sins from them but he no longer remembers them.

Jesus Christ, Our Sin offering

How did Jesus become the sacrifice for our sin? The life that died in Jesus Christ's body on the cross did not serve as the sacrifice for sin. The sinful life of humanity died in the body of Jesus Christ on the cross. Sinful life could not have been a sacrifice for sins of the people. Through the body of Jesus Christ, God destroyed the human life that sinned in the garden in Eden. Eternal or the second death is the wage for our sin. The law requires that the sinner dies forever, with no way out. Jesus laid down his perfect and indestructible life as a sacrifice for our sin. To lay down his life means Jesus separated his perfect life from his body.

> "The reason my Father loves me is that I lay down my life—only to take it up again. No one takes it from me, but I lay it down of my own accord. I have authority to lay it down and authority to take it up again. This command I received from my Father." (John 10:17–18 NIV)

The spirit Jesus received at the Incarnation was the new spirit (the new or re-created humankind's life). Whether perfect or a sinner, the human spirit must have the human brain for intelligent processing of information. The re-created humankind will manage this universe through the intelligent processing of information. Therefore, the separation of the perfect spirit from Jesus' body was the sacrifice for sin.

By this separation of life from the body, Jesus offered his body as the merci seat. God put the sin of the world and the sinful human life on Jesus's body (the Mercy Seat) so he could destroy the sin and the sinful life of humankind forever. The life that died in the body of Jesus is the life that God put in Adam at creation. The perfect spirit (life) of the re-created humankind could not process information without the human brain. Therefore, in human terms if Jesus' body had died on the cross, neither the re-created nor the sinful humankind would ever exist.

Therefore, the separation of the new and perfect human spirit (new human life) from the body of Jesus, represented the most crucial sacrifice of Jesus's body. It embodied a decisive act concerning eternal life for the re-created humankind. Being made sin on the cross, Jesus could not see beyond the death of life in his body. He did not have a shred of tangible evidence that all would work out according to plan. The only thing Jesus could hold on to is God's promise.

> "'Therefore my heart is glad and my tongue rejoices; my body also will rest in hope, because you will not abandon me to the realm of the dead, you will not let your holy one see decay." (Acts 2:26–27 NIV)

Jesus's body did not decay in the grave. The life of re-created humankind lay on a side without the body. Even the perfect and indestructible life could not generate thoughts without the human body that God made on the sixth day of creation. His perfect spirit (life) which he laid down on Friday returned to his body on Sunday morning. The perfect life returned to the body of Jesus after God destroyed the world's sin by removing it from the Mercy Seat—Jesus's body. This act guarantees that the re-created humankind has the indestructible life here and now, in Jesus Christ.

Only Jesus could understand the critical nature of separating the perfect spirit from the sanctified body. On the cross, Jesus's body had the sin of humankind on it. God abandoned Jesus on the cross to destroy the sinful spirit that was in the body of Jesus. God departed from the universe and left Jesus to face the second death alone. We could not comprehend such an act of selfless love. The representative of the re-created humankind knows what it means to be sin on behalf of sinful humanity. The re-created humankind must forever be grateful for such an incomprehensible act of love.

How Did Jesus Become the Scapegoat?

The scapegoat derives from word *ez-azel*, which means the one that goes away. The scapegoat symbolically removed the people's sins from the mercy seat to a remote place of no return. The principal purpose of this symbolic annual purification ritual has been to remind the people that God would permanently remove the sin from them at just the right time. On the Day of Atonement, the high priest would take the blood of the sacrifice for the people's sins and sprinkle it on the cover of the ark of the covenant.

Therefore, the sins of the people had to be removed from the cover (the mercy seat). The high priest would symbolically remove the sins by confessing them on the head of the scapegoat. Thus, the high priest would cleanse the Sanctuary or the mercy seat. The symbolic annual cleansing of the Sanctuary removed (via scapegoat) both the deliberate and the unintentional sins from the sanctuary. The holiest room served as God's residence among his people. The glory of God represented Jesus Christ, as noted earlier in this treatise. The sins of the people that were placed on the mercy seat (Jesus Christ) had to be removed forever.

The Sanctuary's cleansing on the annual Day of Atonement assured the people that the cleansing ritual removed their sins without a trace. The symbolic function of the sacrifice for sins was to remove the people's sins to the Mercy Seat. However, Jews believed that this sacrifice only removed known unintentional sins. Unknown unintentional sins could not be atoned for by the annual sacrifice for sin. They also believed that the intentional sins were indestructible. Therefore, a regular sacrifice for sin could not remove the intentional or deliberate sin from the people.

Removal of the intentional, or deliberate sin, required a process of purging of the sanctuary. Christians generally define the removal of sins from the people with the word *propitiation*. This term may be unfortunate because it does not present what is symbolized. The annual symbolic Temple purification ritual did not remove the sins of the people. It only served as a reminder that God would accomplish it at just the right time through the body of the Messiah.

The annual temple ritual depicted the period of grace, during which God held the punishment for the world's sin in abeyance until the Messiah would remove it permanently. The word *expiate* appears to be a more representative term for describing the removal of people's sins. Whether performed as a part of the shadow or the reality, the sacrifices for sin did not appease God. Sin is utterly offensive to the Holy God. Therefore, the New High Priest had to remove humankind's sin permanently and without a trace. In an ordinary sense, the Messiah could not have only forgiven the world's sin. He had to remove and destroy it forever and without a trace. The real and permanent sacrifice for sin, which was offered by the New High Priest, removed humankind's sin forever. By abandoning Jesus, God forgot our sin and, therefore, it does not exist anymore.

The shadow temple purification ritual was performed annually as a reminder that the Messiah is coming at just the right time. When he comes, he would remove the world's sin, in reality and once for all time. The shadow Atonement ritual had to be performed annually. However, the reality is one time for the whole of eternity. The annual ritual gave hope for the removal of sins. The reality accomplished it and left no trace of our sins. The officiating high priest on the Day of Atonement had to perform the ritual at the beginning of his duty as the high priest. He did not perform it again during his term as the high priest. This practice symbolically pointed to Jesus Christ, who removed the world's sin at the beginning of his service as the New High Priest. He will never again perform the removal of the people's sin because what he accomplished on the cross is sufficient and forever.

> "The priest who is anointed and ordained to succeed his father as a high priest is to make the atonement. He is to put on the sacred linen garments and make atonement for the Most Holy Place, for the tent of meeting and the altar, and for the priests and all the members of the community." (Leviticus 16:32 NIV)

The people believed that regular sacrifice for sin, offered on the Day of Atonement, removed only known unintentional sins. Willful, deliberate sins, the unknown unintentional sins, and known or intentional sins had to be removed by the expurgatory scapegoat, the people believed. However, the annual sacrifice removed only the sins of the people living at the time of the annual purification ritual. The sin of the world was the deliberate decision by Adam in the Garden of Eden. All other sins stem from the first deliberate sin done by an intelligent decision and choice. The Adam's deliberate sin became indestructible. Therefore, the animal sacrifice could not remove it from the people.

The New High Priest could not propitiate or appease God for the deliberate sin that was committed in the Garden of Eden. He had to *expiate* the deliberate sin of humankind. They had to be removed and destroyed forever. Because the deliberate sin is indestructible, the indestructible life was required to remove such sin from the people. The New High Priest has an indestructible life. Therefore, only he had the power to forever remove the deliberate sin committed by humankind in the garden in Eden.

Upon completing the annual atonement ritual, the high priests confessed the people's sins onto the scapegoat's head. This act symbolically moved the sins from the Most Holy Place to the head of the scapegoat. The annual expurgatory ritual served as God's "show and tell" so the people could understand. With it, the officiating high priest assured the people that God will remove humankind's sin forever at just the right time.

> "When Aaron has finished making atonement for the Most Holy Place, the tent of meeting and the altar, he shall bring forward the live goat. He is to lay both hands on the head of the live goat and confess over it all the wickedness and rebellion of the Israelites—all their sins— and put them on the goat's head. He shall send the goat away into the wilderness in the care of someone appointed for the task. The goat will carry on itself all their sins to a remote place; the man shall release it in the wilderness." (Leviticus 16:20–22 NIV)

By placing both hands upon the head of the live goat, the high priest symbolically depicted that the full weight of the people's sins was now on the scapegoat. So, the high priest demonstrated to the people that all their sins, including the deliberate ones, were now removed from them and taken to a place of no return.

By sending the scapegoat into the wilderness, the high priest symbolically ensured the people that their sins and sinful life, that they inherited from Adam, would die the second death, with no chance of the resurrection. The wages for sin were symbolically paid in full. However, the earthly high priest could not have assured the people that their sins had been destroyed. The annual purification ritual served as the shadow, a reminder, not a reality. The ritual demonstrated to the people that God was delaying the punishment for the world's deliberate sin until reality came at just the right time.

> God presented Christ as a sacrifice of atonement, through the shedding of his blood—to be received by faith. He did this to demonstrate his righteousness, because in his forbearance he left the sins committed beforehand unpunished—he did it to demonstrate his righteousness at the present time, so as to be just and the one who justifies those who have faith in Jesus. (Romans 3:25–26 NIV)

The phrase "sacrifice of atonement" above could be translated as the mercy seat. Jesus became the sacrifice of atonement when he laid down his perfect life. He separated his indestructible life from his body to become what he is not, on behalf of sinful humankind. Jesus became sin, not a sinner. By placing on Jesus the sin and sinful life of humankind, God made Jesus a Mercy Seat. By abandoning Jesus, the Mercy Seat, God removed the sin and the sinful spirit from humankind forever. By this Act, God demonstrated that he had expiated or purged our sin from us without a trace. Therefore, God has cleansed the Sanctuary, the body of the new humankind, forever. Consequently, in God's eyes, the re-created humankind (us) stands as if it had never sinned.

On the cross at Golgotha, Jesus represented the sinful and condemned humankind. He did not become our substitute. He offered his body as a means by which God removed our sin and sinful life from us. Therefore, the sinful humankind died the second death in the body of Jesus on the cross at Golgotha. Jesus's body was sanctified, and it could not undergo decay (could not die). The unsanctified body of sinful humankind could not have survived the wonderful exchange on the cross. The moral Law does not allow for a substitution. Therefore, Jesus did not die in the place of sinful humankind. He died as the sinful humankind. The sinful life of all humankind died in the body of Jesus on the cross. The moral Law condemned the deliberate sinner to eternal death; therefore, the deliberate sinner had to die. There was no other way.

No one could take the place of a sinner by nature. Even if a substitute died for a deliberate sinner, he would remain a sinner by nature.

> Parents are not to be put to death for their children, nor children put to death for their parents; each will die for their own sin. (Deuteronomy 24:16 NIV)

Jesus conquered the temptation, and his life became perfect and indestructible. Therefore, his perfect and indestructible life could not have died on the cross. The sinful life had to die as the wages for sin. Some consider that the death of the body satisfied the righteous requirement by the Law. However, the human body did not sin. Therefore, the death of the human body could not pay the wages for sin. The human spirit (life) sinned. Therefore, the eternal death of the human spirit was the wages for sin. The moral Law demands the eternal death of sinners as the wages for sin. A temporary death could not satisfy the righteous requirement by the moral Law. Therefore, had the perfect life of Jesus Christ died on the cross, he would not have risen, and humankind would not exist. Long before Jesus Christ dies, God announced that the sinner must die. The righteous could not die for the sinners.

> "The one who sins is the one who will die. The child will not share the guilt of the parent, nor will the parent share the guilt of a child. The righteousness of the righteous will be credited to them, and the wickedness of the wicked will be charged against them." (Ezekiel 18:20 NIV)

Because all humankind sinned in Adam, in the garden in Eden, it had to die forever as the wages for sin. No one could have taken the place of sinful humanity. Eden's sin was deliberate, and it came from a deliberate, intelligent decision that was made by the human spirit. All members of humankind had the same spirit. Therefore, all members of humankind became a sinner by nature. The apostle Paul asserts,

> Therefore, just as sin entered the world through one man, and death through sin, and in this way death came to all people, because all sinned. (Romans 5:12 NIV)

Certainly, the first humankind had to die for sin committed in Adam. Because of Adam's deliberate, intelligent decision in Eden, the human spirit lost the capability of a subsequent righteous intelligent decision. The sinful spirit (sinful life) could not be rehabilitated. It had to die an eternal death, with no way out. Even if some righteous spirit of the same order died in place of the sinful spirit, the sinful spirit would remain a sinner. A substitutionary death could not change the sinful nature of humanity. Sin could not be transferred from one being to another. The sinner himself must die. Therefore, the re-creation of humankind was the only answer.

Sinful humankind needed both the sacrifice for sin and the expiatory act to purge the sin without a trace. Only the expiatory act could free humankind from the consequences of sin. By separating his indestructible life from his body, Jesus offered a sacrifice for sin. The sacrifice for sin transferred the human sin to the mercy seat, which was the body of Jesus on the cross. By abandoning Jesus on the cross because of sin, God purged humankind of its deliberate sin and, therefore, from all sins. Only the Lamb of God, because he had an indestructible life, could have led the sinful humankind out of slavery to sin and into the kingdom of God's righteousness.

Removal of a deliberate and indestructible sin required a High Priest who was appointed on bases of an indestructible life. The people believed that the annual atonement ritual in the earthly Temple could not remove a deliberate sin. They believed that a deliberate sin is indestructible. Neither by a sacrifice nor anything a sinner did could the deliberate sin be removed from him. The people under the shadow system believed correctly. Their high priest could not remove the deliberate sin. Therefore, Jesus Christ, the representative of the re-created humankind, was the High Priest who removed the deliberate sin of the world forever and without a trace.

Humankind lost its life in the first man Adam, in the Garden of Eden. However, because he loves humankind, God gave humanity a new and perfect life in Jesus Christ. As Jesus Christ has an indestructible life, the yielded believers have a new and indestructible life in Jesus Christ. Because he loves us selflessly, God restored to us much more than we lost in the Garden of Eden. There is no power—past, present, nor future—that could take from us the indestructible life of Jesus Christ.

"The reason my Father loves me is that I lay down my life—only to take it up again. No one takes it from me, but I lay it down of my own accord. I have authority to lay it down and authority to take it up again. This command I received from my Father." (John 10:17–18 NIV)

Therefore, the yielded believers do not have to fear because no one has the power to remove the indestructible life they have in Jesus Christ. They have, here and now, the perfect and eternal life of Jesus Christ. Their old sinful life has died forever in the body of Jesus on the cross at Golgotha. The indestructible life of the yielded believers is secure in God the Father forever.

For you died, and your life is now hidden with Christ in God. When Christ, who is your life, appears, then you also will appear with him in glory. (Colossians 3:3–4 NIV)

Therefore, our body will die; however, our life is secure eternally with God in Jesus Christ. The blessed hope of the Gospel assures us of this. Jesus promised that he would come back to take his own to be with him in his Father's house. Yielded believers can be certain that their Jesus Christ will keep his promise.

How did God remove from us our sin permanently through our scapegoat, Jesus Christ? As stated earlier, Jesus separated his perfect and indestructible life from his body on the cross at Golgotha. Then God put the sin of the world and the sinful spirit of humankind on Jesus's body. By putting our sin on Jesus, God removed that which separated us from him. Our sin created a barrier between our God and us and rendered us utterly helpless. Only God could remove the barrier and restore us to himself. God accomplished it on the cross at Golgotha.

All this is from God, who reconciled us to himself through Christ and gave us the ministry of reconciliation: that God was reconciling the world to himself in Christ, not counting people's sins against them. And he has committed to us the message of reconciliation. (2 Corinthians 5:18–19 NIV)

By separating his perfect life from his sanctified body, Jesus, our High Priest, fulfilled the thing that the shadow symbolized. God removed sin from the people and placed it on the sanctified body of Jesus Christ. Therefore, Jesus became our scapegoat, on whom the full force of our sin rested. However, God did not just remove our sin far from us, as the shadow did. In Jesus Christ, our Scapegoat, God destroyed our sin and our sinful spirit actually and forever, in the body of Jesus, on the cross at Golgotha.

> By oppression and judgment he was taken away. Yet who of his generation protested? For he was cut off from the land of the living; for the transgression of my people he was punished. (Isaiah 53:8 NIV)

God, the Father, put our deliberate sin and our sinful spirit on Jesus while he was on the cross. How did he destroy it forever and without a trace?

> We all, like sheep, have gone astray, each of us has turned to our own way; and the Lord has laid on him the iniquity of us all. (Isaiah 53:6 NIV)

Our sin and our sinful spirit, which God put on Jesus, separated him from the Father. Therefore, God abandoned Jesus on the cross at Golgotha because of our sin. Because God gave us the spirit in Adam at creation, only he could destroy it. God destroyed our sinful spirit by forgetting it. That is why Jesus cried out.

> About three in the afternoon Jesus cried out in a loud voice, "Eli, Eli, lama sabachthani?" (Which means My God, My God, why have you forsaken me?)" (Mathew 27:46 NIV)

By forsaking Jesus Christ on the cross, God destroyed our sins and sinful spirit forever. God does not remember our sins anymore. Therefore, our sinful life (spirit) died the second death, in the body of Jesus on the cross, without a possibility of resurrection. If God, the Creator, forgets it, it must cease to exist forever. Our sinful spirit (sinful life) did not rise on Sunday morning. Jesus' perfect life reentered his sanctified body in the morning of his resurrection. Jesus' body did not begin to decay. It remained the same the entire time in the grave.

Only the unimaginable love of God for humankind could have made the Cross of Christ a reality. God, our Father, willingly abandoned his Son to destroy our sinful spirit in his body.

> Yet it was the LORD's will to crush him and cause him to suffer, and though the LORD makes his life an offering for sin, he will see his offspring and prolong his days, and the will of the LORD will prosper in his hand. (Isaiah 53:10 NIV)

What God has done on our behalf in the body of Jesus Christ on the cross at Golgotha is apart from every law known to humankind. An eternity of study and contemplation will not exhaust all the knowledge contained in what God did for us on the cross at Golgotha.

17

The Dreadful Day

THE BIBLE CALLS Friday that was almost two thousand years ago the dreadful day of the Lord. On the dreadful day of the Lord, Jesus was nailed to the cross at Golgotha. However, the cross did not make it a dreadful day. Friday, the day that Jesus was crucified was dreadful because the darkness ruled.

> "Woe to you who long for the day of the LORD! Why do you long for the day of the LORD? That day will be darkness, not light. Will not the day of the LORD be darkness, not light—pitch dark, without a ray of brightness." (Amos 5:18 20 NIV)

Several prophets either asserted or alluded that the day of the Lord would be darkness. Jesus, at his trial, said that the hour of Jewish leaders was when the darkness rules.

> "Every day I was with you in the temple courts, and you did not lay a hand on me. But this is your hour—when darkness reigns." (Luke 22:53 NIV)

The day of the Lord could also be translated as the day of the Lord's judgment. God judged and punished the world for sin through the body of Jesus on the cross at Golgotha. Jesus told the disciples that his crucifixion was the day of judgment on the world. The dreadful day of the Lord was dark because God punished humankind for the sin that took place in the Garden of Eden; therefore, it was for all sins against the law. On that day, God re-created humankind by destroying the sinful human spirit and removing the sin from humanity through the body of Jesus on the cross at Golgotha.

The judgment of humankind for sin, through the body of Jesus, resulted in an astronomical event that science could not explain. According to the known laws in our universe, such an astronomical event should have destroyed our universe forever on the dreadful day of the Lord. However, the universe survived this incomprehensible event. The earth continued in its place. The re-creation of humankind became a reality. God accomplished it all during the darkness that ruled on the dreadful day of the Lord, when Jesus was nailed to the cross at Golgotha.

> See, the day of the LORD is coming—a cruel day, with wrath and fierce anger—to make the land desolate and destroy the sinners within it. The stars of heaven and their constellations will not show their light. The rising sun will be darkened and the moon will not give its light. (Isaiah 13:9–10 NIV)

Darkness on the dreadful day of the Lord did not come because of a solar eclipse or a very dark overcast. The darkness persisted for three hours; therefore, it was not a solar eclipse. The longest solar eclipse that can occur on the earth is approximately seven minutes and six seconds. However, the darkness on the dreadful day of the Lord lasted three hours while Jesus was nailed to the cross. The darkness on Friday, which was almost two thousand years ago, was extremely dark. Humankind had never seen such darkness.

The darkness persisted throughout the world and the universe. The darkness on that day was not a normal event in our universe. It did not conform to any law known to humankind. Why did it get so dark? The clue is given in the first epistle by the apostle John. We can also deduce an answer from what Jesus felt on the cross at Golgotha during the three hours of dreadful darkness.

> This is the message we have heard from him and declare to you: God is light; in him there is no darkness at all. (1 John 1:5 NIV)

It is true, where God is, there is no darkness at all. The opposite is true also. Where God is not, there is no light at all. The darkness ruled the universe because God abandoned Jesus on the cross at Golgotha. God withdrew from our universe because of humankind's sin; which he had placed on Jesus. The sin separated Jesus (our scapegoat) from the Father (the only source of life). Because the Creator of the universe withdrew himself from it, the whole universe shut down. Every star in it stopped shining. This event was a natural response by the created things when the Creator was not present. When there is no Creator, there is no light and, therefore, no life.

However, according to our universe's known laws, if all the stars in it shut down, the universe's temperature would drop to absolute zero instantly. The universe would cease to exist forever. However, the dreadful darkness lasted for three hours, but the universe survived. Therefore, the dreadful day of the Lord conformed to law that is not in our universe. We cannot know every exhausting detail about the things that transpired on the cross at Golgotha.

With the sin of the world and the sinful human life on him, Jesus Christ experienced the undiluted cup of God's wrath against sin. The Father has left him. The people were against him. The enemy of God tried to distract him from his mission. Even his apostles deserted him. Christ was left alone to suffer the cross of Christ on the Golgotha. King David, in a prophetic spirit, gave us a glimpse of what Jesus might have experienced.

> You know how I am scorned, disgraced and shamed; all my enemies are before you. Scorn has broken my heart and has left me helpless; I looked for sympathy, but there was none, for comforters, but I found none. They put gall in my food and gave me vinegar for my thirst. (Psalm 69:19–21 NIV)

God put the sin of the world and our sinful spirit on Jesus. Therefore, our sinful life received a full blow of God's wrath through the body of Jesus Christ, on the cross. The sinful human life (spirit) suffered the second death, with no possibility of resurrection. Jesus Christ, our scapegoat, took our sin and sinful spirit into eternal abyss from where it could never return and count against us. The removal of our sin, by Jesus, our Scapegoat, was an infinitely greater act than the earthly Temple's scapegoat could was. Jesus Christ, our High Priest, accomplished the unimaginable because he had an indestructible life, which he set aside so he could destroy our indestructible sin forever.

God forgot our sin; therefore, it no longer exists. The only sin that is against us is the sin of our unbelief. Our sin in the Garden of Eden created a barrier between God and us. God removed our sin from us and eliminated the barrier. Now we are free to approach our God in prayer, in the name of Jesus Christ. However, our freedom in Christ requires that we die to ourselves so that Christ can live in us.

The old self was not capable of approaching God by attempting to obey the law. The law was given to sinners and not to the righteous. What Jesus Christ had to endure to restore us to God is simple, yet it is profoundly complex that it is beyond belief. Yielded believers trust that Jesus accomplished everything that they need for an eternity with God. Christ is the only way. Human efforts are useless.

The fallen humankind is the beneficiary of what Jesus Christ accomplished on the cross at Golgotha. The human vocabulary does not contain proper words to accurately describe what God accomplished on our behalf through the body of Jesus Christ. We could not even imagine what it was like for Jesus to separate his perfect life from his body and become sin for us.

What sustained Jesus Christ on the cross while the dreadful darkness ruled? He was made something that he was not, and he was separated him from the Father on the cross. It is very likely he could not have seen beyond the eternal death of the sinful life that was placed on him on the cross. The only thing that he had to hold onto was the promise of the Father. However, the full blow of God's wrath was on him. Will the promise endure?

239

"For a brief moment I abandoned you, but with deep compassion I will bring you back. In a surge of anger I hid my face from you for a moment, but with everlasting kindness I will have compassion on you, says the LORD your Redeemer." (Isaiah 54:7–8 NIV)

Jesus Christ, having no other assurance, held onto the Father's promise. He remained faithful to his mission. By his faithfulness, we stand before our Father as if we have not sinned.

After he has suffered, he will see the light of life and be satisfied; by his knowledge my righteous servant will justify many, and he will bear their iniquities. Therefore I will give him a portion among the great, and he will divide spoils with the strong, because he poured out his life unto death, and was numbered with the transgressors. For he bore the sin of many, and made intercession for the transgressors. (Isaiah 53:11–12 NIV)

By the faithfulness of Jesus Christ, we are justified, sanctified, and glorified in the eyes of our God. We have not contributed anything to it. Even our faith in Jesus does not justify us because it is something that we do. We are a new creation only because of what Jesus Christ has accomplished on our behalf. We are the beneficiaries of God's Grace, not the contributors to it.

Where were we on the dreadful day of the Lord? On the day when God poured the undiluted cup of his wrath on sin in sinful flesh, we were in our sanctuary and our hiding place. God, who loves us, put us in the cleft of the Rock of our salvation. God put us in the pierced side of his Son. Jesus loves us more than he loves himself. Therefore, we were in his heart.

If necessary, Jesus Christ was willing to die and never to live again so that he could secure eternal life for the re-created humankind. Our sinful spirit and our indestructible sin have died forever, in the body of Jesus Christ on the cross at Golgotha. He now shares his indestructible life forever with yielded believers. In him, we are the children of God forever.

Despite the Dreadful Day Jesus Lives

Jesus Chris saw the life of life on the morning of his resurrection. The grave could not hold the body of Jesus for long. The resurrection of Jesus Christ guarantees that the yielded believers will rise when he comes to take his bride, the Church, to his Father's house. Jesus Christ is first among many members of the re-created humankind. Therefore, those who follow him are his offspring.

> Even though the Lord makes his life an offering for sin,
> he will see his offspring and prolong his days, and the will
> of the Lord will prosper in his hand. (Isaiah 53:10 NIV)

The will of the Lord is that all who believe shall be with him forever.

Jesus Christ, our High Priest, has entered the most holy place for us, present himself to the Father, and received all the authority. He spoke in the present tense when he told Mary to tell his brothers what he is about to do.

> Jesus said, Do not hold on to me, for I have not yet ascended to the Father. Go instead to my brothers and tell them, I am ascending to my Father and your Father, to my God and your God. (John 20:17 NIV)

Jesus Christ, our High Priest, offered a perfect and final sin sacrifice for the helpless humankind. Then, as our scapegoat, he removed our sin and our sinful life from us and took it into the eternal abyss, from where there was no return. On the morning of his resurrection, he entered the most holy place to present himself to the Father as a victorious Lamb that was slain. The ascension into heaven on the morning of Jesus's resurrection was the final act concerning humankind's salvation and re-creation.

Jesus Christ sacrificed himself once for all, and he could not be sacrificed again. In the same manner, and on the morning of his resurrection, he entered the most holy place once for all time. He then sat down at the Father's right hand because his service as our High Priest was completed forever. He did not need to enter the most holy place ever again. He offered one sacrifice for all, and he entered the most holy place once for all time.

Because he has completed the service as our High Priest, he now is at the right hand of the Father. He is now sitting and ruling as the King of kings and Lord of lords. He remains our High Priest forever. However, he no longer officiates as High Priest but rules God's dominion.

> For Christ did not enter a sanctuary made with human hands that was only a copy of the true one; he entered heaven itself, now to appear for us in God's presence. Nor did he enter heaven to offer himself again and again, the way the high priest enters the Most Holy Place every year with blood that is not his own. (Hebrews 9:24–25 NIV)

People usually say that God is in heaven. That is how humans could visualize and understand it. However, we should never assign a physical location to God. But we do need to present God in a way the people could understand. When we say that God is in heaven, then we must consider the whole of heaven as the most holy place. Therefore, when Jesus entered heaven to present himself to the Father, he entered the most holy place. Upon entering it Jesus sat down because he has completed his service as the High Priest forever. There was nothing left to be done. Jesus proclaimed on the cross, "It is finished," (John 19:30)and therefore, it is. Now we live as a new creation.

18

The Power of Christ's Cross

THE CROSS OF Christ is the best power. How do we benefit from the power of the Christ's cross? Illustration 9 depicts the undeserved gift that we receive from God, who loves us. We are new creation in Jesus Christ forever.

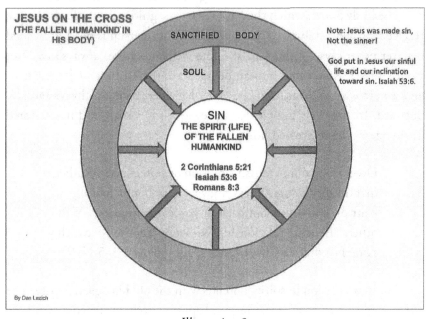

Illustration 9

We still have the old biological nature (the body and the soul). Therefore, we inherit the consequences of sin that we committed in the Garden of Eden. However, yielded believers receive the perfect spirit (perfect life) of Jesus Christ. Therefore, we are new creation in Jesus Christ.

> Therefore, if anyone is in Christ, the new creation has come: The old has gone, the new is here! (2 Corinthians 5:17 NIV)

Yielded believers have a new spiritual nature (new spirit). What we are in Jesus Christ is our unmerited gift from God, who loves us. Therefore, yielded believers have two natures. A newborn person still has the old body that he or she inherited from the first man Adam. However, the newborn person's spirit is the perfect spirit that he or she receives by trusting the Second Man, Jesus Christ. Therefore, in his or her old body, the newborn person has a perfect and eternal life given as a gift from God, in Jesus Christ. The new spirit we receive from Jesus Christ commands and controls the old body that was inherited from the first man, Adam. Therefore, the attitude and the disposition of the yielded believers show the work of the new spirit given through the body of Jesus Christ.

The Holy Spirit, which the Father gave us, guides the perfect spirit we receive from Jesus Christ. The *I* of the newborn person is dead. A yielded believer never says, "I plus Christ." The yielded believes always say, "Not I but Christ." Re-created human beings have the attitude of Jesus Christ and a new way of thinking. The love of yielded believer always radiates outward. In this way, the yielded believer testifies that God has restored his image in the re-created humanity.

> Do nothing out of selfish ambition or vain conceit. Rather, in humility value others above yourself not looking to your own interests but each of you to the interests of the others. In your relationship with one another, have the same mindset as Christ Jesus. (Philippians 2:3–5 NIV)

The new creation in spirit contends with the old biological nature. The old biological nature does not respond appropriately to the commands by the new and perfect spirit that we have in Jesus Christ. The love of self, which is contrary to the desires of the new spirit, sometimes reasserts itself. The opposing force is the daily struggle in the mind of a newborn believer. Accordingly, the perfect life (spirit) that we have in Jesus Christ groans inwardly. The new and perfect spirit that we have in Jesus Christ always desires to do what is right. However, the old body cannot appropriately respond because it is still subject to sin's consequences. The apostle Paul found that it was an ever-present struggle.

> For I do not do the good I want to do, but the evil I do not want to do—this I keep on doing. (Romans 7:19 NIV)

The conflict in a yielded believer's mind is a war between two forces that contend for control of the newborn person's mind. The re-created humankind must still contend with the opposing force while in this world. However, a yielded believer is always certain of the victory in Jesus Christ. Accordingly, the apostle Paul contends.

> So I find this law at work: Although I want to do good, evil is right there with me. For in my inner being I delight in God's law; but I see another law at work in me, waging war against the law of my mind and making me a prisoner of the law of sin at work within me. (Romans 7:21–23 NIV)

The war between the two forces (the two laws) is a daily presence in a yielded believer's mind. However, while this war is in mind, it should not demonstrate itself in the members of a newborn person's body. The experience of the war the two forces wage in the mind of a yielded believer led Paul to exclaim.

> What a wretched man I am! Who will rescue me from this body that is subject to death? (Romans 7:24 NIV)

Every yielded believer feels he or she is a wretched person because of the new knowledge in Jesus Christ. However, a newborn person (a yielded believer) can always be a happy, wretched person. The apostle Paul reminded yielded believers of their victory.

> Thanks be to God – through Jesus Christ our Lord. (Romans 7:25 NIV)

Because of the cross of Christ, yielded believers are victorious in Jesus Christ. Jesus assured us of our everlasting victory in him.

> "I have told these things, so that in me you may have peace. In this world you will have trouble. But take heart! I have overcome the world." (John 16:33 NIV)

Jesus stated the above in the past tense. He has conquered the evil force. Yielded believers do not have to pray and ask for a victory. They should always thank God for the victory they have in Jesus Christ. The Holy Spirit assures the new spirit we have in Jesus Christ.

> The Spirit himself testifies with our spirit that we are God's children. Now if we are children, then we are heirs—heirs of God and co-heirs of Jesus Christ, if indeed we share in his sufferings in order that we may also share in his glory. (Romans 8:16–17 NIV)

Yielded believers will always have a war going on in their minds while they are still in this world. However, yielded believers have a firm assurance that they are victorious children of God with irrevocable right of inheritance through Jesus Christ.

Yielded believers, the children of God, receive all that Jesus has accomplished on the cross at Golgotha. The re-created humankind has an ever-present reminder of its status in Jesus Christ. God sent us the Holy Spirit to remind us that we are newborn children of God through the body of Jesus Christ. Yes, when a yielded believer looks in the mirror, he or she always sees a sinner by nature. However, the Holy Spirit reminds the yielded believer that he or she is a sinner that is saved by Grace—Jesus Christ.

The new creation in Jesus Christ does not sin deliberately, and it does not continue in sin; however, the newborn believers will sin, according to the law, the Ten Commandments. The war between the opposing forces in the mind of a yielded believer is always there. However, the struggle can be made more bearable by total self-surrender to Jesus Christ. A newborn person must join the apostle Paul in the assertion.

> For through the law I died to the law so that I might live
> for God. I have been crucified with Christ and I no longer
> live, but Christ lives in me. (Galatians 2:19–20 NIV)

The cross of Christ is the power that overcomes all doubts and struggles in a newborn person's mind. Newborn believers must always be certain concerning the benefit they have through the power of the cross of Christ. Through the body of Jesus Christ on the cross at Golgotha, God accomplished everything we needed for our salvation and eternity with him. The benefits of the power of the cross of Christ are priceless. The cross of Christ will forever stand as the greatest demonstration of God's selfless love for his enemies. However, studying and contemplating the cross of Christ would be incomplete without a deep appreciation of its power.

To fully appreciate the cross of Christ, we must understand our corporate relation to its power. A summary of what has been presented in this treatise may assist in the proper understanding of the Christ cross's power.

First: God, at the Incarnation, put in Jesus a new spirit (the new life) of the same order as the order of spirit that he put in Adam at creation. However, the body of the representative of the re-created humankind was the body that humankind had at the time of Incarnation. The body of the first man, Adam, was not subject to the consequences of sin before Adam decided to disobey God.

By his deliberate decision and choice, Adam subjected the whole of nature, including the human body, to decay. The Second Adam, Jesus Christ, took on himself our infirmities in the flesh. However, his spirit was good at the time of Incarnation. God promised to give humankind a new spirit in the Messiah. When Jesus Christ returns, he will give us a body that responds well to the new spirit that we have in him.

As the first humankind's representative, Adam made all his descendants utterly helpless sinners by nature. Jesus Christ, the representative of the re-created humankind, is the Savior of the world. Through the body of the Savior of the world, God removed the sin that separated humankind from God.

> And we have seen and testify that the Father has sent his
> Son to be the Savior of the world. (1 John 4:14 NIV)

The sin that humankind committed in the garden of Eden erased the God's image in it. God has restored his image in humankind through the body of the representative of the re-created humankind.

Second: Adam, the first humankind's representative, made a deliberate, intelligent decision to disobey God. Therefore, he and the whole humanity that he represented became sinner by nature. A deliberate, intelligent decision by Adam was a decision by the human spirit that God put in him. Deliberate and willful decisions and choices are irrevocable.

Such a decision makes the person who decides incapable of doing anything to correct the initial decision. A physical act or a verbal expression demonstrates that a deliberate sin has been committed. The human body could not sin, in and of itself. The spirit sins deliberately. When a deliberate decision has been made, the spirit becomes an irrevocable sinner by nature, whether physical activity has been committed or not.

All humankind has one spirit (one intelligence). Therefore, the sin by the first man, Adam, is the sin of the first humankind. By a sinful decision, humankind became utterly helpless to return itself to the pre-decision state. The re-creation of humankind was the only solution possible. The sinful human spirit (life) had to be destroyed and replaced by a new spirit (life) that did not sin. There are no ways to make the sinful human spirit righteous again. It must die forever.

Accordingly, at the Incarnation, God put in Jesus a new human spirit. The spirit that God put in Jesus is of the same order of spirit as the Creator put in Adam at creation. However, the body of Jesus Christ was the body that people had at the time of Incarnation. The body itself did not sin.

Therefore, it did not need to be replaced. Jesus Christ was tempted, and he conquered the same categories of temptation in which the first human pair failed. Therefore, the new human spirit in Jesus Christ became perfect. The Holy Spirit entered his mind and sanctified his body.

Sanctified means that the body of Jesus was designated as the body of the re-created humankind. The body of Jesus also was designated as God's permanent residence with the re-created humankind. By sanctification, Jesus' body became fitting for the great exchange on the cross at Golgotha. By securing a perfect human life, Jesus was qualified to represent the re-created humankind. He was also the Last Adam because there was not another option available. Had Jesus not remained faithful to his mission, humankind would not have existed ever again.

Third: After conquering the temptation and the tempter, Jesus Christ lived a perfect life for three and a half years on the earth. Because Jesus defeated God's enemy, the Father granted him the right to have life in himself. Therefore, Jesus Christ, the representative of the re-created humankind, has an indestructible life. Accordingly, the new creation in Jesus Christ has an indestructible life also. Only the indestructible life could have removed a deliberate sin from the people by destroying the sinful human spirit.

Fourth: On the cross at Golgotha, Jesus set aside his perfect and indestructible life. Then, God put on Jesus the sin of the world and the sinful human life (the sinful spirit). By abandoning Jesus on the cross, God destroyed the sinful life and the world's sin forever. The sin of the world and the sinful human life died the second death. There was no possibility of resurrection. We would be correct in saying that sinful humankind died the second death in the body of Jesus Christ on the cross at Golgotha. The re-created humankind lives forever.

Fifth: Because of what we have become in Jesus Christ, the law has nothing against us anymore. God has destroyed the witness against us, through the body of Jesus Christ on the cross at Golgotha.

> For Christ's love compels us, because we are convinced
> that one died for all, and therefore all died. (2 Corinthians
> 5:14 NIV)

Jesus Christ did not come to change our penalty for sin but to fulfill it. The sinner had to die. There was no way out.

Sixth: In Jesus Christ, God gave humankind a new life (a new spirit). Humanity now has a new history and new identity. The re-created humankind has a holy identity and history of Jesus Christ. By trusting Jesus, yielded believers experience daily the new life and identity that they have in Jesus Christ. Those who do not accept Jesus Christ will lose eternal life because they do not believe and not because they sin against the law. We inherited the decision that first Adam made in the Garden of Eden. However, what we have become in Jesus Christ is our unmerited gif from our God and Father. Yielded believers can have full confidence that they are new creation in Christ Jesus.

> Therefore, if anyone is in Christ, the new creation has come: The old has gone, the new is here! (2 Corinthians 5:17 NIV)

This is the essence of the gospel, the good news for all.

19

Our Gain through the Power of the Cross

THE LAST CHAPTER presented the cross of Christ as a power. What do we gain through the power of the cross of Christ?

First: The power of the cross of Christ made our salvation legal according to the Law. How did it do this? By dying in Jesus Chris, the sinful humankind satisfied the righteous requirement of the Law. The Law does not allow a pardon for sin. A sinner must die. There is no way out. The Law does not allow a substitution either. A sinner himself must die. (Reminder: Law (upper case) refers to the universal moral code, Law. The law (lower case) refers to the Ten Commandments. Humankind violated the Law in the Garden of Eden.)

> "For everyone belongs to me, the parent as well as the child—both alike belong to me. The one who sins is the one who will die." (Ezekiel 18:4 NIV)

In Adam, in the Garden of Eden, all humankind became a sinner by nature. Therefore, the whole sinful humankind had to die an eternal death. No one could have died in place of sinful humanity. The good news is, that the sinful humankind died in the body of Jesus Christ, on the cross at

Golgotha. God has re-created the whole of humankind through the body of Jesus Christ on the cross at Golgotha.

> For we know that our old self was crucified with him so that the body ruled by sin might be done away with, that we should no longer be slaves to sin—because anyone who has died has been set free from sin. (Romans 6:6–7 NIV)

Because all humankind had the one spirit that sinned in the garden, all humankind died in the body of Jesus Christ on the cross at Golgotha.

> "And I, when I am lifted up from the earth, will draw all people to myself." (John 12:32 NIV)

Second: The power of the cross of Christ has destroyed our sin forever.

> For what the Law was powerless to do because it was weakened by the flesh, God did by sending his own Son in the likeness of sinful flesh to be a sin offering. And so he condemned sin in the flesh, in order that the righteous requirement of the law might be fully met in us, who do not live according to the sinful flesh but according to the Spirit. (Romans 8:3–4 NIV)

God destroyed the sinful spirit (life) of humankind through the body of Jesus Christ on the cross. God gave the spirit to humankind, and only he could destroy it. God could destroy the human spirit because it belongs to him and no one else. Not only did God destroy the sinful spirit of humankind, but he also forgot humanity's sin.

> "I, even I, am he who blots out your transgressions, for my own sake, and remembers your sins no more." (Isaiah 43:25 NIV)

By turning his face away from Jesus on the cross, God destroyed our sin, sinful life, and natural inclinations to sin forever.

Third: The power of the cross of Christ has justified us from everything we were powerless to do for ourselves. The power of the cross of Christ has reconciled us to God and made us righteous in his eyes. God justified us in Jesus Chris, the representative of the re-created humankind.

> Consequently, just as one trespass resulted in condemnation for all people, so also, one righteous act resulted in justification and life for all people. (Romans 5:18 NIV)

God reconciled us to himself in the body of Jesus Christ on the cross. We could not reconcile ourselves to God regardless of the willing effort.

> All this is from God, who reconciled us to himself through Christ and gave us the ministry of reconciliation: that God was reconciling the world to himself in Christ, not counting people's sin against them. And he has committed to us the message of reconciliation. (2 Corinthians 5:18-19 NIV)

By destroying the sin that separated us from him, God restored us to himself as his children. And now we are righteous in God's eyes.

> God made him who had no sin to be sin for us, so that in him we might become the righteousness of God. (2 Corinthians 5:21 NIV)

Fourth: The power of the cross of Christ has saved us from the power of sin. Sin is a power. Therefore, a stronger power was needed to free us from it.

> The sting of death is sin, and the power of sin is the law. But thanks be to God! He gives us victory through our Lord Jesus Christ. (1 Corinthians 15:56–57 NIV)

In Adam, sin separated humankind from God, the only source of life. The first man, Adam, made a deliberate decision to disobey God's specific command not to eat fruit from the tree of knowledge of good and evil.

Because of deliberate disobedience, the Law condemned humankind to eternal death. Adam's decision in the Garden of Eden was a deliberate, intelligent decision. The spirit that God put in Adam at creation sinned by a deliberate violation of God's command. Because the spirit in man decided to disobey, mankind became a sinner by nature. Therefore, sinful humankind could not be made good again because deliberate, intelligent decisions are irreversible. Therefore, the sinful mankind had to be re-created by receiving a new human spirit.

The human spirit God put in mankind at creation was good. The deliberate decision by spirit (the intelligence) makes it either perfect or a sinner irrevocably. Humankind could not make a subsequent deliberate, intelligent decision because all options cease to exist. The state of human nature, achieved by a deliberate decision, remains in the achieved state. Only the replacement of the spirit by re-creation could change the state of humankind. Had humankind become perfect in Adam, there would be no need for re-creation. The re-creation of humankind became necessary because the deliberate decisions by the spirit are final.

The apostle Paul stated that the "power of sin is the law." (1 Corinthians 15:56} because the violation of the law is a sin. If there is no command, a violation would not be possible. Therefore, sin would not exist. The Law could not help the sinner change its sinful nature by subsequent careful obedience. Because of a deliberate decision to disobey, the sinner forfeits the ability to obey the Law perfectly. Therefore, the Law and the sinner remain enemies forever. Even the best effort possible by a sinner to obey the Law only increases a sinner's sinfulness by nature.

The only option available to the sinner by nature is victory in Jesus Christ, who represents the re-created humankind. However, to be victorious in Jesus Christ requires a total self-surrender. The old sinful self must die and be replaced by the perfect spirit of Jesus Christ. Jesus Christ does not offer the sinner a victory. He is the sinner's victory. Therefore, to be victorious, a sinner must die to himself so that Christ could live in him. The old, sinful spirit and the perfect spirit of Jesus Christ cannot reside together in humankind's mind. The new birth (the re-creation) is the only way to eternity with God.

God made the whole of sinful humankind die the second death through the body of Jesus Christ on Golgotha's cross. Therefore, the whole of the re-created humankind is victorious in Jesus Christ. The personal experience of victory in Jesus Christ comes by a deliberate personal decision to die to oneself. This type of a deliberate decision and self-surrender becomes irrevocable. Yielded believers irrevocably have eternal life in Jesus Christ, here and now.

The victorious new humankind in Jesus Christ is free from accusation and condemnation by the Law. The new human spirit, given in Jesus Christ, is perfect. Therefore, it is not subject to the Law. By giving us a new spirit in Jesus Christ, God has set us free from the power of sin. Therefore, has set us free from the condemnation by the Law. In Jesus Christ, yielded believers have an assurance that they are free from accusation. The Law does not have the reason or the power to condemn us again. The Law still exists, and is holy. However, the sinner has died, as required by the Law. The new humankind is free from condemnation. Because the sinner has died according to the Law, the re-created humankind lives because of Jesus Christ, who is above the Law.

> Therefore, there is now no condemnation for those who are in Christ Jesus, because through Christ Jesus the law of the Spirit who gives us life has set us free from the law of sin and death. (Romans 8:1–2 NIV)

Those who surrender their self and accept Jesus Christ as their life become subjects to a higher law (not the Ten Commandments). They fall under the law of selfless love. Obedience to the universal law of selfless love is obedience to all laws (including the Ten Commandments). Our efforts to obey the Ten Commandments force us to look at ourselves. The attention to ourselves separates us from Jesus Christ because our old self stands condemned by the Law. We could not serve both, the law that condemned us and Jesus Christ who has justified us and given us eternal life. The universal law of selfless love forces us not to look to ourselves because, we no longer live but Christ lives in us.

Fifth: The power of the cross of Christ saves us from the cheap grace. Historically, some in the Christian Church used the freedom that they have in Jesus Christ as a license for sin. Often, the old self could not realize that Christ's beneficiaries have an obligation because of cross's power.

> Therefore, brothers and sisters, we have an obligation—
> but it is not to the flesh, to live according to it. For if you
> live according to the flesh, you will die; but if by the Spirit
> you put to death the misdeeds of the body, you will live.
> (Romans 8:12–13 NIV)

There are two groups of people who do not understand the power of the cross of Christ. The first ones maintain that, all they need is the faith in Jesus because the works of law cannot save them. Accordingly. they convince themselves that their deeds of the flesh do not count. However, they do not realize that we cannot receive the cross's power if we live according to the flesh. They do not realize that the flesh cannot please God.

> Those who are in the realm of the flesh cannot please god.
> (Romans 8:8 NIV)

The old self belongs to an unconverted person. Such a person is powerless because the Holy Spirit does not reside in him. Only those who have crucified their old self with Christ have the Holy Spirit who guides them.

> Those who live according to the flesh have their minds set
> on what the flesh desires; but those who live in accordance
> with the Spirit have their minds set on what the Spirit
> desires. (Romans 8:5 NIV)

If we are in Christ and he lives in us, through the promised Spirit, we are saved from cheap grace. The power of the cross of Christ made us new creation. The old creation does only what it is accustomed to doing. However, the new creation does what it is accustomed to doing.

Another group would say that faith is not enough. We must repent, ask for forgiveness, and get sanctified. Then we can have the hope in a possibility of salvation. Many Christians are convinced that they must, for their salvation, obey the law in addition to trusting Jesus Christ. Those who believe this do not know that if obedience to the law could set them free from sin, the cross would not be necessary.

A sinner by nature cannot obey the law perfectly. The moral Law demands perfect obedience, with no excuses. However, the sinful human spirit cannot render a perfect obedience. The desire to obey the moral Law counts for nothing. No human effort to obey any law could ever bring the justification, thus do away with the Law's condemnation. The greater the human effort to obey, the greater the fallen human nature's sinfulness.

The sinfulness of the human spirit made the old humankind unable to obey. Old humankind, the descendants of Adam, could not desire to obey. The sinful humanity attempts obedience out of fear of disobedience's consequences. The utterly helpless sinful humanity had to be replaced with the re-created humankind. Therefore, God re-created humankind in Jesus Christ. The new humanity is a beneficiary of the power of the cross of Christ. However, we must be in Christ to receive the benefits of it. To be in Christ, sinner must die to himself. Even the best possible obedience to the law could not give us what we have through surrender to Jesus Christ.

> I do not set aside the Grace of God, for if righteousness
> could be gained through the law, Christ died for nothing.
> (Galatians 2:21, NIV)

By adherence to the cheap grace, we deny the power of the cross of Christ. Its power does not affect those who have not experienced the new birth. The daily living of the new creation in Jesus Christ confirms the power of Christ's cross. Only those who are holy in God's eyes could experience the power of Christ's Cross. Yielded believers are not holy because of the quality of life that they have. Yielded believers become holy by the possession of salvation in Jesus Christ.

No one can be sanctified by the good works of the law. Some believe that their careful performance of what the law requires leads to their sanctification. Those who believe it maintain that sanctification is a lifelong process that leads to holiness. However, the works of the law demonstrate that we are sinners by nature. The law has been given to reveal to sinful humankind that sin is an unconquerable foe.

As good as it is, the law cannot justify the sinner. As designed, the law condemns disobedience, but it cannot help anyone to obey.

> Therefore no one will be declared righteous in God's
> sight by the works of the law; rather, through the law we
> become conscious of sin. (Romans 3:20 NIV)

Our bodies cannot be sanctified by the good works we do. Only what we possess in Jesus Christ could sanctify our body. Yielded believers possess new life (new spirit) through Jesus Christ. Because of the new and perfect spirit of Jesus Christ, the Holy Spirit resides in the yielded believer. Therefore, his body is sanctified and set aside for the Holy Spirit,

> And that is what some of you were. But you were washed,
> you were sanctified, you were justified in the name of
> the Lord Jesus Christ and by the Spirit of our God. (1
> Corinthians 6:11 NIV)

Therefore, we are sanctified by the Holy Spirit, whom Jesus promised to all who trust him. We cannot become sanctified by our good performance regardless, of how sincere it might be. The Holy Spirit comes into the mind of the yielded believer because he has the perfect life (spirit) of Jesus Christ. The Holy Spirit cannot reside in an unsanctified body. Therefore, the Holy Spirit sets aside the body of the yielded believer as his residence. Why is the Holy Spirit in us?

> The Spirit himself testifies with our spirit that we are
> God's children. (Romans 8:16 NIV)

Since we are the children of God, we always represent our Father' However, only if we are not under the Law's condemnation could we be free from the power of sin? The Law cannot free us from the power of sin. We must be free from the power of sin because a sinner cannot please God. Therefore, we must surrender to Jesus Christ, our Grace. The Grace of God is not cheap! To receive Grace (Jesus Christ) and be free from the power of sin, we must die to ourselves.

> What shall we say then? Shall we go on sinning so that
> Grace may increase? By no means! We are those who have

died to sin; how can we live in it any longer? (Romans 6:1–2 NIV)

Sinful humankind had to die to free itself from the Law's condemnation. Only the death to the Law could free us from the power of sin.

For we know that our old self was crucified with him so that the body ruled by sin might be done away with, that we should no longer be slaves to sin—because anyone who has died has been set free from sin. (Romans 6:6 NIV)

Our sinful spirit (our life) has died in the body of Jesus on the cross at Golgotha. Therefore, our sin died also and been removed from us forever. Because our sin and our sinful life have died through the body of Jesus Christ, the Law has nothing against us. The Law could not condemn us even if we were to violate a commandment. This assurance is ours only if we have the power of the cross of Christ as our daily experience. Those who do not accept the perfect life of Jesus Christ remain under condemnation by the Law.

Sixth: The power of the Cross of Christ has freed us from under the Law so that we could be free from sin.

For sin shall no longer be your master, because you are not under the law, but under Grace. (Romans 6:14 NIV)

What is the meaning of Paul's statement above? Why is the Law no longer our master? Paul explains his statement in Romans 7:1–4. Paul employs the law of marriage as an illustration of what he meant by the above statement.

Do you know, brothers and sisters—for I am speaking to those who know the law—that the law has authority over someone as long as that person lives. (Romans 7:1 NIV)

According to the law, marriage is valid as long as both spouses live. The death of one of the spouses dissolves the marriage forever.

> For example, by law a married woman is bound to her husband as long as he is alive, but if her husband dies, she is released from the law that binds her to him. (Romans 7:2) NIV)

Therefore, if a married woman has a relationship with another man while her husband lives, the law condemns her as an adulteress. According to Jesus' definition of the law, even if a married woman would look lustfully at another man, it would make her an adulteress. However, if her husband dies, the woman is free from under the law. Also, if a married woman were to die, she would be free from her marriage. She would not be an adulteress even if, after her death, she were to marry another man.

The message here is that the sinful humankind had to die so that its marriage to the Law would be dissolved and that it would be free her to marry Jesus Christ. The first humankind's husband, the Law, cannot die; therefore, the wife (humankind) had to die.

Traditionally, people thought that physical behavior and deeds are the fulfillment of the Law's requirements. Therefore, if a person behaved in conformity to the Ten Commandments, they thought that such a person was perfect and blameless. However, the people did not realize that the Ten Commandments do not represent the moral Law. The people could not realize that the Ten Commandments were a physical example of what the moral Law demands.

The purpose of the Ten Commandments was to show the people what sin is. Therefore, Jesus reminded the people that a sinner's good behavior was not moral automatically. Violation of the moral Law and thus all laws, occurred in a human being's mind. Human thoughts violate the moral Law and the Ten Commandments, even if the body did not demonstrate the violation. A sinful person continues to sin because he is a sinner by nature.

Human beings do not have to violate the law in deeds to become sinners. Sinful human beings violate the moral Law in their minds with their thoughts, (including the Ten Commandments). From the moral Law's perspective, deliberate, intelligent decisions make us either good or evil. It is so because the sinful spirit could not generate righteous thoughts.

Likewise, the perfect spirit thinks righteous thoughts. The helpless nature of the sinful human spirit can be changed only if it is replaced by re-creation. Accordingly, God destroyed our sinful spirit through the body of Jesus on the cross and replaced it with the perfect spirit of Jesus Christ. When we accept Christ and his perfect life, the new spirit from Jesus guides our minds concerning the righteous requirements. The new spirit we have in Jesus Christ guides our minds with the promised Holy Spirit's help. Jesus' definition of the violation of the Law should be our guide concerning sin.

Paul applied the law of marriage to the wife only. Historically, human societies did not require that men only have one wife. However, human society's law required that a woman marry one man only, with no exceptions. Paul employed the law of marriage in this manner to emphasize a point. Jesus Christ has betrothed to him the whole of the re-created humankind, with its many members. However, there is one Jesus Christ, our husband. He married many members of the re-created humankind. Therefore, according to the law, the re-created humankind could not maintain loyalty to the law and the Grace (Jesus Christ).

The re-created humankind will become one when God restores everything to its original state. However, if yielded believers are one in the Gospel, then Jesus married one woman.

To insist that the Ten Commandments are required for the salvation of sinners, in addition to Grace, violates both the universal moral Law and the Ten Commandments.

At the creation in the first man, Adam, God placed humankind under the Law. God gave the first human pair a simple command.

> "Do not eat fruit from the tree of knowledge of good and
> evil." (Genesis 2:17 NIV)

The command was a test of humankind's loyalty. At the creation, the first human pair was good, not perfect and not evil. Their deliberate, intelligent decision in the Garden of Eden would make humankind perfect or a sinner by nature.

When Adam was confronted with the need to decide, his thoughts and deliberate choice made him and all of humankind a sinner by nature. Eating the forbidden fruit did not make Adam and humankind sinners. Adam ate the forbidden fruit because he had become a sinner. By his deliberate, intelligent decision and willful disobedience of God's command, Adam violated the universal moral Law.

Humankind, in Adam, was married to the moral Law. However, in Adam, humankind violated the Law by choosing to have a relationship with evil while married to the Law. Therefore, humankind's marriage to the Law became unbearable and miserable. The moral Law condemned humankind (the wife) to eternal death, with no way out. The universal moral Law could not die. The wife could not get rid of it by any means. Therefore, humankind could not free itself from marriage to the Law.

The moral Law does not honor sorrow and repentance. No law is capable of doing so. The moral Law, the husband, does not allow divorce. Because her husband (the Law) was indestructible, the wife (humankind) could not free itself from a miserable marriage. The moral Law could not help humankind change its ways and become acceptable to the Law. It was not designed to help the sinner obey its requirements. It only had the power to condemn the sinner to eternal death. Therefore, the sinful wife (the adulteress) had to die.

However in time, the wife (humankind) met another man who loved her as she was. Because he loves humankind, Jesus Christ wanted to marry sinful humankind, with no conditions attached. However, humankind was still married to the universal moral Law. If sinful humankind (the wife) were to marry Jesus Christ, she would become an adulteress. A man who married a married woman would commit adultery also. (Mathew 5:32)

The sinful humankind loved Jesus Christ and wanted to marry him. However, humankind was powerless to dissolve its marriage to the moral Law. What was the solution to this impossible situation?

The only solution acceptable to the universal moral Law was that the wife (humankind) dies. However, how could the dead wife marry another man? She could not in human terms. The wife (the sinful humankind) needed a new life. God loved humankind. Therefore, he implemented a practical solution. On the cross at Golgotha, God destroyed the sinful spirit (life) of humankind and replaced it with the perfect spirit of Jesus

Christ. God's generous act made it possible for humankind to dissolve its marriage to the Law and marry Jesus Christ.

> So, my brothers and sisters, you also died to the law through the body of Christ, that you might belong to another, to him who was raised from the dead, in order that we might bear fruit to God. (Romans 7:4 NIV)

The great exchange on the cross at Golgotha made it possible for humankind to free itself from the miserable marriage to the moral Law. The power of the cross of Christ gave humankind a new life. Because the Holy Spirit guides the new human spirit, yielded believers are equipped to do the works that God requires and not the works of the law.

What works does God wants the people to do? The apostle Paul states that in addition to a new life, God also prepared in advance the works for humankind.

> For we are God's handiwork, created in Christ Jesus to do good works, which God prepared in advance for us to do. (Ephesians 2:10 NIV)

God prepared the good works for humankind he re-created in Jesus Christ, on the cross at Golgotha. The works of the law apply only to the old, sinful humankind. The old and sinful humankind was married to the Law. Therefore, it had to do the works that the Law required. However, no one could become holy and blameless through the works of the law. Only the works of that God requires could make us holy and perfect. What is the works God requires?

> Then they asked him, What must we do to do the works God requires? Jesus answered, "The work of God is this: to believe in the one he has sent." (John 6:28–29 NIV)

Those who asked Jesus about works that God required stated the word "works" in the plural. They had examples of superior performance. However, Jesus spoke in singular, indicating there was one essential work that God required. Jesus did not give them a list of things that they must do. He gave them a simple requirement. However, that may have been much more than some would have liked to do. Those who asked Jesus had the works of the law in mind. The works of the law are many. Jesus gave them one work that was required from the re-created humankind, and it was to believe in him.

The re-created humankind does not do the works of the law because they are not prepared for them. For the new humankind in Jesus Christ, God prepared the work of righteousness, not the works of the law. Even the best works of the law cannot make one righteous. We are righteous by doing one required work of righteousness. We must believe or trust Jesus because we are righteous in him only. Those who are in Jesus Christ are not under the Law's dominion but under Grace. God's requirement conforms with his will.

> For he chose us in him before the creation of the world to be holy and blameless in his sight. In love he predestined us for adoption to sonship through Jesus Christ, in accordance with his pleasure and will—to the praise of his glorious Grace, which he has freely given us in the One he loves. (Ephesians 1:4–6 NIV)

Therefore, if we are in Christ, the Law does not have anything against us anymore. It could not be against us because the re-created humankind is not under the Law's dominion but Jesus Christ. Now we are a new creation for whom only one Law counts. The Law of the re-created humankind is the universal principle of selfless love.

Selfless love fulfills all laws and not only the moral Law. We do not say that the Law is not good. The Law remains as it is. Humankind sinned and became good for nothing. The Law could not help humankind, not because it was not good but because humankind could not do what was good. Because of our sin, the Law could not love us. However, our Grace, Jesus Christ, hates sin but loves the sinners unconditionally.

If we were to insist on having the Ten Commandments as a part of our salvation, we stand condemned. The Ten Commandments are good practical example of appropriate relationship with God and human beings. However, it leads us to look at ourselves, thus, make Grace ineffective.

Additionally, by adding the Law to Grace as a requirement for our justification and salvation, we commit spiritual adultery. The law forbids the wife to have more than one husband. Either we are married to Grace, Jesus Christ, or the Law, but not to both. According to Jesus we cannot look at the law lustfully.

The Law requires an effort far above what sinful beings could do. Even with the new life that we have in Jesus Christ, the Law's requirements are more than we could do perfectly. The re-created humankind still has the old body (old biological nature) which cannot respond properly to the commands by the new spirit we have in Jesus Christ. Therefore, at all costs, we must remain married to the Grace, Jesus Christ. Jesus Christ, our new husband, is willing and able to help us in our shortcomings. The Law could not help the sinner by nature, only condemn him.

However, even though Grace does not require a particular level of physical performance, it requires total surrender. A sinner by nature must always say with Paul, "I no longer live, but Christ lives in me." We are holy in Christ Jesus, but not like him. Through Jesus's body, God removed from us the sin that estranged us from him. Therefore, we are holy in Christ Jesus. Jesus Christ took our sins to the cross at Golgotha. He did not take our sins to heaven. While we are still in this old body, we are sinners by nature. However, in Jesus Christ, we are without sin.

Yielded believers are seated at God's right hand in Jesus Christ. Sinners cannot sit there because God is most holy. A sinner would die instantly in the presence of the Holy God. Therefore, the new creation in Jesus Christ has an obligation. We must be the best lampstands possible from which the Light of the world can shine in the darkness. Yielded believers must turn the world upside down with the good news. God has sent the Savior of the world as promised. The good news is that God has removed our sin from us forever. Now we must surrender to the unmatched power of the cross of Christ.

Printed in the United States
by Baker & Taylor Publisher Services